The Scots and Parliament

Edited by
Clyve Jones

Edinburgh University Press
for
The Parliamentary History Yearbook Trust

© 1996 Edinburgh University Press

Edinburgh University Press
22 George Square
Edinburgh

Typeset in Bembo by WestKey Limited, Falmouth, Cornwall and printed and bound in Great Britain by Page Bros Ltd, Norwich

A CIP record for this title is available from the British Library

ISBN 0 7486 0823 0

1000 666327

CONTENTS

Alan Borthwick is one of the curatorial staff at the Scottish Record Office, Edinburgh. He completed his Ph.D. thesis, 'King, Council and Councillors in Scotland, c. 1430–1460' in 1989. He was editor of *Scottish Local History* from 1989 to 1992. His publications include a contribution of some text and translation to vol. VI of the new edition of Walter Bower's *Scotichronicon* (eds. D.E.R. Watt and others); and (with Hector MacQueen) 'Three Fifteenth-Century Cases', *Juridical Review* (1986). In conjunction with a colleague in the S.R.O., he is preparing an edition of Sir James Darow's notarial protocal book, 1469–84, for the Stair Society.

J.I. Brash is Senior Lecturer in History at the University of Western Australia where he has taught modern British history since 1961. He has held a fellowship at the Institute for Advanced Studies in the Humanities at the University of Edinburgh. He edited *Papers on Scottish Electoral Politics, 1832–1854* (1974) for the Scottish History Society, and has published several articles on Scottish electoral politics.

David J. Brown is Inspecting Officer in the Government Records Branch of the Scottish Record Office, Edinburgh. He completed his Ph.D. from the University of Edinburgh on 'Henry Dundas and the Government of Scotland' in 1989.

William Ferguson was educated at Oxford and Glasgow Universities, and has taught at Glasgow (1952–54) and then at Edinburgh University, retiring as Reader in Scottish History in 1989. Besides many articles and reviews, he has published *Scotland: 1689 to the Present* (1968), being vol. 4 of *The Edinburgh History of Scotland*, and *Scotland's Relations with England: A Survey to 1707* (1976).

Julian Goodare was formerly Research Fellow in the Department of Scottish History, University of Edinburgh, and is now at the University of Sheffield. He is the author of a number of articles on early modern Scotland, including 'Parliamentary Taxation in Scotland, 1560–1603', *Scottish Historical Review*, LXVIII (1989), which won the Royal Historical Society's David Berry Prize; 'The Nobility and the Absolutist State in Scotland, 1584–1638', *History*, LXXVIII (1993); and 'The Scottish Parliament of 1621', *Historical Journal*, XXXVIII (1995). He is co-editor of the forthcoming *James VI: Court and Kingship*, and is currently completing a book, *The Government of Scotland, 1560–1625*.

David Hayton is Lecturer in Modern History, Queen's University, Belfast. Formerly a research assistant, and section editor, at the *History of Parliament*, he remains as Consultant Editor for the 1690–1715 section of the *History*. He is the author of numerous articles and essays on late seventeenth- and early eighteenth-century British and Irish history, and is soon to publish his edition of *The Parliamentary Diary of Sir Richard Cocks, 1698–1702* (Oxford University Press).

John Scally completed his Ph.D. on 'The Political Career of James, Third

Marquis and First Duke of Hamilton (1606–1649) to 1643' at the University of Cambridge in 1992. Since then he has been a Curator in the Department of Printed Books in the National Library of Scotland. He is currently working towards a full biography of the Duke of Hamilton.

PREFACE

This present collection of essays on *The Scots and Parliament* is the third in a planned series of special volumes sponsored by the journal *Parliamentary History*, and published by Edinburgh University Press for The Parliamentary History Yearbook Trust. The series will consist of volumes on particular topics (like the present one) as well as collections of essays covering specific periods. The fourth in the series to be published in early 1997 will be on the late Victorian and Edwardian British Parliaments. Further volumes are planned on 'Parliament and Locality' from the seventeenth to the twentieth century, on the Church and Parliament from the seventeenth to the twentieth century, and on Ireland and Parliament.

As editor of both *Parliamentary History* and the present volume, I would like to thank the contributors to this volume, and to Alasdair Hawkyard who compiled the index.

Clyve Jones
General Editor

Introduction

WILLIAM FERGUSON

The following articles all reflect the new spirit of inquiry that has arisen among students of Scottish constitutional history. Though not iconoclastic in tone, they are at odds with the received establishment view that prevailed until very recently. That traditional view was dominated by the Stubbsian vision of an English Parliament that had steadily grown in importance until it became the main engine of government. The trouble is that the Mother of Parliaments was seen as the model by which all respectable legislatures ought to be judged, and those that failed to measure up were condemned accordingly. Thus, when seen in the perspectives laid down by Bishop Stubbs in his *Constitutional History of England*,[1] the Scottish Parliament appeared as feeble and imperfect—indeed, as something only fit to be scrapped. This was the verdict of R.S. Rait in his influential work *The Parliaments of Scotland*.[2] Earlier a rather similar view was taken by C.S. Terry in a briefer but for its day useful manual.[3] Terry and Rait were unable to resist the powerful influence of Stubbs, and it was beyond their ken to see Scottish institutions and constitutional procedures as worthy of examination in their own right and of assessment in their own terms. Their blinding fixation, plus awkward gaps in the evidence, left their version of the constitutional history of Scotland in a stunted and deformed condition. Nonetheless, theirs remained the standard account, but it is an account that no longer convinces, as Gordon Donaldson, the doyen of late twentieth-century Scottish historians, made clear in one of his last writings.[4]

But, of course, the strait-jacket imposed on English constitutional history by those two great pioneers in the field, Bishop Stubbs and F. W. Maitland, has been loosened by later research carried out in England and elsewhere. The main findings of the revisionists, however, came too late to influence Terry and Rait. Besides, initially revisionist views varied a great deal and there was considerable controversy about the new interpretations of medieval English constitutional history. In the upshot, however, all have renounced Stubbs's notion of a steady and virtually predestined evolution towards a sovereign legislature and parliamentary government. At the same time most of Stubbs's critics have admired his abilities as a historian and venerated him as the founder of a great school of

---

[1] W. Stubbs, *The Constitutional History of England* (3 vols., Oxford, 1874–8).

[2] R.S. Rait, *The Parliaments of Scotland* (Glasgow 1924); for a summary see Rait's pamphlet *The Scottish Parliament* (Historical Association of Scotland, 1925); and see too his early sketch, *The Scottish Parliament before the Union of the Crowns* (1901).

[3] C.S. Terry, *The Scottish Parliament: its Constitution and Procedure 1603–1707* (Glasgow, 1905).

[4] G. Donaldson's posthumous *Scotland's History: Approaches and Reflections*, ed. J. Kirk (Edinburgh, 1995), pp. 42–3.

medieval history at Oxford. His most scathing, and not altogether fair, critics
have been G.O. Sayles and H.G. Richardson. Their misconceived attack on
Stubbs as a historian, however, does not invalidate the fact that their seminal
work has done much to reveal just how fragmented and spasmodic was the
development of the early English constitution.[5] Unfortunately, they produced their
earliest articles too late to make any impression on Rait's work on the Scottish
Parliament. As a consequence the works of Rait and Terry, which are still necessary
works of reference, are seriously flawed in their interpretations. This is the case
with most of the writings on Scottish constitutional history produced in the first
half of the twentieth century. An exception, or at least partial exception, should
perhaps here be made of James Mackinnon's neglected *Constitutional History of
Scotland*, which, though not as elaborate as Rait's *Parliaments*, did show some
independence of mind and made some useful and suggestive points.[6]

Mackinnon, for example, was aware of the importance of ethnic and cultural
differences between England and Scotland. Rait, on the other hand, was intent
on playing them down and stressing the points the two countries had in common.
Thus the Gaelic past of Scotland finds no place in Rait's work. Mackinnon, to
his credit, saw that this would not do, and he tried to assess the influence of
Celtic law and custom in the development of the Scottish constitution. These
played powerfully on one of the most central and important features of the
Scottish constitution, the kingship. The traditions of Scottish kingship stemmed
from the Dalriadic Scots of the sixth century A.D., and were thus of remarkable
antiquity. The kingship was revered by all medieval Scots (whatever their remote
ancestry) as the essential core round which the kingdom of the Scots had been
formed. In other aspects of early law in Scotland, however, Mackinnon was
forced to rely too much upon analogies with ancient Ireland and Wales. Something
like a Celtic system must, indeed, have operated in early Scotland, but it has left
behind it no cohesive body of evidence like the Anglo-Saxon dooms or the laws
recorded in Ireland and Wales. Thus, the imposition of Irish and Welsh norms
on Scotland is highly speculative. Later John Cameron wrote a book on *Celtic
Law* in Scotland, but it also relied too much on analogy and was more interesting
than convincing.[7] Recently, however, Mr Sellar of the Scots Law Department
in the University of Edinburgh has demonstrated, with a wealth of convincing

---

[5] G.O. Sayles and H.G. Richardson, *The Governance of Medieval England from the Conquest to Magna
Carta* (Edinburgh, 1963), and G O. Sayles, *The Medieval Foundations of England* (1948), Chapter 27.
The shortcomings of *The Governance of Medieval England* are pointed out by J. Le Patourel in his
review in *English Historical Review*, LXXX (1965), 115–20. For a summary of revisions of Stubbs
and earlier historians see E. Miller, *The Origins of Parliament* (Historical Association Pamphlet, 1960);
and for a just assessment of Stubbs and his achievements see J.G. Edwards, *William Stubbs* (Historical
Association Pamphlet, 1952).

[6] J. Mackinnon, assisted by J.A.R. Mackinnon, *The Constitutional History of Scotland from Early
Times to the Reformation* (Edinburgh, 1937).

[7] J. Cameron, *Celtic Law: The 'Senchus Mór' and 'The Book of Aicill', and the Traces of an Early
Gaelic System of Law in Scotland* (Edinburgh, 1937). Early Gaelic society in Scotland is now best
studied in the writings of J. Bannerman, notably his *Studies in the History of Dalriada* (Edinburgh,
1974); 'The Scots of Dalriada', in *Who Are the Scots?*, ed. G. Menzies (1971); and 'The King's Poet
and the Inauguration of Alexander III', *Scottish Historical Review*, LXVIII (1989), 120–49.

detail, the debt owed by Scots Law to the Gaelic tradition of Scotland.[8] His findings, however, are not on par with the continuing influence of Anglo-Saxon traditions in England which John Jolliffe so memorably summed up as 'the flow of the broad stream of English custom across the line of the Norman Conquest and into the Middle Ages'.[9]

The salient point here is that recent research into Scottish constitutional history does not, as so disastrously happened in the past, simply mean the foisting of English conclusions onto Scottish questions. Even where direct borrowing can be shown to have taken place, as perhaps in James I's efforts in 1427–8 to widen representation in Parliament, such borrowing was bedded down in a native tradition of which it soon became an integral part. Thus, for example, the freeholder who figures in Scottish county elections from 1587 onwards was not on all fours with the English freeholder.[10] This is so because tenures in England developed in a very different way from tenures in Scotland. There was no Scottish equivalent to the Statute of *Quia Emptores* of 1290 which ended subinfeudation in England and in time led to the concept of freehold as absolute property. Instead feudal principles continued unabated in Scotland, and in particular the concepts of superiority (*dominium directum*) and of property (*dominium utile*) were retained. This became of great importance in eighteenth-century Scottish politics, for the county vote was held to be implicit in the superiority (i.e. tenure-in-capite, or holding directly from the Crown). Shortly after the Union of 1707 it came to be accepted that superiorities could be divided up to produce votes of the requisite valuation. Often such superiorities were naked (i.e. completely devoid of property), and those enrolled on such votes were known as fictitious voters or parchment barons.

In the new approach to the constitutional history of Scotland there is no vestige of chauvinism. The new approach simply aims to come to grips with the realities revealed by the evidence. In other words, it attempts to do what historians ought to do. It also works in the belief that Scottish institutions evolved their own peculiar identities and ways of working. That remains the case even where borrowings from England and the Continent can be clearly demonstrated.[11]

At the moment as far as the early constitutional history of Scotland is concerned we seem to be trying to break an old, fragmented and scarcely decipherable code. We sense that it contains the formulae needed to answer our questions; but much still remains obscure, and the full implications of the new discoveries that have been made still remain to be worked out. Some progress, however, has been made, and, above all, we have freed ourselves from the delusion that we can 'explain' matters by specious and often far-fetched analogies.

[8] D. Sellar, 'O'Donnell Lecture 1985. Celtic Law and Scots Law: Survival and Integration', *Scottish Studies*, XXIX (1989), 1–27.

[9] J.E.A. Jolliffe, *The Constitutional History of Medieval England: From the English Settlement to 1485* (2nd edn., 1947), p. 151.

[10] For fuller details see W. Ferguson, 'The Electoral System in the Scottish Counties before 1832', *Miscellany II* (Stair Society, Edinburgh, 1984), pp. 261–94.

[11] For an instance of this see G.W.S. Barrow, *The Kingdom of the Scots* (1973), pp. 121–3, with reference to the justiciar.

The view taken by Sir Robert Rait was radically different. He tended to measure everything by English standards, and seems, indeed, to have seen the whole history of Scotland and its institutions as a pre-ordained drift towards the Union of 1707 and 'the end o' an auld sang'. He even used Chancellor Seafield's quip on the winding up of the Scottish Parliament as the opening of the pamphlet he published in 1925. People are dazzled sometimes by the wonders of the age in which they live. Such was the case with Rait and Terry who shared the imperial vision of their time and saw manifest destiny at work in making Scotland part of the United Kingdom and a partner (albeit a junior partner) in the Empire on which the sun was never supposed to set. There was, of course, nothing evil or sinister in all this. Nonetheless, such an attitude wreaked havoc on any serious study of Scottish history. Indeed, to venture on a serious study of Scottish history was to invite ridicule.

Times change, and so do perceptions. The Empire has gone and the axioms of Rait, Terry and many others strike us today as misconceived. They were also, in a sense, ironical and perverse. Ironical, because it was precisely the institutions of pre-Union Scotland, save only the Parliament, which were preserved by the Treaty and Acts of Union of 1707. And in the church, law and education they were preserved because they could not be assimilated to their English counterparts. The point here is not whether English or Scottish practice was superior. It is just that they were different and could not be integrated into one British model without unacceptable upheavals and opposition. The Union negotiators wisely recognised the impasse and agreed that specifically Scottish institutions should stand, subject only to such legislation as was needed later to keep them in good repair. Such reforms, however, could only rationally be introduced by measures that made sense in terms of Scots law and administration. Problems could, and did, arise if care were not taken to secure this end, problems that required either remedial legislation or wilful distortion of existing legislation. The latter was not the happiest of outcomes but did occur from time to time. The most mischievous example of this was the scrappy Patronage Act of 1712, which re-introduced lay patronage in the Church of Scotland and which ushered in over two centuries of bitter ecclesiastical strife. The strife and its accompanying animosity, which played a major role in nineteenth-century Scottish politics, continued even after the inadequate Patronage Act of 1712 was finally repealed in 1874. Another prominent example of a measure that was out of step with Scots law and caused undesirable consequences as a result was the Reform Act (Scotland) of 1832.[12]

It must not be forgotten, too, that while the Scottish and English Parliaments united in 1707 to form the British Parliament not every vestige of the work of the Scottish Parliament disappeared. That was very far from being the case, and even today pre-Union Scottish statutes are still sometimes enforced by the courts. The relevant point to note here, however, is that with regard to Scotland the Treaty of Union said nothing about franchises or election procedures. The treaty

---

[12] W. Ferguson, 'The Reform Act (Scotland) of 1832: Intention and Effect', *Scottish Historical Review*, XLV (1966), 105–14.

laid down Scotland's representation in the British Parliament (45 seats in the House of Commons and 16 elected peers in the House of Lords), but the franchises and the legal machinery of elections remained as they had already been defined by the law and custom of Scotland. These differed completely from English practice, and the differences endured right up to the Reform Act of 1832, and, indeed, vestigially thereafter.

Why should this have been so? Would it not have been reasonable to expect one Parliament and one electoral system? The problem really harks back to the earliest history of Parliament in Scotland. Originally all tenants-in-chief could be required to render suit to the King's Council from which at some indeterminate point in the thirteenth century Parliament emerged.[13] Certainly by the end of the thirteenth century an off-shoot of the Council known as Parliament was an established fact though its composition was not then standardised. Gradually representation widened to include the royal burghs and some of the larger episcopal burghs, and gradually, too, a theory of representation defined by law arose. A step forward here was the Parliament of Cambuskenneth in 1326 which came to be regarded in the same light as Edward I's Model Parliament of 1295 in England. But both Scottish and English Parliaments were then inchoate and ripe for development, and in their development they diverged. A major difference was that unlike the English Parliament the Scottish Parliament remained uni-cameral. With no division into an upper and a lower House it came to be regarded as a Parliament of estates, and was, indeed, frequently referred to as 'the estates'. Round this development there arose a theory that Parliament represented the three estates of the realm. The first estate represented the church; the second estate was that of the nobility or, more correctly, the lay tenants-in-chief; and the third estate represented the burghs. This concept of estates, their precise categorisation and even precise number, was to give rise to problems in the late sixteenth and the seventeenth centuries.

But first another matter needs to be touched upon—namely the law that the Parliament served both as legislature and high court. Early medieval law in Scotland was a blend of native customary law and feudal principles drawn from Anglo-Norman sources. Even as early as the thirteenth century Matthew Paris stated that Scotland, like other European countries, had its own customary laws.[14] Much of this would be, in Fritz Kern's famous phrase, 'the good, old law, unenacted and unwritten'.[15] But use was also made of brieves which originated in England, and there was thus in the thirteenth century no great gulf between the two systems of common law that were developing. Had Edward I's designs succeeded, under the Ordinance for the Government of Scotland of 1305 (whereby the kingdom of Scotland was deemed not to exist and was to become, like Ireland,

[13] Rait, *Parliaments*, Introduction; also A.A.M. Duncan, *Scotland: The Making of the Kingdom* (Edinburgh, 1975), pp. 609–10; G.W.S. Barrow, *Kingship and Unity: Scotland 1000–1306* (1981), pp. 126–9; R. Nicholson, *Scotland: The Later Middle Ages* (Edinburgh, 1974), pp. 19–21; and A. Grant, *Scotland 1306–1469* (1984).

[14] H.L. MacQueen, *Common Law and Feudal Society in Medieval Scotland* (Edinburgh, 1993), p. 1, citing M. Paris, *Chronica Majora*, VI, p. 295.

[15] F. Kern, *Kingship and Law in the Middle Ages*, tr. S.B. Chrimes (Oxford, 1939), pp. 156ff.

a lordship held by the English Crown), 'the laws of the Brets and Scots' would have been swept aside, and through the appeal procedures laid down in the ordinance there would have been uniformity of law on the English model.[16] It was not to be, however, and there has been considerable confusion about what actually happened. Some historians believed that after its promising early start the common law of Scotland foundered owing to the upheavals caused by the Wars of Independence and the rise of private heritable jurisdictions. But recent work, notably by David Sellar and Hector MacQueen, have argued that this was a misreading of the situation and that a decentralised court system continued to use the earlier brieves relating to land. Thus, the brieves of right, mortancestry and novel dissasine (Anglicé disseisin) continued in use well into the fifteenth century. They were not, however, as in England, confined to the King's court, but were used in Scotland to enforce actions in the local courts.

It is against this background of hazy and much controverted legal procedures that Alan Borthwick's article must be judged. He shows that Parliament was not, as has been argued by Professor MacQueen, excluded from hearing fee and heritage cases. In spite of paucity of evidence for fifteenth-century practice, he convincingly demonstrates that, in the case of the long-running dispute about trading privileges between the royal burghs of Montrose and Dundee, the judicial competence of Parliament was pre-eminent, for Parliament was, as Dr Borthwick states, the place 'at which and in which justice must be done to anyone with a complaint'. That is rather a sweeping statement, but it does embody a certain truth. To stick to the case at issue, in one phase of this Homeric legal encounter, Montrose argued that, since its case involved fee and heritage, it should be heard by Parliament. In another dispute, against Forfar this time, Dundee took the same view, and averred that the case should be determined before 'the supreme court of the kingdom, that is Parliament'.

Dr Borthwick throughout uses the term 'The Three Estates' without, quite properly given the period with which he deals, troubling to define the term. Later developments confused the issue, and Dr Goodare's article studies the complicated history of the estates of the realm in Scotland and seeks to determine their exact nature and number at any given time, a theme that is also touched upon by Dr Scally. Dr Goodare's sparkling paper might have taken as its title that of the Abbé Siéyès's celebrated pamphlet which had such devastating effects in France in 1789—*Qu'est ce que le tiers état?* In Scotland the traditional three estates later became four, that is, if the freeholders or barons, who were added to the representative system after 1587, are to be regarded as distinct from the estate of the nobles or lords of Parliament who had emerged in the fifteenth century. In the political sense the barons became a significant force in seventeenth-century Scottish parliamentary politics. The Scottish baron, however, differed in essence from his English namesake. In Scotland the term baron was used to describe a small tenant-in-chief of the Crown beneath the rank of lord of Parliament. So, in strict

---

[16] For the text of the Ordinance of 1305 see *Anglo-Scottish Relations 1174–1328. Some Selected Documents*, ed. E.L.G. Stones (Oxford, 1965), pp. 241–59.

theory, the barons, like the lords of Parliament, were represented because of their tenure-in-capite of lands of the requisite valuation held of the Crown.[17] Because of their chronic failure to appear in Parliament efforts were frequently made in the fifteenth century to enforce their attendance. James I tackled this problem and sought to solve it by getting the 40s. freeholders [of Old Extent] in each county to vote for commissioners to represent them. All efforts proved abortive; the flooding of the Reformation Parliament of 1560 by freeholders provoked a crisis, but the matter was not resolved until 1587.[18]

Dr Goodare's article is the most thorough examination to date of the thorny subject of the estates. The term 'Tres Communitates', he informs us, was first recorded in Scotland in 1357. Inveterate borrowers that they were, the Scots seem to have lifted this term from France where it was used to describe the French estates general in 1356. As Dr Goodare notes, the concept of the Three Estates was immortalised by Sir David Lindsay in his splendid pageant-cum-play 'Ane Satyre of the Thrie Estaitis', produced in 1540,[19] and in spite of numerical problems after 1587 'Three Estates' remained the traditional expression. But, argues Dr Goodare, after 1587 there were really four estates—bishops, nobles, burgesses and Commissioners of the Shires. The deposition of the bishops in 1638 and their exclusion from Parliament by the Covenanters preserved the idea of three estates. Thus, it was held that the Parliament of 1640 consisting of nobles, burgesses and barons formed a legally constituted Parliament. But by then, Dr Goodare concludes, the estates were no longer organic communities but constitutional abstractions. He ends by pursuing them right up until 1707. His article, which is thoroughly researched and persuasively written, disposes of many misconceptions, and it gives a clearer picture of the Scottish Parliament in one of its most important phases of development.

Other aspects of the turbulent but creative seventeenth century are considered by Dr Scally. His paper, however, deals more in political analysis rather than in constitutional niceties. An interesting analysis of shifting political allegiances in an age of great turmoil, it studies the growth of factions rather than the growth of ideologies. It argues that Scottish parliamentary politics in the reign of Charles I remained hierarchical and not revolutionary in the social sense. He conducts an illuminating argument, but it seems to me that a close look at the National Covenant of 1638 might have shown the importance of ideas in this imbroglio. After all, the National Covenant demanded not just a free Kirk but also a free Parliament. The ideas that were to cause such a ferment later obviously helped to produce the Covenant of 1638, and throughout this period the works of George Buchanan were extremely influential.

The problem of parliamentary politics and the rise of party intensified and is the subject of Dr Hayton's paper. In surveying early post-Union elections in Scotland he has to take stock of a multiplicity of interacting factors: the pull of Westminster; the virtual collapse of the groups that had operated in the last

[17] See Ferguson, 'Electoral System', pp. 263–71.
[18] *Ibid.*, pp. 263–4.
[19] *The Poetical Works of Sir David Lyndsay*, ed. D. Laing (3 vols., Edinburgh, 1879), II, 8–222.

Scottish Parliament; the scramble for seats in Parliament consequent on the reduction of the number of constituencies after 1707; the rise of a spoils system; early attempts at 'management'; the continuing religious strife between Presbyterians and Episcopalians; Jacobitism and the claims of legitimism; defence of Revolution principles; and not least the steady growth of electoral malpractice as the Union, unwittingly no doubt, removed the legal restraints that had hitherto applied. The politics of influence virtually dictated the growth of 'interests', and the result was a steady decline of ideological commitments. Nonetheless, Dr Hayton is able to detect traces of party politics in early eighteenth-century Scotland; but, as he is bound to conclude, the upheavals following the death of Queen Anne led to the decline of party politics, which survived largely in the rhetoric of political abuse. Dr Hayton thinks that Jacobitism if properly interpreted might qualify that verdict; but it seems to me extremely doubtful if even the closest examination of Jacobitism can do much to overturn it.

The politics of interest is central to Dr David Brown's article, which analyses the general election of 1774. The key to the situation here was the rise and fall of management. Management had become a fine art under Archibald, third Duke of Argyll, who used as his right hand man in rigging the Scottish constituencies a judge, Lord Justice Clerk Milton (Andrew Fletcher of Milton).[20] There was hardly a vestige of party politics in Scotland by the end of Argyll's career. He had the constituencies pretty well secured in support of government. The struggle accordingly was between rival interests vying with each other for the ear of the manager and for the favour of government. On Argyll's death in 1761 the Earl of Bute's brother, James Stuart Mackenzie, acted as political manager, but he lacked Argyll's expertise and was dropped in 1765. Thereafter there was no recognised manager for Scotland, and the way was open for frenzied strife between rival interests which mass created nominal votes. Unfortunately, as one or two of the contributors to this volume have remarked, comparatively little work has been done on Scottish electoral politics in the eighteenth century, though a great deal of source material exists.

To some extent this neglect is attributable to the preoccupying interest with economic and social history that has obtained over the past 30 years or so. The multifaceted nature of history tended to be ignored by the social scientific historians. For most of them politics was just an unprofitable irrelevance. An exception here was Rosalind Mitchison, who as well as being a distinguished social historian, had a wider vision. In her excellent biography of Sir John Sinclair of Ulbster she considered her subject in all his many aspects, including his political activities.[21] But T.C. Smout, in his widely read *History of the Scottish People*, dismissed post-Union political life in Scotland in the eighteenth century with the scornful comment that 'After the Union of 1707, Scottish Parliamentary life as reflected in the careers of Scottish members at Westminster became for a long time so moribund as to be scarcely relevant any longer to a general history of

---

[20] A. Murdoch, *The People Above: Politics and Administration in Mid-Eighteenth Century Scotland* (Edinburgh, 1980); and J.S. Shaw, *The Management of Scottish Society, 1707–1764* (Edinburgh, 1983).

[21] R. Mitchison, *Agricultural Sir John; the Life of Sir John Sinclair of Ulbster, 1754–1835* (1962).

Scottish society.'[22] Too many seem to have too readily accepted this brusque and unsupported assertion. How unsound this has been even from the standpoint of Scottish social history appears from Ronald Sunter's book on *Patronage and Politics*, which shows that the politics of interests afford many revealing insights into the social and economic history of eighteenth-century Scotland.[23]

The most extraordinary feature of the general election of 1774 in Scotland was the fierceness of the contests that raged, a phenomenon also observable in England. That was caused to some extent, as Dr Brown shows, by the snap nature of the election, which by threatening to ruin long term plans led to frantic and desperate electioneering. But in Scotland it was also owing to the absence of a manager who might by expert use of influence have averted some of the contests. Indeed, the general election of 1774 was to pave the way to a new era of management, for it saw the debut of Henry Dundas. His alliance with the Duke of Buccleuch enabled Dundas by stages after 1774 to build up the most powerful interest in his country, which, in fact, laid the basis for the Tory Party in Scotland. Dr Brown's thorough study reveals why the general election of 1774 was so important. In these elections corruption and electoral malpractice increased and sank to new depths. These unhealthy features were to characterise the later 'Dundas Despotism'. But they also shocked public opinion and led to demands for reform. Henry Dundas may have been 'absolute dictator of Scotland' in his heyday, as Henry Cockburn stated,[24] but all the same his position was being undermined by demands for reform. True, Dundas's system outlived him by 21 years, but in spite of ferocious efforts to stamp out demands for electoral reform the Reform Act of 1832 introduced a new era in Scottish politics. A point of great significance here emerges. It was the growing demand for constitutional reform in both England and Scotland which led gradually to the fusion of parties in the two countries. Rather than Scottish politicians being absorbed into English party structures in the early post-Union period, as has been alleged, it was really in the early nineteenth century that this important trend became evident, and it has steadily grown from that period onwards. This political convergence, and the difficulties that impeded it, have been thoroughly dealt with in Dr Hutchison's *Political History of Scotland*.[25]

The Reform Act (Scotland) of 1832 was certainly something of a watershed, but exactly in what way has been variously assessed. It certainly had a more powerful effect on political life in Scotland than its counterpart had in England and Wales. Dr Hutchison gives an apt quotation from one of Sir Robert Peel's advisers in 1835: 'In short, in Scotland, the Reform Bill has produced a more permanent change than anywhere else, amounting to a complete revolution in the Government.'[26] As I pointed out some time ago this was the case even though the act was seriously flawed, indeed, in some ways because it was seriously

[22] T.C. Smout, *A History of the Scottish People* (1969), pp. 217–18.
[23] R.M. Sunter, *Patronage and Politics in Scotland 1707–1832* (Edinburgh, 1986).
[24] H. Cockburn, *Memorials of His Time* (Edinburgh, 1910), p. 79.
[25] I.G.C. Hutchison, *A Political History of Scotland, 1832–1924* (Edinburgh, 1986).
[26] *Ibid.*, p. 3.

flawed.[27] It was a botch that ran counter to the law of Scotland, and its defects allowed fictitious votes to be created within its lax terms. It effectively ended the malpractices of the old system but opened up a new era of corrupt electioneering. Recent work, notably by Dr Brash, has extended and strengthened this interpretation.[28] It can confidently be stated that the old traditional accounts whereby the Reform Act (Scotland) of 1832 was seen as the salve that cured the body politic of the pestilence of corruption and ushered in a period of political good health is no longer accepted, as it was, for instance, rather uncritically by Professor George Pryde.[29]

In the present volume Dr Brash gives the fruits of further research that he has carried out on the subject of the effects of the Reform Act in Scotland. Who, exactly, gained the vote in 1832? By painstaking analysis of the relevant source material he has determined the occupations of most of the new voters. In the areas he has studied he finds that they represented a good cross-section of the population. Their occupations, not surprisingly, varied according to the economies of different regions. The investigation has been very thorough, and the results are thought-provoking. But the political implications of Dr Brash's findings remain to be worked out, though a fair stab could be made at guessing them. The period after 1832 was one of intense political activity which, among many other things, reflected the great social changes that were taking place as a result of economic forces. An unsatisfactory electoral system further complicated matters.[30]

In conclusion, the following articles undoubtedly make valuable contributions to knowledge of Scottish, and indeed, of British history. They are all characterised by deep research into the sources, and each makes a substantial contribution to its chosen theme. They are also a pleasure to read, for, as well as being scholarly and ably argued, they are attractively presented. I have enjoyed reading them, have learnt much from them, and I feel sure that others will as well.

[27] Ferguson, 'The Reform Act (Scotland) of 1832'

[28] J.I. Brash, *Scottish Electoral Politics, 1832–54* (Scottish History Society, Edinburgh, 1974).

[29] G. Pryde, *A New History of Scotland from 1603 to the Present Day* (London and Edinburgh, 1962), p. 193ff.

[30] For a brief summary of these problems see W. Ferguson, *Scotland: 1689 to the Present* (paperback edn., Edinburgh, 1987), Chapter 10, pp. 291ff. They are dealt with in much greater detail in Hutchison, *Political History of Scotland 1832–1924*.

The Estates in the Scottish Parliament, 1286–1707

JULIAN GOODARE

University of Sheffield

> This King gart set ane plane Parliament,
> And for the Lords of his kinrik sent;
> And for the weilfair of his Realme and gyde
> The thrie Estaits concludit at that tyde.
> The King gart cal to his Palice al thrie
> The Estaits, ilkane in thair degrie.[1]

When Scots thought about the nature of their Parliament in the three and a half centuries before 1707, the first thing that was likely to occur to them was that it was a Parliament of estates. Immediately after this, the phrase 'three estates' would have sprung to mind, and the 'three estates' rightly find a place in all histories of Scotland.

But what *were* the 'three estates'? There were, at one time or another, various distinct groups in the Scottish Parliament: titled nobles of various ranks; clergymen (usually prelates); commissioners of burghs; commissioners of shires; and officers of state; not to mention the King himself or his Commissioner. How many of these were 'estates', and how was the number three arrived at (if, indeed, it was)? It is generally accepted that nobles and higher clergy formed two of the estates, but even this is not straightforward. What happened, for instance, when bishops were abolished in 1638? What happened when they were restored in 1661, and abolished again in 1689? The existence or non-existence of bishops at any given date is clear, but did it affect the number of estates?

And what of the third estate? Here, confusion reigns. The editor of the recently-published Scottish counterpart to the English *History of Parliament* writes of 'the personnel representing the royal burghs and the shires, the third estate'.[2] The idea that burghs and shires ever belonged to the same estate is quite wrong, though this author is not alone in believing it. It derives, no doubt, from the English Parliament, where borough and shire representatives sat together in the House of Commons—a House to which Scotland, with its single-chamber Parliament, had no counterpart. The idea of Parliament as a body of 'estates' requires attention.

---

[1] *The Thre Prestis of Peblis*, ed. T.D. Robb (Scottish Text Society, 1920), p. 7. This text dates from the 1480s. 'Kinrik' = kingdom.

[2] *The Parliaments of Scotland: Burgh and Shire Commissioners*, ed. M.D. Young (2 vols., Edinburgh, 1992–3), II, 805.

2

Parliaments emerged in Scotland in the mid-thirteenth century, at much the same time as in many other kingdoms of western Europe; the term 'Parliament' (*colloquium*) is first recorded in 1235.[3] These Parliaments did not consist of estates, but solely of lords, secular and ecclesiastical. Lordship was unitary, and the assembled lords made up the 'community of the realm'. This was a long-standing concept that took more concrete shape in the absence of an effective Scottish monarch for most of the period 1286–1306, memorably evoked by G.W.S. Barrow.[4] It was the 'community' that validated the appointment of the Guardians who ruled Scotland during the interregnums, the 'community' that suspended the authority of King John in 1295, and the 'community' that was present in Parliament.

Early evidence that subdivisions in the 'community' were relevant to Parliament comes on the death of Alexander III in 1286. The kingdom was left without a King, and 'the great men of Scotland elected guardians of the peace for the community, both bishops and magnates'.[5] The Guardians themselves consisted of two bishops, two earls and two barons; it is unlikely that they represented three recognised 'estates', but it was evidently accepted that a diversity of personnel could better command the loyalty of the community. The important Guardians of 1295 also included bishops, earls and barons in equal numbers, as, usually, did their successors until the restoration of the monarchy.[6] The main division in the community that we see here was a conventional twofold one; this was well established in medieval Scotland, encapsulated in the King's salutation in his charters, 'to all good men of his whole land, clerical and lay'.

In 1305, we find a formula which brings us closer to the estates. Edward I, having at last (as he thought) finally conquered Scotland, was advised by a Scot that its representation in English Parliaments should be 'two bishops, two abbots, two earls, two barons, and two for the "commune", one from this side of the sea [the firth of Forth] and one from the other side, who shall be elected by the "commune" of Scotland at their assembly'.[7] Here we have the familiar

---

[3] A.A.M. Duncan, 'The Early Parliaments of Scotland', *Scottish Historical Review*, XLV (1966), 36–58. This seminal article gives references to earlier works on the subject, and supersedes many of them. The best, indeed almost the only, general study of the Scottish Parliament, still of immense value, is R.S. Rait, *The Parliaments of Scotland* (Glasgow, 1924). For a European perspective see A.R. Myers, *Parliaments and Estates in Europe, to 1789* (1975). What follows on the origin of the Scottish estates cannot claim to be definitive, but it may serve to clarify the issues and suggest profitable lines of approach. I have benefited here from the generous help of Professors A.A.M. Duncan and G.W.S. Barrow, though they cannot be held responsible either for the interpretation offered or for any remaining errors.

[4] G.W.S. Barrow, *Robert Bruce and the Community of the Realm of Scotland* (3rd edn., Edinburgh, 1988). See also N.H. Reid, 'The Kingless Kingdom: The Scottish Guardianships of 1286–1306', *Scottish Historical Review*, LXI (1982), 105–29.

[5] '*Majores terrae Scociae elegerunt communitati tam de episcopis quam proceribus pacis custodes*'. *Chronicon de Lanercost*, ed. J. Stevenson (Bannatyne Club, 1839), p. 117.

[6] Barrow, *Robert Bruce*, Chapter 6. The main exception was the sole Guardianship of William Wallace in 1297–8.

[7] '*Deus evesques, deus abbees, deus countes, deus barons e deus pur la commune un de cea la mier e un autre de la, les queux serront esleuz par la commune d'Escoce a lour assemble*'. *Memoranda de Parliamento, 1305*, ed. F.W. Maitland (1893), no. 13. In Edward's subsequent ordinance, the community is given as '*communaulté*': *Anglo-Scottish Relations, 1174–1328*, ed. E.L.G. Stones (2nd edn., Oxford, 1970), p. 240.

prelates (now with abbots alongside bishops), earls and barons, but also a new dual meaning for 'commune': firstly, the non-noble 'commons', from whom there were to be two representatives alongside four prelates and four nobles; secondly, the entire 'community', whose assembly was to elect all ten representatives. The concept of 'commons' was to become significant. It may well be that when Robert I summoned 'earls, barons and other magnates and the community' or 'earls, barons and freeholders and aforesaid community',[8] he was regarding the 'community' as the non-noble remainder rather than as the embodiment of the political nation.[9]

We first hear of the vital formula 'three estates' (*tres communitates*) in Scotland in an assembly of 1357.[10] It followed a celebrated meeting of the French Estates-General in October 1356,[11] at a time when there was much coming and going between Scotland and its continental ally. The term was regularly used in connection with Parliament thereafter. However, we should not necessarily regard 1357 as a new departure. It does seem to have come at the beginning of a period of 'intensive government' caused by David II's return from captivity in England and by the concomitant need to finance his ransom,[12] but this was no sweeping reconstruction of the political community: the burghs, for instance, had already been in some Parliaments for at least a generation, as we shall see. The phrase 'three estates' must already have been a familiar one in 1357, and there was no attempt to explain it. It derived, of course, from the European idea of the 'three orders' of society, a topic illuminated by the work of Georges Duby. He has shown that the eleventh-century concept of a division of society into those who prayed, those who fought and those who worked was pervasive thereafter, although neither static nor all-embracing.[13]

---

[8] Duncan, 'Early Parliaments', p. 54.

[9] It is treated as the entire nation, however, in N.H. Reid, 'Crown and Community under Robert I', *Medieval Scotland: Crown, Lordship and Community*, eds. A. Grant and K.J. Stringer (Edinburgh, 1993). In 1341–2 we find a third idea, that the 'community' were lay freeholders of all ranks. Taxation was accounted for by the 'clergy', 'community' and 'burghs'. *Exchequer Rolls of Scotland*, ed. J. Stuart *et al.* (23 vols., Edinburgh, 1878–1908), I, 501.

[10] *Acts of the Parliaments of Scotland* [hereafter cited as *A.P.S.*], eds. T. Thomson and C. Innes (12 vols., Edinburgh, 1814–75), I, 491. This meeting was not initially a Parliament but a parallel body, a 'Council', though it became a Parliament. Here we might note the term 'General Council', which first occurs in 1368. This body differed from Parliament in minor ways: it was not a court of law, and could be summoned at short notice instead of requiring 40 days. In the sixteenth century the General Council was largely superseded by the Convention of Estates, which again approximated to a Parliament (it could, for instance, tax and legislate). Most of what is said here about Parliaments applies also to these bodies. See R.K. Hannay, 'On "Parliament" and "General Council" ', and 'General Council and Convention of Estates', in *The College of Justice: Essays by R.K. Hannay* (Stair Society, 1990).

[11] P.S. Lewis, *Later Medieval France* (1968), pp. 335–6.

[12] R. Nicholson, *Scotland: The Later Middle Ages* (Edinburgh, 1974), Chapter 7.

[13] G. Duby, *The Three Orders: Feudal Society Imagined*, trans. A. Goldhammer (1980). For cross-cultural comparisons and references to earlier examples of threefold division, see J. Batany, 'Des "Trois Fonctions" aux "Trois États"?', *Annales E.S.C.*, XVIII (1963), 933–8. Note also the worldwide cultural significance of the numbers three and seven, as early prime numbers; prime numbers were uncanny because of their indivisibility, appearing as units in their own right rather than as the products of arithmetical calculation. Five, though also a prime number, tended to acquire a mundane significance as half of ten: D.E. Smith, *History of Mathematics* (2 vols., 1925), II, 2.

All that was happening was that the concept was being applied to Parliament.

The idea of three estates did not wholly supersede the unitary concept—the 'community of the realm'. A writer of the 1390s thought that David II had acted in the 1360s 'with the consent of the community of his kingdom of Scotland'.[14] To the extent that the community was embodied in a singular 'Parliament' at all—and this remained a rather more common term than 'three estates' in the fifteenth century—it was still unified. Even then, we occasionally find a more concrete unitarian phrase like (in 1426) 'the whole kingdom of Scotland to be generally constituted in Parliament'.[15] Instead of a simple contest between unitarians and trinitarians, what seems to have happened is that there were two overlapping sets of *two-fold* divisions in the political community. In 1363, Parliament consisted of 'prelates and magnates of the kingdom'.[16] This division, into clergy and laity, was by now old-fashioned; it is identical to the 'bishops and magnates' of 1286. The other division, that into lords and commons, appears in a 1437 mention of 'all the lords of parliament, ecclesiastical and secular, and also the commissioners of burghs', underlining the burgesses' plebeian position.[17] When people could be divided either into clergy and laity, or into nobles and commons, the overwhelming attraction of the tripartite division into prelates, nobles and burgesses (commons) was that it reconciled these overlapping twofold divisions.

So far, we have seen the three estates as a collectivity. In the Scottish Parliament, which was always unicameral, it is essential to view them thus. But the estates also had their own individual identities, and without a strengthening of these sectional personalities, the shift from a unitary to a tripartite Parliament could not have occurred. The estates represented the distinctive corporate freedoms—or privileges—of sections of the feudal ruling class.[18] In the later middle ages, this class began to include a group—the burgesses—who were not really 'lords'; it was their advent on the scene that perpetuated the division into 'lords' and 'commons'. As traders, burgesses also required a different set of privileges from the landed classes. So it seems appropriate to begin with the Scottish burghs.

The burghs entered politics briefly in 1296 to ratify a Franco-Scottish treaty. Robert I, once he had won his kingdom, developed a close relationship with the burghs, and burgesses may have attended his Parliaments as early as 1312. Burgesses were certainly members of most known Parliaments between 1326 and 1357, because they were to be taxed. The Crown's heavy financial needs during the mid-fourteenth century made their attendance regular, and by 1366,

---

[14] '*Cum consensu comitatum regni sui Scotie*'. 'A Question About the Succession, 1364', ed. A.A.M. Duncan, in *Scottish History Society Miscellany*, XII (1996). *Comitatum* is probably a contemporary mis-transcription for *communitatum*.

[15] '*Totum regnum Scocie generaliter constituendum . . . in parliamento*'. *A.P.S.*, II, 12, c. 22.

[16] '*Prelatis et proceribus regni*'. *A.P.S.*, I. 492.

[17] *A.P.S.*, II, 23, c. 2.

[18] There was also the concept of freedom as *personal* or as *national* freedom; the terms freedom and privilege were not synonyms, however closely they were sometimes related. See G.W.S. Barrow, 'The Idea of Freedom', in his *Scotland and its Neighbours in the Middle Ages* (1992). M.L. Bush, *Noble Privilege* (New York, 1983), Chapter 1, distinguishes between privileges of subjects and rights of lords.

prelates, earls, barons, freeholders and burgesses were being 'summoned and called in due and accustomed manner'.[19]

Town-dwellers formed corporate bodies with defined rights. From the late thirteenth century they began to describe themselves as 'communities'. Their strength in self-government tended to grow. In the early fourteenth century, elected bailies, local magistrates responsible for the daily administration, replaced the provosts, who had been appointed by the Crown or overlord, in power; provosts became head bailies. At the same time, the payment of burgh revenues to the Crown became fixed by the granting of feu-ferme charters to the burghs: henceforth, instead of royal officials collecting tolls, the burgh government took responsibility for collection, paying a fixed annual sum to the Crown.[20]

To be 'estates' at all, the other estates also had to have a corporate identity. That of the church was well defined; if there was a difficulty, it was because it was so much a supra-national body. The national identity of Scottish churchmen was enhanced when, during the Wars of Independence, they had periodically to defy pro-English Popes. Bishops were more politically active than abbots, although the latter were also prelates attending Parliament. Since 1192 the Scottish bishops (who had no archbishop until 1472) had been recognised as a collectivity owing allegiance to the Pope directly, an arrangement that gave them probably as effective a corporate identity as an archbishop would have done.[21] The 'richtis and liberteis' of the church were ratified by many Parliaments.[22] It would be interesting to investigate whether the clergy's identity as an estate derived more from their sacerdotal status or from the position of prelates as tenants in chief of the Crown.[23]

As for the nobles, they found it hard to separate their identity from that of the realm as a whole. The treaty of Birgham (1290), by which the institutional identity of the kingdom was to be preserved after a marriage between the heirs to the Scottish and English thrones, concentrated on the rights of the barons, and has been described as a 'charter of baronial liberties'.[24] The Declaration of Arbroath (1320) was a letter to the Pope on Robert I's behalf by the 'barons and freeholders of the whole community of the realm of Scotland'; it was accompanied by separate letters from the King himself and from the Bishop of St Andrews.[25]

There was originally no titled group enjoying exclusively noble status; every politically-significant lay tenant in chief was a 'lord'. We do find, from at least 1326, quite frequent mentions of 'freeholders' (lesser lords) attending Parliament,

[19] Duncan, 'Early Parliaments', pp. 51–3; Barrow, *Robert Bruce*, pp. 299–302.

[20] E.L. Ewan, 'The Community of the Burgh in the Fourteenth Century', *The Scottish Medieval Town*, eds. M. Lynch, M. Spearman and G. Stell (Edinburgh, 1988), pp. 228–31; cf. E.L. Ewan, *Townlife in Fourteenth-Century Scotland* (Edinburgh, 1990), pp. 147–52.

[21] D.E.R. Watt, 'The Provincial Council of the Scottish Church, 1215–1472', Grant and Stringer (eds.), *Medieval Scotland*; cf. G.W.S. Barrow, 'The Clergy in the War of Independence', in his *The Kingdom of the Scots* (1973).

[22] Sir James Balfour of Pittendreich, *Practicks*, ed. P.G.B. McNeill (2 vols., Stair Society, 1962–3), I, 24–5, gives 22 statutes to this effect from 1328 to 1571.

[23] Rait, *Parliaments*, p. 175, argues for the latter.

[24] A.A.M. Duncan, *The Nation of Scots and the Declaration of Arbroath (1320)* (Historical Association pamphlet, 1970), p. 11. He points out that 'the liberties of other Scots were . . . protected by those of barons'.

[25] Barrow, *Robert Bruce*, p. 304.

but they did not achieve the status of an estate.[26] The gradual emergence in the early fifteenth century of a titled parliamentary peerage[27] underlined the fact that the lesser lords rarely came to Parliament. In 1428, James I promoted a statute enjoining the small barons and freeholders to elect commissioners to Parliament rather than attending personally. They were also to choose a 'common spekar of the parliament' to 'propone all and sindry nedis and causis pertening to the commonis'.[28] But this did not happen, probably because royal tax demands (the reason why James wanted an English-style 'commons') died away after the 1420s. Besides, the small barons did not regard themselves as 'commons'; their identity was more linked with the nobles, and they were unwilling (unlike in England) to be combined with the burgesses.[29]

How far did the concept of three estates represent social reality? Clearly, the categories of prelates, nobles and burgesses do not exhaust the possibilities of social categorisation by today's historians; but nor are they simply cloudy abstractions. They provided a meaningful description of the divisions of the Scottish governing class, and the rise and fall of the concept of three estates relates to the rise and fall of these divisions. In some countries, particularly France, the concept of three estates was pressed further. Creative writers and political theorists (two overlapping groups) developed subdivisions of the estates to categorise the whole people. It has been argued, primarily by Roland Mousnier, that such categorisations, with parallel status groups, are the most appropriate for pre-industrial Europe, but this idea should not be pressed too far.[30] Although they were both estates, burgesses were not really equal to nobles in medieval Scotland. Robert I, who did so much for the burghs, never used burgesses as charter witnesses, even in time of Parliament, even for charters to burghs.[31] Others were not included in the 'estates' at all: women, obviously; peasants, usually. The *Complaynt of Scotland* (1550), an elaborate political allegory based on a French model, discussed the three 'estates'—the orders of society, not the parliamentary estates. These were clergy, nobles and 'Laubir' (peasants); the latter, however, were told that they were not to participate in politics but 'suld be daly dantit

---

[26] Duncan, 'Early Parliaments', pp. 53–6.

[27] A. Grant, 'The Development of the Scottish Peerage', *Scottish Historical Review*, LVII (1978), 1–27.

[28] *A.P.S.*, II, 15, c. 2. This is often stated to be a reversal of a statute of 1426 (*A.P.S.*, II, 9, c. 8) which, it is said, aimed to compel universal attendance by the small barons. This may be so, but the 1426 statute says nothing about them specifically, and seems aimed mainly at limiting the practice of attendance by proxy. The questions of attendance by personal proxy and by elected commissioners are related, but not identical. 'Barons' is a common term because most lesser lords held a barony, the Scottish equivalent of an English manor.

[29] Cf. J. Wormald, 'Lords and Lairds in Fifteenth-Century Scotland: Nobles and Gentry?', *Gentry and Lesser Nobility in Late Medieval Europe*, ed. M. Jones (Gloucester, 1986).

[30] R. Mousnier, *Social Hierarchies: 1450 to the Present*, trans. P. Evans (1973). The book fails most obviously in its purpose of discrediting Marxist classifications, since most of the 'hierarchies' discussed fall within what a Marxist would regard as the ruling class. However, for our purpose—to understand divisions within Parliament—the discussion is still useful. Cf. W. Outhwaite, 'Social Thought and Social Science', *The New Cambridge Modern History*, XIII (Companion Volume), ed. P. Burke (Cambridge, 1979), 274–83; *Social Orders and Social Classes in Europe since 1500*, ed. M. Bush (1992).

[31] *Regesta Regum Scottorum* (8 vols. to date, Edinburgh, 1960–), V, ed. A.A.M. Duncan, 116.

and haldin in subjectione, be cause that your hartis is ful of maleis, ignorance, variance and inconstance'.[32]

3

By the time of the Reformation, the three estates had long been entrenched as the constituent parts of Parliament, and had gained literary immortality in Sir David Lindsay's 'Satyre of the Thrie Estaitis' (1540).[33] But change was at hand. John Knox conceptualised the body politic without much reference to the three estates, and even envisaged a role for the common people. In 1558 he appealed to 'the quene regent, estates, and nobilitie, as . . . the chiefe heades (for this present) of the realme', and, separately, to 'the communalitie and bodie of the same'.[34] So there was a world beyond the traditional estates. The common people remained excluded; but if the fourteenth century saw an expansion of the political nation to include burgesses, the sixteenth century took the process further, with lairds being differentiated from the nobles and acquiring independent representation.

The Reformation Parliament of 1560, dominated by a party of insurgent lords who had just seized power, recognised this new world. It enacted a confession of faith which began by greeting it: 'The estaitis of Scotland, with the inhabitantis of the samyn professing Christ Jesus his holy evangell, to their naturall cuntrey men and to all utheris realmes and natiounis professing the samyn . . .'[35] Membership of the party of revolution was avowedly not limited to 'the estaitis'. But despite the unprecedented presence in Parliament of just over a hundred Protestant lairds, there were still 'thre estatis of parliament', constituted in the traditional way.[36]

As yet, it was unclear how the new class would be incorporated in the body politic. In 1567 Queen Mary was deposed in a palace coup, sparking off a civil war between a more radical 'King's party' and a 'Queen's party' who refused to accept the deposition. The outstanding ideologue of the King's party, moderator of the General Assembly of July 1567, and from 1570 tutor to the young James VI, was George Buchanan. His tract, *De Jure Regni Apud Scotos*, written in 1567 or 1568 to justify the proceedings of the King's party, became an internationally-known text on resistance theory. Since resistance was often held to be legitimate if sanctioned by the estates, we need to consider Buchanan's views carefully.[37] What he wrote on this was:[38]

[32] *The Complaynt of Scotland*, ed. A.M. Stewart (Scottish Text Society, 1979), p. 110.

[33] Sir David Lindsay, 'Ane Satyre of the Thrie Estaitis', in his *Works*, ed. D. Hamer (4 vols., Scottish Text Society, 1931–6), II.

[34] John Knox, *A Letter Addressed to the Communalty of Scotland*, in his *Works*, ed. D. Laing (6 vols., Edinburgh, 1895), IV, 523.

[35] *A.P.S.*, II, 526, c. 1.

[36] *A.P.S.*, II, 535, c. 3.

[37] Calvin had the 'three estates' legitimising resistance to a tyrant; indeed they were *required* to act. But action by the people, unsanctioned by their authority, was condemned. Jean Calvin, *Institutes of the Christian Religion*, ed. J.T. McNeill (2 vols., 1960), II, 1518–19 (para 4.XX.31).

[38] George Buchanan, *De Jure Regni Apud Scotos, Dialogus* (Edinburgh, 1579), p. 32. My translation is a modified version of that by D.H. McNeill in *The Art and Science of Government Among the Scots* (Edinburgh, 1964), p. 41.

I would give the people the right to prescribe the limits of the authority which they have vested in him [i.e. the King], and I would ask that he, as king, should abide by these limits. And I would not have these laws applied by force, as you understand it, but I think that what affects the joint safety of all should be decided by an open general council acting with the king. . . .

I have never thought that a matter like this should be left in the hands of the common people. Roughly according to our custom, selected people from all estates should meet with the king in council. Then when they have agreed on a measure, it should be referred to the judgement of the people.

This call for referendums on legislation sounds like subversive stuff, and we are not surprised to read it from the pen of one of the great European 'monarchomachs'. What is more surprising is that we have recently been told by Roger Mason that Buchanan was merely describing the traditional practice of Parliament, by which legislation was formulated by the Lords of the Articles (a sub-committee of Parliament) and ratified by the full Parliament—the latter process constituting the 'judgement of the people'. However, I believe that the older and more straightforward view—that the 'judgement of the people' amounted to a referendum among the wider political classes—is correct.[39] Buchanan was

[39] Dr Mason's argument has two strands. Firstly, Buchanan used the phrase 'roughly according to our custom' (*prope ad consuetudinem nostram*), and thus could not have been advocating referendums or other such radical innovations. Then, the 'people' (*populus*) to whom reference were to be made were distinguished from the 'common people' (*universus populus*): 'It seems most likely that this distinction corresponds to one between the people and the political nation—in terms of sixteenth century Scotland between the mass of the peasantry and a relatively small but extremely powerful nobility': R.A. Mason, '*Rex Stoicus*: George Buchanan, James VI and the Scottish Polity', *New Perspectives on the Politics and Culture of Early Modern Scotland*, eds. J. Dwyer, R.A. Mason and A. Murdoch (Edinburgh, [1982]), pp. 19–20. Although this article is essential reading on sixteenth-century Scottish political thought, this particular argument is more ingenious than convincing. The phrase 'roughly according to our custom' relates to the way in which the estates 'meet' or 'assemble' together with the king (*ad regem . . . coirent*) (an expression, incidentally, more likely to refer to the physical coming-together of the Members of Parliament than to the *election* of the Lords of the Articles from among their number), and need not be applied also to the next sentence about submission to the people. Here, a distinction between 'people' and 'common people' was certainly implied. But few in sixteenth-century Scotland, certainly not Buchanan, would have written about the *nobility*, however powerful, as the 'people'. The *three estates* could have been the 'people' to some; but not to Buchanan. We have seen that the changes of regime of 1560 and 1567, which Buchanan was writing to justify, had brought new men into the corridors of power, previously frequented only by the traditional estates. The 'people' surely included the lairds and wider propertied classes who had supported the revolution of 1560 but who had not hitherto been represented in Parliament. Had Buchanan merely been endorsing the restricted traditional constitution (and thus, be it noted, disenfranchising these supporters of his party), his subsequent passage (*De Jure Regni*, pp. 32–3), in which he argued eloquently that the 'people' could and should be entrusted with the responsibility of political decision-making, would have been inexplicable.

All this proves that Dr Mason is unlikely to be right; what proves him wrong is that Buchanan has the 'selected people from all estates' (*ex omnibus ordinibus selecti*)—which Dr Mason takes to mean the Lords of the Articles, and I to mean Parliament—assembling to 'meet with the King in Council' (*ad regem in consilium coirent*). Counselling the King, or acting as his Council, was *not* a function of the Lords of the Articles, whose role, as a sub-committee, was purely to prepare a report for Parliament; but it was, of course, the central function of Parliament itself. James VI sometimes attended the deliberations of the committee in the 1590s, and even claimed a vote, but he had no formal role and was not the focus of the committee. See Rait, *Parliaments*, p. 371. There is no mention of any earlier monarch doing such a thing, and I know of no evidence for Dr Mason's

Notice to Subscribers

Please note that this is a
special issue of
Parliamentary History.

The issue is
Volume 15, part 1.

willing to continue with the three estates, and did not envisage a hundred lairds being added to Parliament on a permanent basis; but this was only because he proposed to subject the estates to regular scrutiny from the political nation. It would be interesting to know whether this programme for periodic referendums was ever put forward as a concrete legislative proposal. But in the event the widening of political participation was to be accomplished by other means.

Even as Buchanan wrote, these means were being created. A commission framing legislation for Parliament in December 1567 approved a proposal that 'of law and reason the baronis of this realme aucht to haif voit in parliament as ane part of the nobilitie and for saulftie of nowmer'; the barons were to elect representatives.[40] No legislation emerged on this. However, the lairds sustained their claim to attend in September 1571 and November 1572, in Conventions of Estates that elected new Regents. In the list of Members of Parliament they were placed in a separate category at the end, with the note 'The remainder claimed the favour of attendance'. But they did not just attend; they voted, all 81 and more of them. The election of the Regent was recorded as 'be pluralitie of voces of the saidis estattis *and uthers* abouewrittin'.[41] This continues the usage of 1560, whereby the lairds were included in decision-making, but not recognised as part of the 'estattis'.

Parliamentary taxation at this time was apportioned by estates: half on holders of benefices, a third on nobles and secular freeholders, and a sixth on royal burghs. From the 1580s onwards, there was a great deal more taxation; this gave the institutional identities of the estates a sharper focus.[42] The growth of regular taxation was also linked with the lairds' winning of their place in Parliament. As lay freeholders, they had always been liable for taxation on the same basis as nobles, but their growing independence from the magnates meant that they had to be called to Parliament directly in order to secure their consent. The burgesses had been given a voice two centuries before for a similar reason. But the lairds were keen to come: they even paid for their place in Parliament with a heavy tax on themselves. The act of 1587 creating a system of elected shire commissioners mentioned 'how necessar it is to his hienes and his estaittis to be trewly informit of the nedis and caussis pertening to his loving subjectis in all estaittis, speciallie the commonis of the realme'.[43] The lairds had become separate from the nobles.

The only lairds to gain a voice were those holding their lands in freehold from

---

[39] *(contd.)* belief that the committee met 'in closed session with the king'. Many members of the Articles were, in practice, Privy Councillors wearing different hats; but that they *were* wearing different hats is indisputable. This conclusion accords with the views of J.H. Burns, 'The Political Ideas of George Buchanan', *Scottish Historical Review*, XXX (1951), 60–8, where a broader discussion of these matters may be found.

[40] *A.P.S.*, III, 40. Some writers have erroneously treated this proposal as a statute: Rait, *Parliaments*, p. 203; C.S. Terry, *The Scottish Parliament: Its Constitution and Procedure, 1603–1707* (Glasgow, 1905), p. 24.

[41] *A.P.S.*, II, 65, 77. Italics added. For the full attendance list, see *Calendar of the State Papers Relating to Scotland and Mary Queen of Scots* [hereafter cited as *C.S.P. Scot.*], ed. J. Bain *et al.* (13 vols., Edinburgh, 1898–1969), IV, 433, 434.

[42] J. Goodare, 'Parliamentary Taxation in Scotland, 1560–1603', *Scottish Historical Review*, LXVIII (1989), 23–52.

[43] *A.P.S.*, III, 509, c. 120.

the Crown.[44] There were some lairds, however, with other, newer, species of property. Significant here were feuars: heritable proprietors who were technically vassals of others, particularly benefice-holders, since the 'feuing' of benefices was the means whereby the property of the Scottish church passed into lay hands. There were also wadsetters (moneylenders in temporary possession of land held as security) and tacksmen of teinds (anglice, impropriators of tithes). None of these were, as yet, represented. The 1587 act, passed to modernise the body politic, did so in a way that was already becoming old-fashioned.

As for the other estates: the burghs were maintaining their corporate identity, though under pressure from Crown interference.[45] It was the institutional identity of the church that was most in flux at this time. The General Assembly of the church developed as a new central organ, consisting mainly of ministers but with some burgesses and lairds.[46] The Assembly was not itself an estate: it even divided into three estate-like groups in 1588—lairds, burgesses and ministers—to discuss the Spanish invasion threat.[47] Meanwhile, the bishops were declining drastically. By 1592 they had lost virtually all ecclesiastical functions, and few even titular bishops existed. The clerical estate in Parliament had virtually to be rebuilt from scratch, a task to which James VI devoted over a decade from 1596 onwards, in the teeth of vigorous Presbyterian resistance.[48] In the process, the clerical estate began to be spoken of as the prospective 'third estate in the kingdome', although they had always been the first estate before the Reformation.[49]

4

With the formal admission of shire commissioners, how many estates were there? The obvious answer is four. However, it is sometimes argued that three estates continued after 1587, the lairds becoming a separate estate only in 1640. The argument is that lairds and nobles, both lay tenants in chief of the Crown, were technically one estate, the 'barons'. Only after the covenanting revolution abolished bishops were the nobles and lairds separated, to allow 'three estates' to be preserved.[50] This account has several points to recommend it. It seems to explain why we hear so little about 'four estates' between 1587 and 1638, the date of the abolition of bishops by the revolutionary Glasgow Assembly. It also harmonises with some contemporary explanations of the constitution. I shall deal later with

---

[44] They were often referred to as 'small barons', although there was no requirement for them to hold a barony. They merely had to possess, in chief from the Crown, land valued at 40 shillings of old extent (a traditional valuation).

[45] M. Lynch, 'The Crown and the Burghs, 1500–1625', *The Early Modern Town in Scotland*, ed. M. Lynch (1987).

[46] D. Shaw, *The General Assemblies of the Church of Scotland, 1560–1600* (Edinburgh, 1964), Chapters 10–11 and *passim*.

[47] *Acts and Proceedings of the General Assemblies of the Kirk of Scotland*, ed. T. Thomson (3 vols., Bannatyne Club, 1839–45), II, 704. I am grateful to Dr Alan MacDonald for this point.

[48] D.G. Mullan, *Episcopacy in Scotland, 1560–1638* (Edinburgh, 1986).

[49] John Row, *History of the Kirk of Scotland*, ed. D. Laing (Wodrow Society, 1842), p. 187; cf. *A.P.S.*, II, 603, c. 9.

[50] For a sensitive exposition of this case, see M. Lynch, *Scotland: A New History* (2nd edn., 1992), pp. 252–3.

what happened in 1640; here we need to consider the evidence for the period 1587–1638.

Our first witness is James VI. He ought to have known how many estates he had; and his account was straightforward. 'The whole subjectes of our country (by the auncient and foundamental policie of our kingdome) are devided into three estates'. The first two were the church and the nobility. 'The third and last estate . . . is our burghes (for the small barrones are but an inferiour part of the nobilitie and of their estate)'.[51] The statute of 1606 restoring the lands of the bishops, an act close to the King's heart, spoke of the 'ancient and fundamentall policie consisting in the mantenance of the thrie estaittis of parliament', which the renovation of the bishops would guarantee.[52] There are various sources which mention 'three estates' in passing.[53]

Taxation was one area where the number of the estates was always three. No division into greater and lesser nobles was recognised; all secular freeholders were assessed alike. Nor, indeed, was there any distinction in assessment between prelates (the clerical estate) and holders of lesser benefices.[54] There was, however, the difference that lairds who were taxed were also (except the very smallest) represented in Parliament, whereas benefice-holders below the rank of bishop or abbot were taxed without representation. An additional complication was that in the 1590s and 1600s most holders of monasteries received titles as secular nobles, but continued to be taxed (at a higher rate) with the benefice-holders. The 'estates' were becoming entangled with one another.

The evidence for the continuation of three estates after 1587 seems strong. But in fact it cannot be accepted as it stands. Within Parliament the straightforward definition of an estate was a group with its own representatives on committees. From the first Parliament to include shire commissioners onwards, they regularly had their own representatives on parliamentary committees, including the most important committee of all—the Lords of the Articles.[55] In 1587 it had been

---

[51] King James VI, *Basilicon Doron*, ed. J. Craigie (2 vols., Scottish Text Society, 1944–50), I, 73, 80, 89.

[52] *A.P.S.*, IV, 282, c. 2.

[53] James had mentioned in a proclamation of 1605 that he intended to take the advice of his 'thrie estaittis': *Register of the Privy Council of Scotland* [hereafter cited as R.P.C.S.], eds. J.H. Burton *et al.* (38 vols., Edinburgh, 1877–1970), VII, 126. For another such proclamation, in 1606, referring to the 'soverane and high court of parliament, consisting of 3 estaites', see *ibid.*, p. 224. It seems as though the restoration of bishops made the King particularly sensitive to the issue at this time. In 1594, an act of a rather small Convention of Estates was said to be as authoritative as if it had been passed by the three estates: R.P.C.S., V, 167. There is passing mention of the Parliament of 1594 as the 'thre estaits': B.L., Add. MS. 35844, f. 92v, 'A Historical Discourse on Scotland, 1031–1600'. The continuation of the *Historie of King James the Sext* described an act of Parliament of 1597 as 'maid be advyce of the thre estaits': *The Warrender Papers*, ed. A.I. Cameron (2 vols., Scottish History Society, 1931–2), II, 432. (For the act see *A.P.S.*, IV, 124–30, c. 1; it does not enumerate the estates.) Mr John Colville has sometimes been claimed as the author of this work; in 1602 he mentioned 'the high parlament, vhar the king and thre estats of the realme ar assembled': 'The Names and Titles of Erles and Lords of Scotland . . .', 1602, in *Estimate of the Scottish Nobility During the Minority of James the Sixth*, ed. C. Rogers (Grampian Club, 1873), p. 80.

[54] Goodare, 'Parliamentary Taxation', p. 45.

[55] The change can be traced in the *A.P.S.* index, which includes a section on 'Representation of Each Estate on Committees': *A.P.S.*, XII, 933–4.

ordained 'that the nowmer of the lordis of the articles be equall *in ilk estait* and that the fewest nowmer of everie estait be sex and the maist number ten'.[56] The shire commissioners were always represented separately, usually (like the nobles) having eight representatives.

One of the decisive pieces of evidence for a change in the number of estates is the enacting clause of a parliamentary statute. In 1587 it contained, as it had done for over a generation, the phrase 'Oure soverane lord and his thre estaitis convenit in this present parliament' or 'Oure soverane lord with avise of his thre estaitis in this present parliament'.[57] However, the first Parliament to include shire commissioners met in 1592, and an original act (the copy used in its passage through Parliament) survives. Comparison with the parliamentary register shows that the clerk who compiled the latter silently altered the original act's traditional phrase 'thre estaitis' to the new, uneasily non-committal, 'estaitis'.[58] Thereafter, the phrase 'thre estaitis' virtually disappeared from view; the typical phrase in the enacting clause was now 'Oure soverane lord and estaitis of this present parliament'.[59] It must be stressed that this change would not have occurred if nothing had happened; if people had really believed that there were still three estates, they would have continued to use the traditional phrase.

But why, if there *were* 'four estates', did people not say so? Why leave things vague? Obviously, they were reluctant to make too clean a break with immemorial tradition. As recently as 1584, Parliament's constitution had been defended as 'the auctoritie of [the] supreme court of parliament continewit past all memorie of man unto thir dayis'.[60] The change had happened; but that was no reason to shout it from the rooftops. Charles I's Lord Advocate, Sir Thomas Hope, referred uncomfortably to 'four degrees of persones', seemingly a conscious effort to avoid the term 'four estates'.[61] John Spalding, after describing the 'riding' of the 1633 Parliament (its formal opening ceremony) in such a way as to make a tripartite division almost impossible to perceive, was happy to refer to 'the king, and his thrie estaitis'. However, Spalding later provided an illustration of how the idea of 'three estates' had been detached from concepts of enumeration. He described an Anglo-Scottish plot in 1637, 'to root out the bishopis of bothe kingdomes cropt and root, quhairby his majestie sould loiss ane of his thrie estaitis'.[62] In what realistic sense were bishops one of the three estates in England? Surely we have here a mere rhetorical device, similar to modern expressions such as the 'Third World'.

[56] *A.P.S.*, III, 443, c. 16. Italics added.

[57] *A.P.S.*, III, 429–30, cc. 3, 6.

[58] Scottish R.O., PA7/1/43 (misc. parliamentary papers); *A.P.S.*, III, 559, c. 32.

[59] *A.P.S.*, III, 584, c. 87.

[60] *A.P.S.*, III, 293, c. 3. The intention was to reinforce the shaky position of the bishops.

[61] See his notes on the composition of the Lords of the Articles at various dates. In 1526, there had been '9 of every estait'; in 1543, '7 of the clergie, 7 of the barrons all earles and lords, and 6 burgesses'. But: 'Anno 1600, Articles chosen, 8 for the clergie, 8 for the earles and lords, and 8 for the small barrons, and 8 for the burrows: Anno 1604, 8 chosen upon the articles for every on[e] of the saids four degrees of persones'. Sir Thomas Hope, *Major Practicks*, ed. J.A. Clyde (2 vols., Stair Society, 1937–8), I, 14–17.

[62] John Spalding, *Memorialls of the Trubles in Scotland and in England, 1624–1645*, ed. J. Stuart (2 vols., Spalding Club, 1850–1), I, 40, 77.

Given this reluctance to enumerate four estates, what is significant is that some people did in fact do so. We have had James VI in the witness box already, testifying that nobles and shire commissioners formed a single estate. But let us call him back, to tell us about an occasion when he had all the estates in front of him. A Convention of Estates refused him a tax in 1600, the opposition ringleaders being shire commissioners and burgesses. 'The king raged,' and threatened the shire commissioners that 'he should remember them and be even with them and call a Parliament and displace them of vote in Parliament and Convention, saying he gave them vote and made them a 4th state, which he should undo again.'[63]

This was two years after James had written the passage on Parliament, quoted earlier, in *Basilicon Doron*. In that book, he also told his son that by re-establishing diocesan episcopacy 'ye shall also re-establishe the olde institution of three Estates in Parliament, whiche can no otherwise be done'.[64] Taken literally, this would imply the existence of only *two* estates at the time he wrote. James's belief that there were three estates operated only at a high level of abstraction.

Views on the number of estates sometimes depended on political expediency. The shire commissioners were not entirely welcome to nobles or burgesses, representing as they did a dilution of their influence. (The bishops' influence derived entirely from the Crown, so it did not bother them.) But seeing that they were there, how would each estate regard them? It would not have been obvious to the nobility whether lairds belonged with them or not. The burghs, however, did have a clear view: they wanted to see only three estates, since that made them a notional third of Parliament instead of a quarter. The burghs' commissioners in 1613 told the Privy Council that they were one of the 'three esteatis'.[65] By contrast, in 1623, the 'gentlemen and barronis' of East Lothian thought of 'ane conventioun of the haill four estaittis'.[66]

However, there was also something of a *rapprochement* between burgh and shire commissioners, both suspicious of the Crown's increased demands. The Earl of Angus in 1604 saw the 'commons' as the main opponents of taxation.[67] Lairds and burgesses made common cause in a number of Parliaments against the Court.[68] A combined delegation of lairds and burgesses sent to London to negotiate on a wool-exporting scheme were 'chosen as weele affectit gentlemen to thair countrey and commounweele'.[69] Lairds and burgesses alike were 'gentlemen'. It was no doubt with this in mind that Archbishop Spottiswoode, writing in the 1630s, described the admission of shire commissioners in 1587:[70]

---

[63] George Nicolson to Robert Bowes, 29 June 1600, *C.S.P. Scot.*, XIII, 663. Cf. Goodare, 'Parliamentary Taxation', pp. 43–5.

[64] James VI, *Basilicon Doron*, I, 81.

[65] *R.P.C.S.*, X, 191–3.

[66] *R.P.C.S.*, XIII, 774.

[67] Angus to James, 20 Nov. 1604, *Letters and State Papers During the Reign of King James VI*, ed. J. Maidment (Abbotsford Club, 1838), pp. 58–9.

[68] For an example, see J. Goodare, 'The Scottish Parliament of 1621', *Historical Journal*, XXXVIII (1995).

[69] *R.P.C.S.*, XIII, 172.

[70] John Spottiswoode, *History of the Church of Scotland*, ed. M. Russell (3 vols., Spottiswoode Society, 1851), II, 377.

An act was made in favour of the small barons, giving them by their commissioners a voice in Parliament and conventions with the other estates. The earl
of Crawford did strongly oppose, and in name of the nobility protested against
their receiving. That which the king intended by this was, to free the barons of
their dependence upon noblemen, and have the estates more particularly
informed at their meeting of the abuses in the country. But so far was he from
obtaining these ends, as to the contrary they did work him great business in all
the ensuing Parliaments.

Most of the witnesses for three estates were writing about the constitution in the
abstract. But some even of those who did so could count up to four. An account
of the Scottish constitution, written for an English reader probably around 1603,
described the estates, including shire commissioners, and specifically stated that
the 'three estates' were a thing of the past now that they were present. It did
not specifically say that the shire commissioners were an estate, but in describing
the election of the Articles (in which they had their own representatives) it said
that 'the number of everye estate must be eight'.[71]
    There is at least one clear case where Parliament itself placed the existence of
four estates on its own record. The parliamentary commission of 1617 to revalue
ministers' stipends, one of the most important government operations of the
period, consisted of representatives from each estate—all four of them. The
quorum of the commission was set at 'fyve of everie ane of the saidis four
estaittis'.[72] The conclusion must be that the virtual disappearance of the term
'three estates' after 1587 shows that there were really four estates; the few occasions
when the term 'three estates' was used were rhetorical.

5

The anomalous situation created by the introduction of shire commissioners was
thrown into further constitutional confusion by the covenanting revolution of
1637–8. This was made by organised groups of disaffected nobles, lairds, burgesses
and ministers. Representatives of these four groups met in Edinburgh late in
1637, ostensibly to petition the King against the new prayer book and other
grievances, but eventually to form what became a provisional government.[73] The
ministers, of course, had never been an estate, although they sometimes behaved
like one. The three lay groups in the so-called 'Tables'—the steering committee
of the petitioning campaign, and thus of the revolution—closely paralleled the
three established estates. But although most of the lairds were freeholders qualified
to sit in Parliament, a minority had heritable but non-freehold property.[74] A
crack had opened which would eventually (in 1661) allow this non-feudal group
into Parliament.

    [71] 'Relation of the Manner of Judicatores of Scotland', ed. J.D. Mackie and W.C. Dickinson,
Scottish Historical Review, XIX (1922), 254–72.
    [72] *A.P.S.*, IV, 531, c. 3. Before parting with this subject, it may be worth noting the opinion of
a leading constitutional historian that there were four estates: W.C. Dickinson, 'Freehold in Scots
Law', *Juridical Review*, LVII (1945), 140.
    [73] D. Stevenson, *The Scottish Revolution, 1637–1644* (Newton Abbot, 1973), Chapter 2.
    [74] W. Makey, *The Church of the Covenant, 1637–1651* (Edinburgh, 1979), p. 23.

Allan Macinnes, discussing the Scottish constitution in this period, simply regards the four 'Tables' as 'estates'.[75] There is certainly some justification for this. In December 1637, the Tables' commissioners told the Privy Council that they 'represented the body of the Supplicants of everie Estate'. But there was a distinction: 'This answer seimes to have been ill reported, as thogh they had called themselves the representative body of the whole Estates.'[76] Here we see a distinction between estates as orders of society, and as estates of Parliament. Still, when the King's Commissioner proposed to make a proclamation against the Covenant in Edinburgh in June 1638, there were covenanters waiting 'to protest for the Four Estates'.[77]

In August 1639, a Parliament assembled; one of its traditional estates, the bishops, had been abolished the previous December. What did this mean for the idea of the 'three estates'? According to one recent writer, Peter Donald: 'As a replacement for the bishops, an estate might be formed by the lairds in their own right, instead of their being counted alongside commissioners for burghs; thus there would still be three estates to elect representatives on to the Articles.'[78] Dr Donald is clearly under the impression that burgh and shire commissioners somehow formed a single estate; he also seems to think that the lairds could not elect representatives to the Lords of the Articles before 1638. The errors in this passage need no elaboration. However, no final decisions on the matter were reached in 1639; a temporary compromise was reached over the election of the Lords of the Articles (the bishops had formerly chosen the nobles' representatives, and the royal commissioner now did so instead). Nevertheless, despite the abolition of bishops, there were still three estates; when a prorogation of Parliament was ordered, it refused to dissolve, 'in name of the thrie estatis'.[79] The existence of these estates—nobles, lairds and burgesses—should be borne in mind when we come to consider the constitutional changes that followed.

The covenanters now pressed for a Rescissory Act to ratify the abolition of episcopacy by the General Assembly of 1638. This is how they justified this:[80]

That it is impossible without passing the Rescissory Act, and Act of Constitution, to have a valid Parliament to ratify the conclusions of the Assembly, is manifest; seeing by former constitutions of the Parliament, no act of Parliament can pass without the consent of the three Estates, of which the kirk was the third (as is to be seen by the act of Parliament 1609), and any act of ratifying the conclusions

---

[75] A. Macinnes, 'The Scottish Constitution, 1638–1651: The Rise and Fall of Oligarchic Centralism', *The Scottish National Covenant in its British Context, 1638–1651*, ed. J. Morrill (Edinburgh, 1990), pp. 107–8.

[76] John, Earl of Rothes, *A Relation of Proceedings Concerning the Affairs of the Kirk of Scotland, from August 1637 to July 1638*, ed. J. Nairne (Bannatyne Club, 1830), p. 37.

[77] Robert Baillie, *Letters and Journals*, ed. D. Laing (3 vols., Bannatyne Club, 1841–2), I, 84.

[78] P. Donald, *An Uncounselled King: Charles I and the Scottish Troubles, 1637–1641* (Cambridge, 1990), p. 206.

[79] *A.P.S.*, V, 256.

[80] *Historical Collections*, ed. J. Rushworth (8 vols., 1659–1701), II, ii, 1007–8. For a draft 'Act of Rescission' see Edinburgh University, New College Library, BAILL 4/1, ff. 210v.–211v, Robert Baillie's letters and journals.

of the Assembly, or for any other cause whatsoever, which can be put in this Parliament, till the Parliament be lawfully constitute without prelates, or any other representing the kirk, cannot be valid, but may be quarrelled and annulled upon that formal and fundamental ground of the former constitution of Parliaments, which stands established by acts of Parliament, *anno* 1584, 1587, 1597, and 1606. By all which it is clear that the Parliament was constitute of the three Estates.

Clear indeed. But, given the King's hostility, this is what they were obliged to say. They did not yet dare to tell the King that he had no power to veto acts of Parliament (although that came next year); but they could plausibly argue that he had no such power in the General Assembly. The argument ran, therefore: episcopacy has been abolished for good by the General Assembly, so this decision *has* to be confirmed by Parliament, whatever the King may think. Otherwise, Parliament's own constitution will be invalid.

When Parliament reassembled on 2 June 1640, an act was passed that was central to our study, and shows the covenanters abandoning their earlier argument. It confirmed the abolition of bishops, and declared 'this present Parliament holdine be the nobilitie, barones and burgesses and thair commissioneris, the trewe estatis of this kingdome . . . and ordeanes all Parliamentis heireftir to be constitute . . . of the noblemen, barronis and burgesses as the memberis and thrie estatis of Parliament'. The act of 1606 'anent the restitutione of the estat of beshopis and thair representing the third esteat' was repealed.[81]

So what exactly had happened? According to David Stevenson:[82]

> Though technically forming a single estate the tenants in chief had in practice long been divided into the nobles or greater barons, with personal rights to attend, and the shire commissioners, lesser barons or lairds, who sat by right of election. . . . by sleight of hand one estate was excluded from parliament but three remained, as tradition demanded. The 'lesser barons' were promoted to be 'the barons', an estate in their own right.

This interpretation rests heavily on the assumption—shown above to be dubious—that there had been 'three estates' before the change. The decision of 2 June did *not* say that the 'lesser barons' were being 'promoted'; in fact it said no more about them than about the other estates. Nor was there any suggestion that an estate (that of the 'barons' or nobility) was being divided.[83] Indeed, the act did not actually *do* anything: it was declaratory and confirmatory in form, carefully worded to avoid speaking of the bishops as a genuine estate and to give the impression that the three surviving estates had *always* been the 'trewe estatis'. It was *possible* to think that one old estate had been divided into two new ones; but nobody said this. All we can say for certain—and it is, surely, the straight-

[81] *A.P.S.*, V, 259–60.

[82] *The Government of Scotland under the Covenanters, 1637–1651*, ed. D. Stevenson (Scottish History Society, 1982), pp. xxii–xxiii.

[83] The term 'barons' had before 1639 been used only for the shire commissioners; we also find 'small barons', less frequently.

forward interpretation—is that one estate had been abolished and three remained.

There was, however, something happening to the status of the shire commissioners. Previously, they had had one vote per shire; most shires sent two commissioners, and now they claimed—and, it seems, were granted—one vote each. These issues were actually separate, but an act of the Edinburgh Council of 4 June 1640 shows how they could be linked, writing of 'the procedor of the barrones of this kingdome in this Parliament craeving theme selffis to be declaired the thrid estaitt and to have ilk ane of thair commissioners ane decessive voice in all Parliaments'.[84] Similarly, an English observer wrote in 1641: 'Wheare as before ther weare 2 knights of shire too one voice, they have (since the bishops weare thrown out) eache a voice'.[85] This change survived the Restoration to become established practice.

6

The old constitutional forms returned with the monarchy in 1660. But although bishops were not reinstated immediately, the first Parliament, in 1661, did have three estates: the Lords of the Articles consisted of 'tuelff of each estate', nobles, barons and burgesses.[86] When the estate of bishops was restored in late 1661, there was no suggestion that any of the other estates was being modified; it is evident that there were four estates once more.

In 1662 new seating arrangements were made: 'non presume to sit upon the benshes save the nobilitie and clergie', officers of state were to sit on the steps of the throne, and 'commissioners of shires and burrowes sit in the furmes appointed for them'.[87] It does not look as though any attempt was being made to assimilate nobles and shire commissioners; if anything the shire commissioners were being bracketed with the burgesses. The blurring of the distinction between these latter estates extended to their own representatives. In the past, the combined influence of Crown and Convention of Royal Burghs had successfully restricted burgess representation to practising local traders; but we now see signs of the kind of invasion by the gentry that had taken place in sixteenth-century England. Sir John Dempster of Pitliver sat in his first Parliament, in 1681, as a 'burgess' of Inverkeithing, but after 1689 was elected commissioner for Fife.[88] It would be interesting to know how typical he was. English forms are also indicated in the King's 1663 letter to 'the lords spirituall and temporall, the commissioners of shires and burrowes assembled in our Parliament of Scotland'.[89] This formula, which thereafter became standard, could almost have been used for the English Parliament.

The Restoration period saw two traditional functions of the estates finally

[84] *Extracts from the Records of the Burgh of Edinburgh, 1626–1641*, ed. M. Wood (Edinburgh, 1936), pp. 241–2.
[85] *The Nicholas Papers*, ed. G.F. Warner (4 vols., Camden Soc., new ser. XL, L, LVII, 3rd ser. XXXI, 1886–1920), I, 24, Sir Henry Vane to Sir Edward Nicholas, 23 Aug. 1641.
[86] *A.P.S.*, VII, 9, c. 4.
[87] *A.P.S.*, VII, 371.
[88] Young (ed.), *Parliaments of Scotland*, I, 181.
[89] *A.P.S.*, VII, 467.

buried. Firstly, the covenanters had superseded the old tax system, in which the estates were taxed separately, with an assessment on all property shire by shire. There was one attempt to revive the old system in 1665, but it was a fiscal failure.[90] Secondly, the feudal idea of shire representation was killed off in 1661, when representation was broadened beyond the tenants in chief of the Crown. Hereafter, feuars of church or Crown land—heritable proprietors with a non-feudal title—gained the vote if they possessed lands valued at £1,000.[91] This, incidentally, was likely to undermine the vestigial idea of the nobles and shire commissioners forming a single estate on the basis of their common land tenure.

After 1661, however, the question 'Three estates or four?' arises once more. Sir Robert Gordon wrote a memorandum 'Anent the government of Scotland as it wes befor the late troubles'. The first three estates were prelates, nobles and royal burghs; the shire commissioners had been admitted under James VI 'to attend the Parliament, and thair to make up the fourt estate'.[92] Since this situation, formally, had been restored in 1661–2, he must have thought that there were four estates.

According to another writer, however, Parliament consisted of three estates. The bishops and burgesses were straightforward. Then: 'The Second Estate is the Nobility, who were antiently divided into the Greater Barons and the Lesser.' This is all very well; however, the author continued by saying that lesser barons had been introduced 'to ballance the Nobility'.[93] The contradictory usage of the term 'Nobility', to mean both the peerage alone *and* the combined peers and shire commissioners, is obvious.

In 1678 the lord advocate, Sir George Mackenzie,[94]

alleged, that it had been decided that a nobleman's eldest sone and appearand heir, though he have a 40 shilling land in the shire, yet he cannot be choisen, because he is of the Estate of the nobility, and not of the small barons, and one man . . . cannot be of 2 Estates.

But he later wrote that it was treason to impugn the dignity or authority of the Estates, 'as if one contended that Parliaments were not necessary, or that one of the three Estates may be turned out'.[95] Like James VI, Mackenzie could count

---

[90] Rait, *Parliaments*, pp. 499–500.

[91] *A.P.S.*, VII, 235, c. 253. This was a current valuation. Proprietors with the traditional valuation of 40s of old extent, held of the Crown in chief, retained the vote until 1832. See W. Ferguson, 'The Electoral System in the Scottish Counties Before 1832', *Stair Society Miscellany*, II (1984), 267, and on old extent, T. Thomson, *Memorial on Old Extent*, ed. J.D. Mackie (Stair Society, 1946).

[92] Sir Robert Gordon, 'Anent the Government of Scotland As it Wes Befor the Late Troubles', *Geographical Collections Relating to Scotland*, ed. W. Macfarlane (3 vols., Scottish History Society, 1906–8), II, 393–4.

[93] A[lexander] M[udie], *Scotiae Indiculum: Or the Present State of Scotland* (1682), pp. 75–6. This is substantially the same as an account of Scotland, probably by Mudie, appended to the 1677 edition of Spottiswoode's *History*: see John Spottiswoode, *History of the Church and State of Scotland* (1677), Appendix, p. 32.

[94] Sir John Lauder of Fountainhall, *Historical Observes of Memorable Occurrents in Church and State, 1680–1686*, eds. A. Urquhart and D. Laing (Bannatyne Club, 1840), p. 276.

[95] Sir George Mackenzie, *The Laws and Customes of Scotland in Matters Criminal* (Edinburgh, 1678), p. 47.

up to four estates when he had them ranged in front of him, but when it came to abstract theory he reverted to the idea of three estates.

In the Parliament of 1681, during a debate on an act regulating funerals, 'the nobility and barons had some discord, why the small barons should be aequalized with them, in the number of mourners. Yet Tarbet, in some passion, replyed, The Lords ought to remember, they ware all one state.'[96] This passage was cited by Rait to show that 'it was always recognized that the two groups of Lords of Parliament and commissioners of shires formed, strictly, one estate'.[97] But does it really show that? It only shows that the issue was a debatable one, and could be argued either way for party advantage. In fact, in the statute, nobles and shire commissioners were *not* 'aequalized'.[98] Similarly, in 1685, during a dispute over the riding of Parliament, 'the Nobility grudged that the Commissioners of Shires have silver and gold mixed in the freinges of their foot-mantles. The Barons answered, They made one Estate in Parliament with the Peers, *et magis et minus non variant speciem*.'[99] But as for what the nobles thought, we learn in 1682 that 'the nobility grumbled in ther bosome' because a laird was appointed chancellor.[100]

One final piece of evidence may be cited. Nicolas de Gueudeville's *Atlas Historique* of 1720 included an illustration of the Scottish Parliament with a description of it as it had been between about 1680 and 1685. 'The nobility', it said, 'are divided into two classes', lords and lesser barons, of whom the latter are elected by their fellows; while 'the people is represented in the Parliament by the deputies of towns and burghs'. With the bishops, this might perhaps make three estates; but when describing elections to the Lords of the Articles, it is clear that the committee represents 'the four estates [*ordres*] of the kingdom'.[101]

In the revolutionary Convention of Estates of March 1689, there was a brief but remarkable new development: the idea that *nobles and clergy* formed a single estate suddenly emerged. Presumably it had been incubating during the revolutionary and Restoration periods, when there had been some assimilations to English forms, such as the introduction of 'sessions' of Parliament and demands for separate readings of proposed legislation.[102] The commission for controverted elections consisted of 'fiftein persones, wherof fyve to be named by each estate'. The 'nobility and clergie' nominated one set of five (an archbishop and four nobles), and the 'commissioners for shyres and burghs' nominated five each. The Convention, hostile to bishops, debated 'Whether the Lords Spiritual were a distinct Estate, or only a part of the same Estate with the Lords Temporal?'[103]

[96] Sir John Lauder of Fountainhall, *Historical Notices of Scottish Affairs*, ed. D. Laing (2 vols., Bannatyne Club, 1848), I, 318.

[97] Rait, *Parliaments*, p. 166.

[98] *A.P.S.*, VIII, 350, c. 80.

[99] Lauder of Fountainhall, *Historical Notices*, II, 634: 'And greater and lesser do not change the species'.

[100] Lauder of Fountainhall, *Historical Observes*, pp. 68–9.

[101] The illustration is reproduced in Young (ed.), *Parliaments of Scotland*, I, between pp. xii and xiii.

[102] Rait, *Parliaments*, pp. 341–5, 428–30.

[103] *An Account of the Proceedings of the Estates in Scotland, 1689–1690*, ed. E.W.M. Balfour-Melville (2 vols., Scottish History Society, 1954–5), I, 1–2.

The result of the debate is not recorded, but two days later, the act declaring that they would not dissolve until they had secured 'the Protestant religione, the government, lawes and liberties of the kingdome' was subscribed by 'The Clergy and Nobility' together, then the barons, then the burgesses.[104]

This was not anglicisation for the sake of anglicisation; it was carefully chosen, for the dominant party wished to abolish bishops. It was desirable to evade the possible objection that they constituted an estate, for the abolition of an entire estate (as we have seen from Mackenzie) was liable to be quarrelled as being against the fundamental laws of the kingdom. The revolutionary party were particularly vulnerable to this charge, since they were justifying the deposition of James VII by claiming that he had subverted those same fundamental laws.

However, bishops still existed. On 11 April, the Claim of Right included the statement that episcopacy was 'a great and insupportable greivance . . . and therfor ought to be abolished'.[105] When the Convention reconvened, on 5 June (having been turned into a Parliament), they were explicitly a meeting 'consisting of the Noblemen, Barons and Borroughs'.[106] The abolition of bishops took place only on 22 July.[107] Again, the measure was not accompanied by any change in the status of the other estates.

And that, essentially, is that. From 1689 on, it was accepted that there were three estates until the abolition of the Scottish Parliament in 1707; there were no more constitutional changes relevant to our study. There is little evidence of institutional solidarity among the post-Revolution estates. One possibility is the unsuccessful proposal of 1704 that 'when a nobleman shall be created, a baron shall be added to the representation of the shires'.[108] But although it could indicate rivalry between two cohesive estates, it is more likely to reflect suspicion of the Crown's influence. Meanwhile, the Convention of Royal Burghs in the 1690s loosened its collective control over the parliamentary behaviour of individual burghs.[109] The blurring of distinctions between estates continued: the politicians of the 1690s were politicians first and foremost, and nobles, shire commissioners or burgh commissioners only incidentally.[110] The same was true in the debate on the Act of Union in 1706–7.[111] Although there were different voting patterns in different estates—there certainly seems to have been stronger support for the Union among the nobility—there is little suggestion of corporate consciousness or action by individual estates.

The way was open for the truth about the estates to be forgotten. Sir John Clerk of Penicuik, one of the negotiators of the Union of 1707 and a Member of the first United Kingdom House of Commons, anticipated the error of some

---

[104] *A.P.S.*, IX, 6, 9–10.
[105] *A.P.S.*, IX, 40.
[106] *A.P.S.*, IX, 79, c. 80; 98, c. 1.
[107] *A.P.S.*, IX, 104, c. 4.
[108] *A.P.S.*, XI, 174, and App., 59.
[109] Mackie and Pryde, *Estate of the Burgesses*, pp. 49–53.
[110] P.W.J. Riley, *King William and the Scottish Politicians* (Edinburgh, 1979), *passim*.
[111] The historiographical literature is surveyed by C.A. Whatley, '*Bought and Sold for English Gold'? Explaining the Union of 1707* (Scottish Economic and Social History Society, Glasgow, 1994).

of our modern authors in the 1720s by saying that Parliament in 1689 had separated the barons and burgesses to make up three estates.[112] Along with this new confusion, an old one survived: the ancient idea that nobles and 'small barons' were really one estate was used by William Forbes, a writer on election law, in 1710.[113]

7

From 1286 to 1707, this study has taken us from unity to quaternity, and back again. A unitary ruling class of magnates, the medieval 'community of the realm', gave way to a more complex political nation, expressed in a Parliament of three estates, and eventually (though the fact was rarely acknowledged) of four.

The idea of 'three estates' developed gradually, and the older concept of 'community of the realm' remained to unite the political *élite*. In the fifteenth century, we still do not see individual estates with a strong corporate personality.[114] The estates as corporate bodies were probably strongest in the mid-sixteenth century. The development of the system of estates is an example of the way that medieval ideas on political and administrative institutions reached their apotheosis in that century, before the emergence of a strong state which would inevitably tend to curtail the estates' capacity for independent corporate action.[115]

Cracks began to appear in the system when an attempt was made to adapt it to changing conditions—the growing importance of the lairds. But even when the estates did not actually number three, the Scottish constitution provided people with meaningful status groups. Thus the system survived despite the unsightly intrusion of a fourth estate in 1587: people wanted it. The lairds, naturally, were glad to gain a voice; but in particular, among the people who wanted the system, we find the King and the supporters of the Court. It was they who wanted taxation, something that could only be obtained by consulting the lairds (and sometimes not even then). Then the claim that each individual estate was essential to Parliament provided them with one of the best constitutional arguments for episcopacy. After the Reformation, bishops were always in Scotland an adjunct to royal power—and always, for that reason, controversial. Any weapon that came to hand would be seized upon to defend the royalist view of the constitution.

This weapon, however, buckled when the covenanters succeeded in ejecting bishops from the parliamentary quaternity. Again, they used any arguments that came to hand—claiming in 1639 that the bishops had been a third estate (in order to underline the need for parliamentary ratification of their ejection), and in 1640 that the true estates had always been nobles, barons and burgesses. By now the estates were less important as organic status communities, having become

---

[112] Sir John Clerk of Penicuik, *History of the Union of Scotland and England*, ed. D. Duncan (Scottish History Society, 1993), p. 174.
[113] Ferguson, 'Electoral System', p. 264.
[114] A. Grant, *Independence and Nationhood: Scotland, 1306–1469* (1984), pp. 167–8.
[115] S.G.E. Lythe, 'The Economy of Scotland Under James VI and I', *The Reign of James VI and I*, ed. A.G.R. Smith (1973), p. 57.

constitutional abstractions. It is interesting that the continental genre of literature discussing the 'estates' of society died out in the mid-seventeenth century, as the focus of attention shifted to the sovereign state.[116]

After this, things could never be the same again. Parliament became more of a single integrated whole, and remained so at the Restoration. It began to look and behave more like the Parliament of England. There was occasional use of the concept of estates, but more out of respect for tradition in general than because of a feeling that this particular tradition spoke powerfully to the present. The supporters of the unreformed House of Commons in the early nineteenth century did not believe that it was vital *per se* for the green fields of Old Sarum to return two Members of Parliament. They liked Old Sarum not for what it was, but for what it symbolised: a polity validated by tradition rather than abstract reason. They knew that its loss would presage more serious changes. Nobody attacked the concept of estates in the late seventeenth century, but it was now a dignified, rather than an efficient, part of the constitution. In 1689, new constitutional arguments against bishops were invented in an offhand way, presumably because nobody could be bothered to check the precedents of 1638–40. Anyone who had had to justify the system of estates at this time would have found it difficult to argue that it was essential to the Scottish constitution in the way that it had been before 1587, and even before 1638.

---

[116] R. Mohl, *The Three Estates in Medieval and Renaissance Literature* (New York, 1933), p. 383.

Montrose v. *Dundee* and the Jurisdiction of Parliament and Council over Fee and Heritage in the Mid-Fifteenth century*

ALAN BORTHWICK

Scottish Record Office

In recent years research into legal procedure in later medieval Scotland has significantly altered the accepted view of a 'Dark Age' in Scottish legal history, an age deemed to have begun in the early fourteenth century following the foundation of a legal system in Scotland based on English models which had emerged during the Anglo-Norman period. This development, so the old view had it, was halted in its tracks by the Wars of Independence, and the legal system went into decline for at least 200 years. Historians of Scots law and administration have been successfully picking away at this edifice, and have shown that the system as it evolved in the late thirteenth century continued to operate well into the fifteenth century.[1]

Professor Hector MacQueen has been particularly to the fore in revising the old views. In his recently published book, he has drawn together the strands of a number of articles illustrating the interaction of law and society in medieval Scotland.[2] MacQueen deals with civil procedure particularly with regard to litigation over property. He shows that there were three pleadable brieves (of novel dissasine, mortancestry and right) which initiated action before judges ordinary (the justiciar, sheriff, provost and bailies of burghs and their equivalents in regality jurisdictions) which alone could be used to settle the matter of right to property. These brieves were introduced to or developed in Scotland in imitation of English models. A rule emerged compelling their use in property disputes. Associated with that rule there arose a restriction on the judicial competence of Parliament and the King's Council which, if asked to adjudicate on

---

* I am very grateful to Professor H. MacQueen for his comments on an earlier draft of this. Quotation from unpublished MSS. is made with the approval of the Director of Libraries and Museums Service, Angus District Council, and of the Archivist, Dundee District Archive and Record Centre.

[1] On the 'Dark Age', see particularly T.M. Cooper, 'From David I to Bruce, 1124–1329: The Scoto-Norman Law', *An Introduction to Scottish Legal History*, ed. G.C.H. Paton (Stair Society, Edinburgh, 1958), pp. 3–17; T.M. Cooper, 'The Dark Age of Scottish Legal History, 1350–1650', in his *Selected Papers, 1922–1954* (Edinburgh and London, 1957), pp. 219–36; T.M. Cooper, *Select Scottish Cases of the Thirteenth Century* (Edinburgh and London, 1944). A good review article of the topic is W.D.H. Sellar, 'The Common Law of Scotland and the Common Law of England', *The British Isles 1100–1500: Comparisons, Contrasts and Connections*, ed. R.R. Davies (Edinburgh, 1988), pp. 82–99.

[2] H.L. MacQueen, *Common Law and Feudal Society in Medieval Scotland* (Edinburgh, 1993).

right to property, were compelled to remit the matter to the ordinary. There the matter would be settled by use of one of the brieves, which could not be used to initiate an action before a central court. Clear evidence of the operation of these two rules can be seen at least into the late fifteenth century.

Much of MacQueen's earlier work, and of other recent authors, was case-based. This article examines a long-running dispute between the burghs of Dundee and Montrose which centred on their trading privileges and particularly the right to indict forestallers at chamberlain ayres, which they had been granted by the Crown. The present author has already studied the case in some depth in an unpublished thesis; there are no known previously published studies.[3] The appearance of Professor MacQueen's book has encouraged a fresh look at the pleadings submitted during and other documentation of this case. Some arguments adduced by either side in the case, when put into a wider context, appear to conflict with some of MacQueen's views, particularly about the judicial competence of Parliament and the King's Council in fee and heritage matters. But are appearances deceptive?

A major problem confronts every writer on medieval Scottish history, even on so late a period as the fifteenth century: the lack of consistent source material. The old view of the development of Scots law held sway because, in part, there seemed to be a dearth of evidence to show that there had been an active legal system. The increasing quantity of material, mainly estate papers of the landed families of Scotland, which has become available in Scottish archive offices in the last 50 years or so has allowed considerable advances in our knowledge of events and the period in general. It cannot, however, entirely make good the loss of records of what might be loosely called central government: a very incomplete register of the great seal, no privy seal register before 1488, Exchequer rolls whose existence is patchy well into the later fifteenth century, no Treasurer's accounts until 1474, no contemporary rolls of Parliament until 1466, and no political records of the Privy Council at all in the fifteenth century (or earlier).

The picture is little better when we turn to local authority archives, much used in this article. The matter has been well covered by Flett and Cripps, who wrote that: 'no continuous urban archive survives which predates the very end of the fourteenth century and most begin or expand to a useful degree only a century later'.[4] Montrose's and Dundee's archives fit into this pattern. Dundee has only a small collection of charters available to inform us about the case. Montrose's archive has survived better, as we have some burgh court minutes for the 1450s and 1460s, although of no value in elucidating this case, and a much wider selection of loose documents ranging from major charters to administrative precepts. Yet this survival is apparently due largely to the industry of the late 19th century local antiquarian J.G. Low, who rescued some of the 'rubbish

---

[3] A.R. Borthwick, 'The King, Council and Councillors in Scotland c. 1430–1460' (University of Edinburgh Ph.D. thesis, 1989), Chapter 7.

[4] I. Flett and J. Cripps, 'Documentary Sources', *The Scottish Medieval Town*, eds. M. Lynch, M. Spearman and G. Stell (Edinburgh, 1988), pp. 18–41, the quotation being from p.18.

papers' from a rag store to which they had been sent.[5] It is largely because of Low's interests that no less than 40 documents at least now survive which allow us to build up a picture of how this case, the best documented one now known in the period up to 1460, was conducted between *c.* 1432 and 1462.

Before examining the contentious points in the case, I shall sketch in the economic background as well as the history of settlements of disputes between burghs. This context should help us appreciate why the administration favoured one burgh against the other, as seems to have happened. Both Dundee and Montrose were royal burghs, and there was therefore much pressure on the Crown to be even-handed in this dispute. If the judgement resulted in a loss of privilege, the burgesses of either of the disputants, or of any burgh in Scotland, might wonder who would protect their privileges if the grantor did not?

Of the two, Montrose had greater antiquity as a royal burgh. It is likely that David I (1124–53) had granted the burgh a major charter, but well before this dispute arose it seems that the charter was already lost, and all that remained was a spurious version confirmed by David II in 1352 and again by Robert II in 1385. In this spurious charter, the bounds within which Montrose enjoyed trading privileges were carefully plotted, so that they would not conflict with the areas within which the older royal burghs of Aberdeen and Perth could claim similar privileges. Barrow writes that, 'the sphere assigned to Montrose is what we might expect for an important king's burgh and port on the Angus coast in the reign of David I'. To judge by the repeated references to their old charters, Montrose's burgesses clearly felt that history was on their side.[6]

At the time of its foundation in the twelfth century, Dundee was not a royal burgh, its superior instead being the Earl of Huntingdon. It did not attain the status of royal burgh until some point in the thirteenth century, but its development of international trade was already under way. Its early charters were also lost, and in 1325 Robert I had to commission his Chancellor and Chamberlain to hold an inquest into its liberties. The result Duncan regards as 'entirely unsatisfactory' for Dundee, because its rights were not clearly defined. Almost three years were to pass before the King issued a charter in favour of Dundee resulting from this inquest, and when he did the charter seems to have been a patchwork of liberties culled from other burghs' charters.[7]

Despite Dundee's relative juniority as a royal burgh, it is clear that it was better

---

[5] Montrose's archive is now split between the Scottish Record Office, Edinburgh (mainly sasine records but including some court papers) and the Archive Department of Montrose Library, where the bulk of the burgh records are kept. In this article the holdings in Montrose are footnoted as Montrose B.R. Low's comments about the burgh MSS. are found in a number of volumes now amongst the burgh's records in Montrose, for example in 'Inventory of the Books, Papers and Charters in the Record Room, Town Hall, Montrose, compiled by me James G. Low 8/9/1885'.

[6] The David II confirmation is *Regesta Regum Scottorum* (henceforth *R.R.S.*), eds. G.W.S. Barrow *et al.* (4 vols. Edinburgh, 1960–88), VI, no. 122; the spurious David I charter is *R.R.S.*, I, no. 19, with Barrow's comments at pp. 92–5 (the quoted sentence is on p. 95).

[7] The Robert I commission is *R.R.S.*, V, no. 278, and the subsequent charter *ibid.*, no. 336. Useful comments on the process of obtaining the charter are A.A.M. Duncan's in *ibid.*, pp. 27–31 and E.P.D. Torrie, *Medieval Dundee: A Town and its People* (Abertay Historical Society Publication no. 30, Dundee, 1990), pp. 22–4, 31–3.

able to establish itself as a trading burgh than Montrose. But in the fifteenth century, the economy was in a poor shape. Professor Lynch has written that for Scottish towns then:[8]

> The basic context . . . is, as revealed by custom records, one of a lingering economic decline which was exaggerated by periodic short-term crises. Few towns outside the four great burghs escaped the cycle of urban decay or outright decline.

In the mid-fourteenth century there were four burghs recognised by Bruges as being the chief ones in the realm: Edinburgh, Aberdeen, Perth and Dundee. Customs returns give point to this: in the 1370s 58 per cent of the customs revenue was paid by them, a proportion which rose to 81 per cent by 1500. A 'league table' compiled by Lynch shows Montrose lying eighth in the 1370s, and slipping to ninth by 1500, comfortably lower than Dundee.[9] This indicator of Montrose's status is neatly reinforced by a one-off set of figures, available after a tax on moveables was levied in 1373, which reveals that Montrose was the seventh wealthiest burgh, well behind Dundee.[10] In the fifteenth century, Edinburgh asserted its dominant role in the export of wool (albeit in a declining market), and others were left to jockey for the minor positions in the trade of hide and skins. Dundee appears to have maintained its share of the trade, and moved up the table of exporters. Montrose lost much ground to Dundee, but was able to notch up a noticeable, though possibly short-lived, success in respect of a revival in fish exports from the late 1460s.[11]

Given this background, if called upon by James II to advise him how to deal with the matter, the King's Council could surely only have recommended him to favour Dundee if it came to the crunch. Dundee's importance to the Crown had been underlined by the deal concocted to engineer the release from captivity in England of James I in 1423–24. The King issued letters by which he obliged himself to keep the four burghs unharmed in respect of the sum of 50,000 marks which they undertook to pay for his release. The four burghs were Edinburgh, Perth, Dundee and Aberdeen. There was the vague hope expressed that the other burghs in the realm would help in this ransom payment. Montrose can only have been one of the other burghs.[12]

Inter-burgh disputes were not uncommon in the medieval period, often arising from charters of privileges, of which burghs still commonly sought simple confirmations, granted by the Crown. The patchy evidence does not make it clear if on the whole the burghs were prepared to live with anomalies in their charters,

---

[8] M. Lynch, 'Towns and Townspeople in Fifteenth-Century Scotland', *Towns and Townspeople in the Fifteenth Century*, ed. J.A.F. Thomson (Gloucester, 1988), pp. 173–89 at 177–8.

[9] *Ibid.*, p. 176; see also Torrie, *Dundee*, pp. 34–5.

[10] A.W.K. Stevenson, 'Mediaeval Commerce', *The Port of Montrose: A History of its Harbour, Trade and Shipping*, initiated by D.G. Adams, eds. G. Jackson and S.G.E. Lythe (Tayport, Fife, and New York, 1993), p. 21.

[11] Lynch, 'Townspeople', p. 176; Stevenson, 'Commerce', pp. 23–4; A.W.K. Stevenson, 'Trade with the South, 1070–1513', Lynch, Spearman and Stell (eds.), *Scottish Medieval Town*, pp. 180–206.

[12] E.W.M. Balfour-Melville, *James I, King of Scots 1406–37* (1936), pp. 94–105.

except when major rows erupted, or if there were frequent niggles which brought constant underlying tension. It is not unusual for a dispute to be apparently settled but in fact resurface months or years later.

In essence the problem in this case was that Montrose's privileged area seemed to cover all the area between Perth's liberty in the south and Aberdeen's in the north; but Dundee was then inserted, and furthermore there were close at hand Brechin, an episcopal city a few miles up the South Esk from Montrose, and Forfar and Inverbervie, also royal burghs, as well as a number of smaller settlements with trading interests but lacking royal burgh status. Dundee had an additional protagonist in the form of Perth, for both claimed rights to oversee water traffic on the Tay. A decision in Dundee's favour in 1402 seems to have settled the matter in the fifteenth century, however, and allowed it to concentrate on its role in Forfarshire.[13]

When they occurred, the stand-offs amongst the three main towns here, Dundee, Montrose and Brechin, were quite dramatic. Brechin was a particular thorn in the flesh for both Montrose and Dundee. In the reign of David I, a weekly market on Sunday had been established there, under royal protection. Later royal confirmation and an inquest showed that 200 years later the market was still going strong, but in the reign of David II Montrose struggled, at first successfully, to curb Brechin's rights. In 1370, however, the Bishop of Brechin was able to obtain a charter allowing merchants of Brechin free entry and exit to the waters of the Tay and the South Esk with their goods, with a particular instruction to the burgesses of Montrose and Dundee not to harm the Brechin merchants. Two years later the merchant guilds of Montrose and Forfar attempted to counter this by granting each other reciprocal trading rights and specifically excluding Brechin.[14]

Little further is known until 1450, when in the midst of the Dundee/Montrose case the King had an inquest consider Brechin's customs, which found that its market continued, with free entry and exit to the Tay and the South Esk for the merchants, and that the bishop was accustomed to holding his own chamberlain ayres. A confirmation of privileges, which now included the right of Brechin merchants to free entry and exit in Montrose's port of Strumnay, followed in September 1451.[15]

This extension of privileges would be alarming to both Dundee and Montrose. Dundee in particular made a rapid response, delivering a formal protest at a chamberlain ayre in January 1452 about the possible harm to its prior infeftment

---

[13] Torrie, *Dundee*, fig. v on p. 32 for the liberties; Inverbervie's charter is *R.R.S.*, VI, no. 483; Torrie, *Dundee*, p. 33 and *Charters, Writs and Public Documents of the Royal Burgh of Dundee*, ed. W. Hay (Dundee, 1880), facsimile facing p. 18, cover the *Dundee v. Perth* dispute.

[14] For information about Brechin's privileges and problems caused by them, see *R.R.S.*, II, no. 115; V, no. 191; VI, nos. 120, 334, 369, 464; E. Ewan, *Townlife in Fourteenth-Century Scotland* (Edinburgh, 1990), p. 143; H.M.C., *2nd Report* (Montrose Burgh MSS.), p. 206.

[15] *Registrum Magni Sigilli Regum Scottorum* (henceforth *R.M.S.*), eds. J.M. Thomson *et al.* (11 vols., Edinburgh, 1882–1914), II, nos. 493, 494; for identification of Strumnay as Montrose's port see G. King, M. King and D.G. Adams, 'Montrose: Basin and Burgh', Jackson and Lythe (eds.), *Port of Montrose*, p. 8.

from the Crown in its bounds and freedoms, which in turn could affect the King's and its own fee and heritage. It is not clear if Dundee took any further action, as it may have intended to do. As part of the settlement of *Montrose* v. *Dundee* in 1462, however, the burghs united to restrict the rights of Brechin citizens to load or unload vessels within their bounds. Montrose took direct action to implement this. There is a King's Council decree in 1464 noting that Brechin's privileges were to be maintained, and that Montrose's provost and bailies were to enter the King's ward when charged for their part in casting out Brechin's goods and stopping of their merchandise, apparently when in Montrose harbour.[16]

Other cases illuminate how contemporaries tackled the problem of burghs in dispute. An interesting case, in that it was also about disputed trading privileges and bounds, was that of 1431–32 between St Andrews, an episcopal city, and Cupar, a royal burgh. Because of the importance of St Andrews as an episcopal see, it had obtained significant trading privileges for its citizens, which had already been the subject of dispute in the late 1360s. The lords auditors, later to be discussed, twice considered the matter, in Parliaments in 1431 and 1432. Both cases ended with St Andrews being confirmed in possession of its existing boundaries, notwithstanding any charter for Cupar. At the second of these hearings, St Andrews was also confirmed in its privileges with regard to the liberties of Crail.[17]

At the General Council of February 1444 a dispute between Ayr and Irvine was settled, this time by means of electing all other burgess representatives present to consider the matter. The issue here was specifically whether or not burgesses of Irvine had the right to sell various goods in Ayr on market day. It was decided that they could only do this on fair days, according to the old privileges.[18]

In 1469, the lords auditors heard a case between Glasgow and Dumbarton, after burgesses of Dumbarton had prevented some citizens of Glasgow buying wine from a Frenchman whose vessel was on the Clyde, this being contrary to Glasgow's 'priviliges fredome and thair ald infeftment grantit to thaim be oure souverain lordis predecessouris'. The auditors decreed that Dumbarton should be punished at the King's will for this injury.[19]

The King's Council also dealt with burgh disputes. For example, in 1448–49 the Council considered a dispute between Inverkeithing and Kinghorn about the latter's boundaries. After the Council decreed that the boundaries should be those of the constabulary of Kinghorn as described in 'King David's' charter, an inquest took place locally, before the Council, to determine what then these boundaries really were. In 1473, a further case between the burghs took place before the Council, this time concerning the indictment of Inverkeithing's inhabitants to chamberlain ayres held in Kinghorn. (The case therefore has similarities to *Montrose* v. *Dundee*.) The lords decerned that the boundaries of each burgh should be

[16] *Registrum Episcopatus Brechinensis cui accedunt cartae quamplurimae originales*, eds. P. Chalmers and C. Innes (Bannatyne Club publication no. 102, 2 vols., Aberdeen, 1856), II, no. 276; Scottish R.O., GD1/176/1 (Auldbar House writs); Dundee District Archive and Record Centre (henceforth D.D.A.), TC/CC 1/40 (Town charters); Montrose B.R., M/WI/10/2.

[17] *R.R.S.*, VI, no. 462; St Andrews University Library, B65/22/23, 27 (St Andrews Burgh MSS.).

[18] *Charters of the Royal Burgh of Ayr*, ed. W.S. Cooper (Edinburgh, 1883), no. 18.

[19] *The Acts of the Lords Auditors of Causes and Complaints*, ed. T. Thomson (Edinburgh, 1839), p. 19.

preserved as in their former state; and that if any Inverkeithing inhabitants without the constabulary and parish of Kinghorn had been indicted to the Kinghorn ayre, Kinghorn should refund the costs thereof to Inverkeithing.[20]

Not all disputes would merit the formality of a hearing before Council or Parliament. In 1424, Dumbarton and Renfrew reached an agreement on how to settle future disputes between them. Six representatives of each burgh, with an oversman, would be chosen to arbitrate. Only if the matter lay outside their power would the case be transferred elsewhere, with a view to the quickest possible settlement. One such case arose in 1429, heard by the Chamberlain at the King's request, concerning certain fishings and freedoms of the burghs. An assize of local barons and gentlemen was selected, and the possession of the disputed fishings seems to have been amicably settled.[21]

Having sketched in the general context of the economic standings of the burghs, their own disputes with neighbouring burghs and how other burghs sought to settle disputes, we can now turn to the *Montrose* v. *Dundee* case itself. Before we examine the contentious points in the case, we must first review its proceedings. In the form as now known, there are five stages, punctuated by (at times) lengthy spells when there are no extant documents.[22]

The first stage is represented by a single document bearing to have been compiled at Parliament on 10 March 1432. Twelve men, whose personnel formed a powerful commission, delivered their counsel to the King concerning debates between burghs for the 'commune profyt of the kyng and of the contre and quiete of the land'. The commission recommended that each should continue to use the bounds and freedoms contained in their charters, but that Dundee should have the privilege of indicting forestallers throughout the sheriffdom of Forfar excepting within Montrose's bounds. It is unclear if this recommendation was ever formally ratified by the King, as the document is clearly not a product of the King's Chancery.[23]

Silence falls for 15 years, but in 1447, after a chamberlain ayre hearing, James II issued a letter stating that he wished the issue to be dealt with by Parliament or General Council, and this letter seems to have prevented the matter being raised before the Court of the Four Burghs later that year.[24]

Nevertheless, there was a flurry of activity in early 1448, at the time of a general chamberlain ayre in Dundee. One of Montrose's inhabitants was to be accused there of forestalling, but Montrose was determined to use this as a test case. It employed a forespeaker, one of whose main arguments was that the trial could not take place in Dundee as it meant ejecting Montrose from its fee and heritage,

---

[20] Scottish R.O., B34/20/2 (Inverkeithing Burgh MSS.); GD172/145, 146 (Fordell Muniments).

[21] *Descriptions of the Sheriffdoms of Lanark and Renfrew, compiled about MDCCX, by William Hamilton of Wishaw*, eds. J. Dillon and J. Fullarton (Maitland Club publication no. 12, Glasgow, 1831), pp. 282–4.

[22] A fuller discussion of the course of the dispute is Borthwick, 'King, Council and Councillors', pp. 329–39.

[23] D.D.A., TC/CC 1/27.

[24] Montrose B.R., M/WI/14, 'Trading bundle', no. 1; CR2/10; 1/10/7 (Charter Chest inventory), p. 375.

which was bad enough on its own but much worse when the ejection was to be accomplished without pleadable brieves. The arguments put forward by the forespeaker were apparently too weighty to be dealt with by the Great Chamberlain and his deputes, and the matter seems to have rested there until 1450.[25]

The third stage begins with one of the high points for Montrose, a decision by a special commission of 12 (four from each of the three Estates) appointed by the January 1450 Parliament to investigate the dispute. Montrose would be permitted to indict forestallers within its bounds as outlined in its old charters, and Dundee would have perpetual silence imposed upon it. But the King and Council seem to have refused to accept this decision, despite protests by Montrose in August and October that year.[26]

The fourth stage commenced when both burghs were summoned to the March 1458 Parliament for a hearing before the King and his councillors, auditors of causes. The brieve of summons specifically comments on how a lack of a previous settlement meant prejudice to the liberties of the burghs and no little harm to the King because of the prevention of holding of chamberlain ayres. When Parliament gathered, the only result was to continue the case to the second day of the Perth justice ayre, where it was further continued to the Exchequer audit in June/July, and there to a formal King's Council meeting in August. Montrose was determined to obtain execution of the decree of the commission appointed in the 1450 Parliament, and was particularly concerned about the council interfering in a fee and heritage matter. The council seemed equally determined to proceed, leading Montrose to lodge a series of complaints about its action, and place itself in the King's protection.[27]

All this was to no avail, as in October (probably at the time of an unrecorded meeting of the Court of the Four Burghs), the King issued a charter in favour of Dundee which (although allowing Dundee and Montrose to continue trading as before) appointed Dundee as the place for indicting all forestallers in Forfarshire.[28]

Despite this apparent conclusion, the final stage began when Montrose managed to obtain a further hearing at Parliament in October 1459, continued to the next meeting, which took place in July 1460. Montrose had achieved a notable feat in first re-opening the affair, and second in persuading the administration to have summoned the surviving members of the 1450 commission to this 1460 Parliament, in order to determine the case. Inconclusive proceedings occurred then and in the following four months (partly because of the death of James II in August 1460), until in Parliament in March 1461 the lords auditors rejected Dundee's efforts to halt further proceedings, and furthermore seem to have annulled the August 1458 decree which had fallen against Montrose.[29]

Almost 18 months passed with no known action, until the Crown issued a

---

[25] Montrose B.R., M/WD/1; M/WI/14 'Trading bundle', no. 2; M/WI/15; CR2/11(4).

[26] Montrose B.R., M/WI/15; M/WC/7/1; M/WD/1; National Library of Scotland, MS. 15471, f. 95 (Chalmers of Audlbar papers).

[27] D.D.A., TC/CC 1/33, 36; Montrose B.R., CR2/10; M/WI/14, 'Trading bundle', no. 7.

[28] *R.M.S.*, II, no. 628.

remarkable document: a licence to the two burghs permitting them to reach a settlement as long as it did not prejudice the Crown. The settlement quickly followed, at Arbroath on 9 November 1462. For the purposes of indicting forestallers Forfarshire was effectively split in half between the two burghs; and the chance was also taken to restrict the rights of Brechin citizens to load or unload vessels within the bounds of Dundee or Montrose. After what must have been a very strained 30 years or so, the settlement could with some justification comment that it was made for the common profit of the King and of the burghs, and to produce full friendship and tenderness between the burghs.[30]

The conclusion to be drawn from the disputes earlier covered, and the *Montrose v. Dundee* case, is that there were five possible means of settling a debate: by putting the matter in the hands of the King's Great Chamberlain, presenting a case to the Court of the Four Burghs, approaching the King and Council, submitting a petition to Parliament where either the lords auditors or a special commission would deal with the matter, or finally seeking an arbitrated settlement, which need not involve any of the four other agencies mentioned. These were typical pieces forming the jigsaw of civil dispute settlement in medieval Scotland, with due allowance made for non-burgh cases.

The Chamberlain's close connection with burgh affairs is well-known, and until the reign of James I he was also the King's supreme financial officer. At that time, much of his financial powers were lost to the newly-instituted Comptroller and Treasurer, but his burgh interests appear undiminished. In particular, he was obliged to pass on ayre from burgh to burgh, holding a court which was both judicial and administrative: appeals from the burgh court lay to the ayre, first instance business could be raised there as well, and the Chamberlain would also enquire into the affairs and administration of the burgh, to ensure that the Crown revenue was not subject to fraud. Disputes between burghs could be (and were) referred to him.[31]

The Chamberlain was apparently appointed in 1426 to head a body capable of settling disputes of a type normally heard by the King's Council, but nothing is known of this body in action in this form. (Its link to the Council will be later noticed.) The Chamberlain's involvement may have been short-lived, as by 1431 the Chancellor probably replaced him. Although Duncan sees the burghs as the source of pressure for this body, there is only one passing reference to it in *Montrose v. Dundee* and none in other known cases, and it may then not have been the ideal forum for burgh disputes. The Chamberlain on ayre certainly

[29] Montrose B.R., M/WD/1; M/WI/15; M/WI/10/1; M/WI/14; 'Trading bundle', nos. 8–10; D.D.A., TC/CC 1/39. Some uncertainty surrounds the terms of the 1461 decree as the document is damaged.

[30] Montrose B.R., CR2/10; D.D.A., TC/CC 1/40; Scottish R.O., GD1/176/1 (Auldbar House writs).

[31] A.L. Murray, 'The Comptroller, 1425–1488', *Scottish Historical Review,* LII (1973), 1–29; W.C. Dickinson, 'A Chamberlain's Ayre in Aberdeen, 1399x1400', *Scottish Historical Review,* XXXIII (1954), 27–36; *Early Records of Aberdeen, 1317, 1398–1407,* ed. W.C. Dickinson (Scottish History Society [henceforth *S.H.S.*], 3rd ser., XLIX, Edinburgh, 1957), esp. pp. lxxxi–ii, cxlii–iv; 'The Scottish King's Household', ed. M. Bateson, *S.H.S. Miscellany, II (S.H.S.,* 1st ser., XLIV, Edinburgh, 1904), pp. 7–8, 32, 38.

became involved in 1447–48, but evidently felt unable to cope with the arguments raised by the Montrose forespeaker. It seems, therefore, that the Chamberlain on his own was least likely to be able to deal with this dispute.[32]

More effective should have been the Court of the Four Burghs headed by the chamberlain. As a body which, could hear appeals from burgh courts and from chamberlain ayres, as well as dealing with disputes between burghs, this court would seem to have been the ideal forum for a case of this nature. The four burghs from which it derived its title were at first Berwick, Edinburgh, Roxburgh and Stirling, but in 1369, because of continued English possession of Berwick and Roxburgh, Lanark and Linlithgow were substituted for them. Its first regular meeting place was Haddington, but in 1454 James II, in confirming a decree of James I, appointed Edinburgh as the seat of the court, which was to meet annually on the day following Michaelmas. Significantly, the court is styled Parliament of the Four Burghs in these letters patent, and it is clear that the court had power to determine finally causes laid before it.[33]

Duncan, in a brief study of the reign of James I, has attempted to show that the court was a regular feature in the late 1420s and 1430s, and that following its deliberations various new statutes were accepted by a full Parliament or General Council. This suggestion apart, there has hitherto been little evidence to show any activity on the part of the court in the reigns of James I or II at the least.[34]

We can now show, however, that the court was directly involved in efforts to settle the *Montrose* v. *Dundee* case. Early in 1447 there had been an attempted indictment of forestallers at a chamberlain ayre in Dundee. After Montrose protested, the matter had been held over to the next Court of the Four Burghs, but in the interim the King instructed that as the matter had been left undecided in a Parliament of James I it must be left either to Parliament or General Council to determine the issue at stake. On 9 October 1447, the Court or Parliament of the Four Burghs, sitting in Edinburgh, was evidently about to proceed in the matter in the presence of commissioners of both burghs when the King's interdict was presented. The Montrose commissioners duly protested again, but the sole document which records this provides no more illumination about proceedings.[35]

We hear no more about efforts to resolve the matter in the Court of the Four Burghs, and must assume that both burghs accepted the need to have the matter brought before Parliament or General Council. It certainly seems strange that the court's dealings in the case were so restricted; yet our review of other burgh

---

[32] *The Acts of the Parliaments of Scotland* (henceforth *A.P.S.*), eds. T. Thomson and C. Innes (12 vols., Edinburgh, 1814–75), II, 11 c. 19; with revisions in I.E. O'Brien, 'The Scottish Parliament in the Fifteenth and Sixteenth Centuries' (University of Glasgow Ph.D. thesis, 1980), Chapter 1, esp. pp. 26–8 and Appendix C; and A.A.M. Duncan, *James I, King of Scots, 1424–1437* (Glasgow, 1984), pp. 3–4; Montrose B.R., CR2/10; Borthwick, 'King, Council and Councillors', pp. 244–6.

[33] Dickinson (ed.), *Aberdeen Records*, pp. cxlii–cxlv; H.L. MacQueen and W. Windram, 'Laws and Courts in the Burghs', Lynch, Spearman and Stell (eds.), *Scottish Medieval Town*, p. 214; *Charters and Other Documents Relating to the City of Edinburgh, A.D. 1143–1540*, ed. J.D. Marwick (Edinburgh, 1871), no. 33.

[34] Duncan, *James I*, pp. 9–11, 21.

[35] Montrose B.R., M/WI/14, 'Trading bundle', no. 1; CR2/10; 1/10/7 (Charter Chest inventory) p. 375 (the source for the King's interdict, which is a late, fragmentary copy only).

disputes shows that they too were settled outside the court's ambit, as if it were quite unable to settle these disputes adequately. The continuing sparse references to the court suggest that it had great difficulty maintaining its status. Full Parliaments or Councils General frequently gathered in the fifteenth century until the end of the reign of James III, and it may be that the burghs found these occasions more than adequate to deal with their needs.

The failure of either the Chamberlain or the Court of the Four Burghs to solve the dispute meant that, unless an arbitrated settlement was reached, the burghs would have to approach the King and Council, or Parliament. Parliament was the first to encounter the cause, in 1432 when the dispute may have been aired for the first time, and then with great regularity from January 1450. The King's Council was not involved until 1450, but thereafter was as much involved as Parliament. (The Council would, however, almost certainly have been involved earlier in advising the King about the matter, particularly when the signet letters inhibiting the Court of the Four Burghs from dealing with it were issued.)

The work of both the King's Council and Parliament in a judicial capacity is difficult to elucidate before the consistent record of their activities begins in 1478 and 1466 respectively. For knowledge of events prior to then we must turn to decrees formally extracted from now lost registers plus some precepts consequent on the decrees surviving amongst the legal papers of landed families, or of institutions such as the royal burghs as in this case. Because only a few dozen are known to exist, conclusions about the procedure adopted by either body must be tentative. In the 30 years the case lasted, however, the record shows that both Parliament and the King's Council certainly made particular developments in processing judicial business. On its own, the case may not have affected these developments, but it does illustrate some of the problems faced by such central courts which had to cope with a surge in business as the fifteenth century wore on.

Given the fifteenth-century legislation touching on its role which appears to show that the Council was under pressure, there is strangely little to show that this was the case. We have already noticed that a 1426 statute had accorded to the Chamberlain or the Chancellor headship of 'certane discret persons of the thre estatis' to be chosen by the King who were to determine finally all causes and complaints which could be determined before the King's Council. It is normal to see in this the origins of what would become the present-day Court of Session. Further legislation of 1439, 1456, 1458 and 1468 apparently touching on it suggests that it was seen as a way of providing a regular forum for consideration of the type of petitions normally presented to the King's Council. This body would be available to hear cases left unconcluded after Parliaments or Councils General, on which occasions many brought forward cases to be considered which tended to prolong the sittings of the Estates.[36]

This legislation certainly refers to a body other than the King's Council,

---

[36] For a general review of the 'session' as set up by this legislation see Borthwick, 'King, Council and Councillors', pp. 243–53 and other works cited there. The legislation mentioned is *A.P.S.*, II, 32, 46 c.8, 47–8 cc. 1–5, and 92 cc. 2, 4–7; cf. also *A.P.S.*, XII, 31 (undated but c.1463).

although apparently sharing its competence. There would, however, still be a need for the Council to hear judicial matters. A 1487 statute refers to cases 'pertenyng in speciale to our soverane lord', which were 'accions and complaintis made be kirkmen, wedowis, orphanis and pupillis, accions of strangearis of uther realmis and complaintis made apone officiaris forfalt of execucioun of thair office'. To the King therefore fell the task of protecting the vulnerable or needy, and of dealing with maladministration of his ministers (which is particularly emphasised in fifteenth century legislation). Further, the King would expect the Council to deal with cases touching upon his royal rights which might affect his income. There is no difficulty in illustrating cases of this nature, even before the Council's consistent record begins in 1478.[37]

Despite the legislation mentioned above promoting the concept of a regular session, it is clear that during the reigns of James I and II the Council itself underwent procedural initiatives which give it the air of being a body accustomed to dealing with judicial matters. The evidence of this is first, that study of the personnel of the judicial Council shows considerable overlap with the daily Council for more general business, but frequently at times of judicial business the Council was able to call on men with significant experience. Second, by 1448 there was a clerk of Council, although it is not clear that at this stage the post was permanent. Finally, analysis of the extant Council decrees compared to those of the lords auditors, the lords of the Three Estates or the session, shows that while the Council's own record is hard to pin down even as late as 1460, we can be confident that it differed particularly from that of the parliamentary bodies. It can therefore be concluded that the records of the Council were not under the control of the clerk register, in other respects the guardian of the Crown's administrative records. Indeed the Council's records were probably independent of the clerk register until 1483, when the then clerk of Council became clerk register as well.[38]

With hindsight, we can see that the trend in the 1450s and onwards was for the Council to be increasingly concerned with judicial matters, a process which may have been enhanced by the sudden death of James II in 1460 while his son and heir was still a minor. It is therefore surprising that the reasonably consistent Council record showing a regular involvement with judicial business begins as late as 1478, although there may have been a register of cases for late 1455 which was only to be lost in the late seventeenth century. The trend might have surprised contemporaries, as the statute evidence bears that it was wished to deflect judicial business from the Council.[39]

One of the prime functions of the medieval Scottish Parliament was that the King's subjects might be 'servit of the law'. It was the place 'at which and in

---

[37] *A.P.S.*, II, 177 c.10. For a case of maladministration, see Scottish R.O., GD211/3 (Sheriff McPhail papers) (1474); of royal rights, see GD16/2/5 (Airlie muniments) (1473); and of protecting the vulnerable, see W.C. Dickinson, 'Our Signet of the Unicorn', *Scottish Historical Review*, XXVI (1947), 147 (1460).

[38] Borthwick, 'King, Council and Councillors', pp. 258, 266–7, 288–301; *Acts of the Lords of Council*, III (1501–1503), ed. A.B. Calderwood (Edinburgh, 1993), pp. xix–xx.

[39] *Ibid.*, p. xix.

which justice must be done to anyone with a complaint'. A glance at the recently-published table of assemblies from 1290 onwards shows just how frequently Parliaments or Councils General were convened. For a fair number there is no surviving legislation, but from extract decrees we do know that judicial activity occurred. Parliament had first appointed commissioners to deal with judicial business at latest by 1341, and similar appointments can be found in subsequent Parliaments. Committees might be appointed separately for first instance business and for falsed dooms (appeals from lower courts), and at first it looks as if the committees may not have had full power themselves to give the final decree, but had to report back to Parliament for this purpose.[40]

There is much more evidence for the judicial workings of Parliament from 1424, probably the result of the greater survival rate of documents from that period, although, as with the Council, record-keeping was increasingly better organised. The record shows that, as well as the falsed dooms committee, a body was regularly elected to deal with first instance judicial business, styled the lords auditors of causes or lords auditors of causes and complaints. An equal number (usually three or four) was elected from each Estate. These committees were empowered to bring cases before them to any conclusion open to them, which would not necessarily finally end the case.

A second body is sometimes encountered to which Parliament entrusted some judicial business; the lords of the Three Estates. It was a much larger body than the auditors, although only occasionally are its members (amongst which burgesses can be found) identified. As we find both auditors and the lords of the Three Estates making decrees in the January 1450 Parliament, they must be separate. Rait suggests that this body was one instructed to continue Parliament after most of those attending had left.[41]

Here, then, in Parliament and Council were two bodies increasingly used to dealing with judicial business, which had available to assess the disputes some experienced clergy and laymen. In 1450 and 1459–61 particularly the *Montrose v. Dundee* case was frequently led before them. But Montrose was just as certain that Parliament was the only forum in which the case could proceed as it was that the Council had no competence. What underlay its certainty, and was it reasonable?

The basis of Montrose's arguments was that, if the indictment for forestalling of an inhabitant of Montrose proceeded at a chamberlain ayre held in Dundee, it was being ejected from its fee and heritage. This could only be done by use of a pleadable brieve which, as mentioned earlier, had to be led before the ordinary and not before either Council or Parliament.

The first expression of this rule (as Montrose saw it) in the case arose in 1448, during the chamberlain ayre proceedings. Montrose instructed its forespeaker to

---

[40] *A.P.S.*, I, 557 (1389), 573 (1399); for table of assemblies see *The Parliaments of Scotland: Burgh and Shire Commissioners*, ed. M.D. Young (2 vols., Edinburgh, 1992–3), II, Appendix 1; discussion of judicial functions of Parliament in P.J. Hamilton-Grierson, 'The Judicial Committees of the Scottish Parliament, 1369–70 to 1544', *Scottish Historical Review*, XXII (1925), 1–4; R.S. Rait, *The Parliaments of Scotland* (Glasgow, 1924), Chapter 7.

[41] Borthwick, 'King, Council and Councillors', pp. 253–4; Rait, *Parliaments*, pp. 349–61.

argue, if the Chamberlain intended to proceed with the indictment as he had letters thereanent from the King,[42]

> [to] say he is not holding of his office to suffer any uncoursable letters that are against the common law nor in prejudice of party as the king's statutes bears witness in the book of the king's majesty where he sees this statuit dominus rex quod nullus iusticiarius vicecomes nec aliquis alius minister eius faciet petitione alicuius mandati sibi directi sub quocunque sigillo magno secreto vel parvo aut signeto in preiudicium partis vel contra communem formam iuris sed si quod tali sibi directi fuerint indorse et indorsate remitte scribendo in dorso rationabilem causam quare dictus iudex adimplere non possit etc.

This argument and others against any action prejudicial to Montrose's fee and heritage were duly employed by the forespeaker, evidently to the Chamberlain's consternation. All he could do was to recommend approaching the King and Council for a remedy.

In 1458, Montrose again played the fee and heritage card, in the course of a wide-ranging appeal against the manner in which the case had proceeded. In effect, Montrose threw itself at the King's mercy, thus showing how important the case was to it. One of the planks of its protest now was that there had not been a lawful summons of it to a hearing, only the King's signet letters on paper which by law could not force a party to enter litigation on a fee and heritage matter, and thus the whole process was invalid. On this occasion, it does not look as if Montrose's plea cut much ice, as within two months the King granted the charter in favour of Dundee, including the provision about indictment of forestallers. Despite this, Montrose was able to reopen the case next year, and in due course obtain a satisfactory resolution, as we have seen.[43]

From other contemporary sources, we can show that the rule that a pleadable brieve was needed to eject a party from its fee and heritage was well-known, and further that this rule has a long history. MacQueen traces the rule compelling their use in land disputes to certainly the thirteenth century, although it was given its clearest expression in a statute of Robert I in 1318: 'no-one is to be ejected from his free holding of which he claims to be vest or saised as of fee without the king's pleadable brieve or some similar brieve nor without being first reasonably summoned to a certain day and place for his free holding'.[44] From fourteenth and fifteenth century examples, there is no doubt that this rule was generally thought to be operative. Indeed, apart from the citation by Montrose in the course of the case against Dundee, there is a nice example from 1456 in Montrose's own court book. During a chamberlain ayre held in Montrose that year, Janet Ichmedan complained that a man (surname illegible) had detained a

---

[42] Montrose B.R., M/WD/1. The original instructions are in Scots, with the exception of two Latin paraphrases, but here the Scots has been changed to English. The 'book of the king's majesty' referred to here is the Scots law book *Regiam Majestatem.*

[43] Montrose B.R., M/WI/14, 'Trading bundle', no. 7. The protest is reproduced in full in Borthwick, 'King, Council and Councillors', Appendix E.

[44] R.R.S., V, no. 139 c.25. The translation of the statute is from MacQueen, *Common Law,* p. 106, and see generally Chapter 4.

tenement unjustly from her. He asserted that he had held it in fee and heritage for a certain (unstated) time, and that he did not have to answer for it without a pleadable brieve. The court held his plea to be valid.[45]

But according to MacQueen this pleadable brieve rule was only half of the restrictions on the means of settling property disputes in the central courts. The other half was the restriction on the jurisdiction of the King's Council and Parliament, which meant that when actions of fee and heritage occurred they would have to be remitted by these bodies to the judge ordinary, that is, the judge having jurisdiction at common law over the land in issue.[46] This rule finds particularly good expression in an undated, but probably mid to late fifteenth-century, petition of William, Richard and Henry Graham after their summons before the King's Council to show charters and other documents by which they held the lands of Hutton:[47]

> [W]e clame the sayde landis wyth thair pertynence our fee and herytage, and haf beyne this hundreth yeris and mare, and we in pesabyll possessioun this xx yeris, and we understande that he that is yere and day in peseabyll possessioun in any lande clamande it of fee and herytage he aucht nocht to ga owte of his possessioun forowte the kyngis brefe pledabyll We understande that our soverayne lorde the kyngis counsale is na cowrte to plede fee na herytage na lyfe na lym in Quharfor we beseke our soverayne lord the kyng for the lufe of Gode that of his mychty maieste that he walde kepe us as we that ar his pure legis unwrangyt otherwayis [in] oure lyfis and in oure lande in ony other wayis bot as the course of commoune law wyll and at we may byde befor our jugegis ordynare as the ordure of law of Scotlande wyll.

As MacQueen comments, this petition implies a connection between the brieve rule and the fee and heritage rule, but he goes on to argue that the 'true origin of the fee and heritage rule lies in the exclusion of the jurisdiction of Parliament and Council where there was an ordinary common-law remedy'. This position was, however, abandoned in the fifteenth century, and the exclusion of Parliament and Council came to be expressed in terms of a refusal to act in cases touching fee and heritage, which remained those where action by pleadable brieve was competent. Despite in general an increasing amount of judicial business for Parliament and Council landownership cases therefore remained quite distinct.[48]

Although the *Montrose* v. *Dundee* case did not actually touch on landownership, it did concern fee and heritage as Montrose's pleas show. We would therefore expect that the parties would view any hearing by Parliament or Council to be wrongful. But this did not quite happen.

---

[45] Scottish R.O., B51/10/1, p. 5 (Montrose Burgh MSS.); Borthwick, 'King, Council and Councillors', pp. 344–5.

[46] MacQueen, *Common Law*, pp. 216–8, 236.

[47] H.M.C., *Various Collections*, V, 77 (Edmondstone of Duntreath), with corrections from a microfilm of the original (now sold and current whereabouts not known) in Scottish R.O., RH4/124/1.

[48] MacQueen, *Common Law*, p. 228, and generally Chapter 8.

Both burghs seem to have accepted that Parliament had jurisdiction in their case. Montrose, indeed, in the course of a protest about the dealings of the Council in the case in August 1458, specifically stated: 'we refer us to the parliament quhar debatis off bondis of burowis off fee and heritage aucht off law to be determyt'. Dundee for its part accepted that the dealings of Parliament represented the most likely way of obtaining a settlement, although once Montrose had taken action against its new charter in 1458 Dundee itself became irritated with the course of proceedings. It lodged a protest in the March 1461 Parliament, in particular that it did not want to have put under review its new charter, as it was insistent that any argument about boundaries had been fully concluded with the authority of Parliament.[49]

Montrose was much less content with the hearings by the King's Council. Both burghs had consented to the election of a special commission of Parliament in 1450 to settle the dispute, and we know that this commission did fulfil its task with a verdict favourable to Montrose. But for some reason the decree was not executed, and Montrose protested three times in 1450 alone about this when it was summoned before the King's Council for a consideration of the affair. Then, and again in 1458, its commissioners were appointed solely to seek execution of the 1450 decree.[50]

When the case resurfaced in 1458, there was an unsuccessful effort at an extra-curial settlement before it was taken up again by Parliament, this time by the lords auditors. Both burghs evidently agreed to this, and to the continuation (with the full power of Parliament) to the second day of a justice ayre at Perth. Thereafter, however, there were continuations to the Exchequer audit and to a hearing before the King himself. Although the document recording this asserts that all these continuations were with the parties' consents, Montrose insisted that the continuations could not now have the full force of Parliament. Certainly the body referred to in the interlocutor providing a summary account of the proceedings in 1458 which concluded the affair looks as if it must have been the Council under some guise. In March 1461 the lords auditors seem to have accepted Montrose's arguments about the validity of the continuations and final verdict of 1458 and annulled that decree, to Dundee's dismay.[51]

We can see therefore that while particular events might anger each side, neither wished to deny that in principle Parliament was entitled to consider the matter. The greater informality of the Council, which could have led to a decree issued by those who happened to be present on a particular day, worried Montrose more than Dundee. But it is likely that Montrose would have agreed with an argument put forward by Dundee in 1463 in the course of a dispute with Forfar: that after hearings before the justiciar and the Chamberlain it had been taken 'to the supreme court of the kingdom, that is Parliament, before our supreme lord the king and the three estates', and what was 'once before the supreme court of

[49] Montrose B.R. CR2/10; D.D.A., TC/CC 1/39.

[50] Montrose B.R., M/WD/1, M/WI/14, 'Trading bundle', nos. 4, 7; Nat. Lib. Scotland., MS. 15471 (Chalmers of Audlbar papers), f. 95.

[51] Montrose B.R., M/WI/14, 'Trading bundle', nos. 3, 10; D.D.A., TC/CC 1/36, 39.

the realm must not and could not be turned back afterwards to any inferior court'.[52]

A protest lodged in a separate case in 1471 supports this contention. Thomas Allardice of that ilk, in protesting that his dispute with John Dempster ought in fact to be heard by the judge ordinary and not before the Council, stated that 'it is agane the comoune law and consuetude that ony mater or questioune decidit and decretit be a generale counsale or Parliament suld resort or remain to be deliverit in a laware court'.[53]

The text entitled 'The Scottish King's Household', thought to be of late 13th-century date, also supplies evidence for Parliament's supremacy. In discussing offices of fee and how claims to hold one should be tried, there is the comment: 'let this be done in full Parliament and not by a less council'.[54]

It seems that it is unwise to link Parliament and the Council too closely. The Council was specifically charged with catering for causes which the King wished it to deal with, including those where parties having the King's ear obtained the privilege of taking their cases to Council; while Parliament would have to deal with the rest. Chalmers and Duncan have commented that unconcluded cases could not automatically be continued from sessions of the auditors to the Council once the auditors had returned home. If this had been possible, there would have been little need to make special extensions of auditors sittings, as the Council could have assumed the backlog.[55]

One reason for this difference is surely that Parliament was, as Duncan reminds us, a proper court, while Council was not. Not only was it a court, but the supreme court, in which dooms might on occasion be pronounced in presence of the King 'with the crown on his head and sceptre in his hand sitting in the throne of justice in Parliament'. On the other hand, cases were theoretically brought before the King and Council, but it is rare to hear in the record of a decree of the King's presence during a Council hearing. As for the finality of verdicts, we have seen in this case how the auditors in 1461 annulled a 1458 decree as not being a true one of Parliament, which accords with Chalmers' comment that appeals from the auditors to full Parliament was possible but only in the event of 'blatant technical irregularity'; whereas Council decrees may have been 'more routinely appealable in Parliament'.[56]

Despite this air of supremacy of Parliament, the Council may have had a more secure role in certain landownership matters. Recognition following unlicensed alienation has long been appreciated as a tool for increasing income for later fifteenth-century monarchs. In the reigns of James III and (more particularly) James

[52] D.D.A., TC/CC 1/41 (my translation, from the original Latin).

[53] H.M.C., *5th Report*, (Barclay Allardice MSS.) p. 630 (corrected using the original, now Scottish R.O., GD49/7 (Barclay Allardice muniments).

[54] Bateson (ed.), 'Scottish King's Household', pp. 37, 43.

[55] T.M. Chalmers, 'The King's Council, Patronage and the Governance of Scotland, 1460–1513' (University of Aberdeen Ph.D. thesis, 1982), pp. 160–3; A.A.M. Duncan, 'The Central Courts Before 1532', Paton (ed.), *Scottish Legal History*, p. 337.

[56] Duncan, 'Central Courts Before 1532', pp. 323, 328; *A.P.S.*, II, 114 (1476 doom): cf. also *A.P.S.*, XII, 28–9 (no. 50) (1463) for similar expression about presence of the King; Montrose B.R., M/WI/14, 'Trading bundle', no. 14 (decree annulled, 1461); Chalmers, 'King's Council', p. 162.

IV, the Crown demanded compositions from its vassals for re-entry to their lands recognosced following wrongful alienation. This was a new avenue for patronage, and the benefit for the Crown of pursuing the matter vigorously was clear.[57]

Until recently, it has escaped notice that recognition was relatively common at least half a century earlier. Then, however, it is possible that the reason for it was not necessarily as punishment, but to encourage settlement of a dispute. What is commonly found, as MacQueen shows, is that when parties were in dispute over a right to property held of the Crown, the Crown would have its officers recognosce the property preparatory to a decision as to the last lawful possessor, which would be made before, if not necessarily by, lords of the King's Council. When this had been reached, the property was relaxed to that person on his giving security, and (if necessary) a contest could then begin as to the actual ownership of the heritage. Not all recognitions were carried out by Crown officials; some were done by subject superiors exercising authority over their vassals.[58]

It is important to note that only the King or his Council could relax a recognition carried out by the King's officers. The auditors could not. The Council would on occasion have to act on the King's behalf (particularly during minority rule), as the superior of the ground, as numerous examples show. This did not stop people presenting petitions to the lords of Council during a session of Parliament, but this may simply have happened in an effort to publicise their cause, and because the session of Parliament was a known fixed event, whereas Council met irregularly.[59]

Patronage and punishment were certainly possible here too. A good example is the *Skene* v. *Keith* case. The case is full of interest, but the essential details are that the son of the original grantor of the lands involved, James Skene, obtained a brieve of right against the niece of his cousin, and subsequently asserted that he had been found to have greater right to the lands. Yet the property was recognosced by the Crown about 1457, and Skene had to petition the King in Parliament on at least three occasions in the next four years for return of the lands on giving security. In this case in particular, one suspects that political pressure demanded that the King favour the defender more than the pursuer, despite his successful use of the brieve of right, which ought to have awarded him the lands outright to the exclusion of any other claim.[60]

[57] The basis for most recent comment on recognition as the consequence of wrongful alienation is two articles: R.G. Nicholson, 'Feudal Developments in Late Medieval Scotland', *Juridical Review*, new ser., XVIII (1973), 1–21; and C. Madden, 'Royal Treatment of Feudal Casualties in Late Medieval Scotland', *Scottish Historical Review*, LV (1976), 172–94.

[58] MacQueen, *Common Law*, esp. pp. 228–31. There are many more examples of recognition prior to settlement of a dispute than MacQueen mentions. A fine example is *Muniments of the Royal Burgh of Irvine* (2 vols., Edinburgh, 1890–1), I, no. 9 (1417).

[59] The examples cited by MacQueen, as above, imply that the auditors had a definite role in recognition. Although I do not accept this, it is clear that at particular times (e.g. during the Albany governorships or during the minority of James III) Councils General or Parliament would encounter cases in which a recognition had occurred. These are surely to be explained by the incapacity of the monarch, for whatever reason, and the consequent enhancement of the role of the Three Estates.

[60] MacQueen, *Common Law*, pp. 203–4, 230; Borthwick, 'King, Council and Councillors', pp. 216–7.

Whatever the cause, it would certainly not suit vassals for their lands to be in Crown hands for any length of time, as loss of income would result, and their tenants' security would also be threatened. In the process of regaining their property, if simply by petition to the Crown, some right to the property would have to be exhibited, and here we can perhaps see how the Council might become accustomed to hearing heritage issues by what could be called 'the back door'. MacQueen indeed wonders if the brieve of novel dissasine fell into desuetude because of the Council acting in this way. It would still be open to disputants to purchase a pleadable brieve to have the matter of right declared before the ordinary, but perhaps possession was all that mattered on many occasions—which could be secured before the Council.[61]

Although the auditors' role in recognition was very limited, Parliament as a whole might be faced with fee and heritage matters on appeal. It was quite possible that the doom awarding ownership of property after the execution of a pleadable brieve could be falsed all the way to Parliament. (Council had no role in the falsing of dooms.) In 1471, for example, Parliament had to consider the case of Andrew Bisset against John Dishington of Ardross, occasioned by the falsing of a doom upon a bieve of mortancestor. And there is the paradox that Parliament, in adjudicating treason cases, could award forfeiture of life and land, but could apparently not deprive a person of his heritage in the course of a simple dispute. Parliament had to be no less flexible than Council. Apart from dealing with simple judicial matters, and treason cases, it might even have to convene in the form of a trial by peers, as in 1452 to acquit the King of duplicity in the murder of the eighth Earl of Douglas.[62] The *Montrose* v. *Dundee* proceedings demonstrate this flexibility. At first a special commission of 12 was elected, then the lords auditors were to deal with it, quickly becoming the Exchequer auditors, then any lords being present with the King, then back to the special commission (most of whom were by then dead), so back to the lords auditors again—and the case had not changed.

We might conclude, then, that MacQueen's views on the disability of Parliament and Council with respect to fee and heritage cases are not mistaken, but that the rule restricting their role was not strictly applied. A plus for litigants was that each could strip the case down to its essentials even if it decided that the matter should then proceed before the ordinary. It is unfortunate that generally we do not know how cases proceeded after the decree by the auditors or Council. In particular cases, however, litigants might be more inclined (or were instructed) to accept the jurisdiction of Parliament or Council; and in due course, as MacQueen has shown, the role of the ordinary in fee and heritage matters was completely forgotten.

What is likely is that litigants were becoming confused about the right forum for their case. Legislation directed them to the ordinary, rather than to the Council, and in respect of fee and heritage cases this was where they ought to have gone. Pleadings display this theory well. But litigants in the fifteenth century were attracted to active central courts to whom they brought their cases, and their

[61] MacQueen, *Common Law*, pp. 237–8, 256–7.
[62] *Ibid.*, p. 179; *A.P.S.*, II, 73 no. 33 (acquittal of King).

pleadings then altered to argue against the thrust down to the ordinary, as the Allardice example in 1471 just mentioned seems to show. The confusion was heightened by the readiness of Parliament or Council to deal with cases, on occasion because both parties assented to this course, but on others because the court determined that it could hear the matter notwithstanding objections by one party. MacQueen cites a case of this nature in 1430 in Parliament, to which can be added another similar one in 1453 (*Glamis* v. *Fleming*). In the case examined here, both burghs did assent to the hearings by Parliament, which certainly explains why so much was conducted before it, but it looks very unlikely that either would have assented to hearings by Council.[63]

This case also neatly shows how local and national politics were intertwined. Dundee had risen to prominence in international trade to an extent that Montrose, as the longer-established royal burgh, found hard to bear. When there was the possibility of its liberties being infringed by the indictment in Dundee of one of its inhabitants, it clearly decided to use this minor case as a test of principle. For the Crown, this at first minor irritation grew to dominate the late 1450s, as it realised that chamberlain ayres could not readily be held without a decision being reached about the principle. Strangely, despite it being ready to have inquiries conducted into the privileges of Brechin and Forfar in the 1450s and 1460s, there was no such inquiry here. Instead, the Crown attempted to force through its own settlement which favoured Dundee, but the manner of its doing so stung Montrose into further protests. Yet this settlement may have contained the seeds of the Crown's defeat. The Bishop of Brechin was the Chancellor, and Montrose was so disgruntled by his handling of the case before the Council in 1458 that it threw itself at the King's mercy. The bishop had, of course, primary responsibility for his own city of Brechin, whose long-running dispute with Montrose has already been mentioned. It is therefore not surprising that after the bishop ceased to be Chancellor in 1460 Montrose began to make headway. It is interesting to reflect on the apparent inability of the Crown to maintain its stance, given the status of James II who had seen off all his internal enemies in the nobility by that time.[64]

No less important is the light shed by proceedings on the development of means of dealing with judicial business in Council and Parliament. The traditional method of conducting landownership cases before the ordinary was no longer in such demand, as Council and Parliament were better organised for the conduct of judicial business. Local courts most certainly continued to operate, but litigants were prepared to take their chance at a central court. It was becoming increasingly

---

[63] For legislation directing litigants to the ordinary, see *A.P.S.*, II, 8 c.24 (1425), 94 c.2 (1469) (although note the final sentence in this statute which emphasises that the King may continue to have any action brought before him at his will), 177–8 c.10 (1487); MacQueen, *Common Law*, pp. 232, 238 (1430 case); Nat. Lib. Scotland, Ch. 16060; and Strathmore MSS. (Earl of Strathmore and Kinghorne, Glamis Castle, Angus), Box 2, no. 46, both cover the 1453 case, but the latter is very badly damaged.

[64] *R.M.S.*, II, no. 494; Montrose B.R., M/WI/10/2 (for Brechin's privileges inquiries); D.D.A., TC/CC 1/41 (for Forfar's); Borthwick, 'King, Council and Councillors', p. 488 (dates of holding of chancellorship by the Bishop of Brechin).

difficult to cater for the large number of cases brought to one or other of these central courts, and the Crown's advisers and the Three Estates realised that to deal with complex issues a more certain judicial framework had to be created, by maintaining the session's sittings. But the death of James II in 1460 brought a strong measure of conciliar government again. As the Council sat for political purposes more regularly more judicial business came before it, while the session, the innovation of the earlier fifteenth century, though not dropped as yet seems to have been shaded out. Would this have happened if the King had not been killed?

A consequence of regular sittings of the Council, and of the auditors, was a myriad of cases, some of a minor nature. *Montrose* v. *Dundee* was in one sense a minor case. One wonders how many contemporaries realised that all the effort we have outlined here arose from a case where the fine levied on a guilty person would have been a few shillings.[65]

---

[65] According to the 'Leges Burgorum' (*A.P.S.*, I, 347 c. 72) the fine for forestalling was 8*s.*, but a swift check of published burgh court minutes suggests that no uniform fine was levied in practice.

Constitutional Revolution, Party and Faction in the Scottish Parliaments of Charles I*

JOHN J. SCALLY

National Library of Scotland

In the last few months of 1649, Sir James Balfour of Denmylne, Lord Lyon King at Arms to Charles I, recorded in a tortuous sentence the refusal of John, Earl of Crawford-Lindsay, recently deposed Lord Treasurer of Scotland, to acknowledge that the last full parliamentary session in the reign of Charles I was illegal:[1]

> My Lord wes ever contentit to give the churche all resonable satisfaction, bot to declare that sessione of parliament quherby the engagement for the King's liberatione against the perfidious hereticks and faithbreake[r]s of England, wes unlawfull, being commandit by parliament, and him to acknouledge the last sessione of parliament, quho had no uther warrant for their meitting, bot the indiction of that wich they disannulled; that he wold not doe one aney tearmes, for if he should so doe, then he behoved to ratiffie that sessione of parliament, that had quyte altered the goverment established by the former session of parliament, quherin wer above 65 of the nobility, and in this, not above 3.

Crawford-Lindsay's refusal to subscribe to the illegality of the Engagement Parliament of 1648 rested upon the fact that the nobility were not adequately represented at the rump session which followed it and declared the Engagement Parliament illegal. Without the presence of the noble estate in adequate numbers, the authority of Parliament was severely diminished.

Crawford-Lindsay was one of the leading Covenanters throughout the 1640s along with Archibald, first Marquess of Argyll, John, first Earl of Loudoun, John, sixth Earl of Cassillis, James, second Lord Balmerino, Robert, second Lord Burleigh, and Sir Archibald Johnston of Wariston. He was also the brother-in-law of James, third Marquess and first Duke of Hamilton, who, along with Hamilton's brother, William, first Earl of Lanark, Secretary of Scotland, was the architect of

---

* I am grateful to Dr John Morrill and Professor Keith Brown for their comments on and criticisms of drafts of this essay.

[1] *The Historical Works of Sir James Balfour of Denmylne and Kinnaird* (4 vols., Edinburgh, 1824) [hereafter Balfour, *Works*], III, 435. The second session of the second Triennial Parliament commenced on 4 Jan. 1649, and Charles I was executed on the 30th of the month while the session was in progress. It appears that about 14 to 16 of the nobility attended the first day of Parliament on 4 Jan. See, *The Acts of the Parliaments of Scotland* (12 vols., Edinburgh, 1884) [hereafter *A.P.S.*]; VI, ii, 124–156; Balfour, *Works*, III, 373; *The Memoirs of Henry Guthry, late Bishop of Dunkeld* (2nd edn., Glasgow, 1747), pp. 301–302.

the Engagement of 1647–8. At the height of the Engagement preparations, Crawford-Lindsay, with Lanark as his second, had been involved in a duel with Argyll, the chief opponent of the Engagement.[2] The Earl of Crawford-Lindsay's behaviour at the end of the Parliaments of Charles I encapsulates the central theme of this essay: that despite a rebellion against the King's authority in 1638, despite a constitutional revolution focused in Parliament between 1639 and 1641, despite a war against the King between 1643 and 1646, and despite a war to save the King in 1648, the operation of politics, particularly in Parliament, followed an established pattern based on the social hierarchy.

2

Of course, certain groups enjoyed a higher profile than hitherto, notably the barons in Parliament, who replaced the clerical estate in 1640 and had their voting power doubled,[3] but their political role, whilst greatly enhanced, did not lead to a breakdown in traditional political relationships based on the landed and social hierarchy. In fact the barons were an integral part of the landed hierarchy being, like the higher nobility (or peerage), tenants-in-chief of the Crown and the elected representatives of the shires.[4] Even during the most vociferous phase of the Covenanting period between 1644 and 1646 their traditional identity changed little—they were described in the sederunt roll as the 'Commissionaris for the Barrones', occasionally as the 'Commissionaris for the Shyres', and were referred to in the Parliamentary Registers not as the gentry, nor the shire commissioners, but as the 'Barons' with all the associations with the noble estate that this implies.[5] Behind the scenes, the barons and burgesses packed the numerous committees of Parliament during the 1640s and shouldered the bureaucratic workload of that tumultuous decade. But, although impressive in numbers, they did not occupy the political cockpit during this period. Moreover, they did not seek to overturn, or in most cases to challenge, the political hierarchy. Commissioners for the

---

[2] Balfour, *Works*, III, 395–396. When the parties convened at Musselburgh Links for the duel, Argyll refused to fight.

[3] Barons were the elected representatives of the shires. Traditionally each shire had a single vote in Parliament even though they were entitled to send two representatives. But in 1640 the two barons who represented a shire were given a vote each, which effectively doubled the voting power of the estate. See, D. Stevenson, *The Government of Scotland under the Covenanters, 1637–1651* (Edinburgh, 1982), p. xxiii.

[4] The nobles, higher nobility or peerage were tenants in chief along with the lesser or small barons, but they had long been divided; the former attended Parliament by personal right, the latter by election. The most accurate assessment of this group is provided by James VI who, in *Basilikon Doron*, observed 'the small barronis are but ane inferioure pairt of the nobillite & of thaire estait', *The Basilikon Doron of James VI*, ed. J. Craigie (2 vols., Edinburgh, 1944), I, 88–89; see also, J. Wormald, 'Lords and Lairds in Fifteenth-century Scotland: Nobles and Gentry?', *Gentry and Lesser Nobility in late Medieval Europe*, ed., M. Jones (Gloucester, 1986), p. 181; A. Grant, 'The Development of the Scottish Peerage', *Scottish Historical Review*, LVII, (1978), 1–27 *passim*.

[5] For 1640–41 see for example, *A.P.S.*, V, 258–261, 279, 312, 313, 384. For 1644–46 see *A.P.S.*, V, i, 60–61, 71, 83–84, 93–94, 95–96, 284, 429, 440–441, 474–475, 612–613. In the roll of the Convention of Estates on 25 Jan. 1644, the nobility and barons are listed together, with the 'burgess' [sic] listed below, *A.P.S.*, V, i, 73. For 1646–48, see Scottish R.O., PA 7/24, f. 200r; PA 11/5, ff. 3–218; PA 11/6, f. 1r-v. The term 'Commissionaris for the Barronis' was first used in July 1593, see *A.P.S.*, IV, 6–7.

barons such as Sir Archibald Johnston of Wariston and Sir Andrew Fletcher of Innerpeffer were important spokesmen both for their estate and on the floor of the House, but they were always in the shadow of their political superiors and collaborators, Archibald, Marquess of Argyll, and James, Duke of Hamilton, respectively.

It is within this context that the politics of party and faction determined how individuals behaved in Parliament—and it was these labels which were used by contemporaries to describe political groups. In the years 1647 and 1648, for example, Robert Baillie, although often bewildered by the machinations of 'our great men' in the Committee of Estates and Parliament over how to respond to the treatment of the King in England, described political alignments in terms of 'party' and 'faction'.[6] As with most political labels,[7] they carried with them derogatory connotations, especially 'faction', which, in the hands of hostile commentators, often denoted a group intent on undermining the body politic to gain an advantage.[8] However, a more striking feature of the use of these contemporary labels was the naming of a party or faction after its leader, in particular the two dominant figures in parliamentary politics of this period, Archibald, eighth Earl and first Marquess of Argyll, and James, third Marquess and first Duke of Hamilton. And this was a telling indicator of the hierarchical nature of Scottish parliamentary politics in the reign of Charles I.

Patterns of allegiance to a parliamentary party were complex, and difficult to recover with any certainty given the absence of parliamentary division lists, records of debates or diarists' scribblings, though Henry Guthry's observation on the reasons for following Hamilton's Engagement in 1648, albeit from a hostile source, are revealing: 'so absolute was duke Hamilton's power, that he could carry what he pleased, many adhering to him upon interest of blood and friendship; and others conceiving him to be for the king'.[9] It was the mixture of traditional kin and blood ties harnessed to a national issue, in the above case the fate of the King, that defined parties in the Scottish Parliaments of the 1640s. Indeed the regular sitting of either Parliaments, Conventions of Estates or Committees of Estates throughout the decade 1639–49 permitted the establishment of loose parties, with a committed core, and led by a noble magnate, which articulated a policy on national issues such as the constitutional settlement

---

[6] *The Letters and Journals of Robert Baillie*, ed. D. Laing, (3 vols., Edinburgh, 1841–2) [hereafter Baillie, *Letters and Journals*], III, 18, 20, 34, 35, 38. See also, Guthry, *Memoirs*, pp. 262–5; P. Gordon, *A Short Abridgement of Britane's Distemper*, ed. J. Dunn (Spalding Club, Aberdeen, 1844), pp. 206, 223. For the earlier 1640s, cf. J. Gordon, *History of Scots Affairs, 1637–1641* (3 vols., Spalding Club, 1841), III, 78, 133; Gordon, *Britane's Distemper*, p. 146. In 1643 Baillie talks of 'faction' and Gilbert Burnet recorded the contemporary labels, 'Argyle's party' and 'Hamilton party', Baillie, *Letters and Journals*, II, 59; G. Burnet, *The Memoirs of the Lives and Actions of James and William Dukes of Hamilton* (Oxford, 1673), p. 262. See also, *The Diplomatic Correspondence of Jean De Montereul and the Brothers De Bellievre, French Ambassadors in England and Scotland, 1645–1648*, ed. J.G. Fotheringham (2 vols., Edinburgh, 1898–9), *passim*. Charles I also viewed parliamentary factions in Scotland in the same way, see below.

[7] A.I. MacInnes, 'The First Scottish Tories?', *Scottish Historical Review*, LXVII (1988), 56–66.

[8] See, for example, Baillie's venomous description of the Independents in England, Baillie, *Letters and Journals*, III, 26–31. See also Guthry, *Memoirs*, p. 263.

[9] Guthry, *Memoirs*, p. 262.

of 1639–41, the Solemn League and Covenant of 1643–4 and the Engagement of 1647–8.[10]

3

Traditionally, Scottish Parliaments were both infrequent and short-lived, the exception being the period 1639–51 when Parliament or one of its mutated forms—a Convention or Committee of Estates—was regularly in place in Edinburgh.[11] Yet the overarching characteristic that defined the Scottish Parliament before 1640 was not that it had three estates,[12] nor that it was unicameral, but that on convening it promptly surrendered its legislative and deliberative function to a committee, the Lords of the Articles.[13] The procedure for choosing members of the Articles, and the number of them, changed over time until a precedent was set in the early seventeenth century whereby the nobles chose eight of the clergy, the clergy chose eight nobles, and then these two estates jointly elected eight each from the Commissioners for the barons and burghs. Finally the King or his Commissioner, elected eight officers of state to complete the membership of the Articles.[14] At the Coronation Parliament of Charles I in 1633 this was all done by the nobles, clergy and the King away from the chamber.[15] Immediately

---

[10] At least two streams are evident in recent writing on the nature of the political nation in Scotland 1560–1637; the first, championed by Maurice Lee *jr.* argues for a conservative and declining nobility engaging with an innovative Crown allied to a rising middling sort, *John Maitland of Thirlestone and the Foundation of Stewart Despotism* (Princeton, 1959) and *idem, Government by Pen, Scotland under James VI and I* (Urbana, 1980). This view has also been influential in J.M. Goodare, 'Parliament and Society in Scotland, 1560–1603' (2 vols., University of Edinburgh Ph.D, 1989); *idem* 'The Nobility and the Absolutist State in Scotland, 1584–1638', *History*, LXXVIII (1993), 161–82. The second stream, of a powerful nobility working with a robust Crown, can be recovered from J. Wormald, 'Bloodfeud, Kindred and Government in Early Modern Scotland' *Past and Present*, No. 87 (1980); *idem, Court, Kirk and Community* (London, 1981), pp. 151–2, 157; K.M. Brown, *Bloodfeud in Scotland, 1573–1625* (Edinburgh, 1986), *idem, Kingdom or Province? Scotland and the Regal Union, 1603–1715* (1993), pp. 33–51, esp. pp. 42–5. For the 1640s, the key role of the gentry in Parliament—a Scottish Commons, in fact—is powerfully argued in J.R. Young 'The Scottish Parliament, 1639–1661: A Political and Constitutional Analysis' (3 vols., University of Glasgow Ph.D., 1993); A.I. MacInnes, *Charles I and the Making of the Covenanting Movement, 1625–1641* (Edinburgh, 1991); *idem,* 'Early Modern Scotland: The Current State of Play', *Scottish Historical Review*, LXXIII, (1995), 37–40, 42. This article argues for a continuation of elements of the second stream into the parliamentary politics of the 1640s.

[11] K.M. Brown, *Kingdom or Province*, pp. 13–14; D. Stevenson, *The Government of Scotland under the Covenanters, 1637–1651* (Edinburgh, 1982), Appendices, pp. 174–98; Young, 'The Scottish Parliament, 1639–1661', *passim*; Goodare, 'Parliament and Society in Scotland 1560–1603'; R.S. Rait, *The Parliaments of Scotland* (Glasgow, 1924); C.S. Terry, *The Scottish Parliament: Its Constitution and Procedure, 1603–1707* (Glasgow, 1905).

[12] It was accepted *de facto* by some contemporaries that with the division of the lords temporal or nobles into higher nobility, or peerage and lesser barons there were unofficially four estates in Parliament, see Stevenson, *Government under the Covenanters*, pp. xxii–xxiii.

[13] The historical context of the Lords of the Articles is best described in *A.P.S.*, I, 15–18.

[14] The numbers varied between six and ten for each Estate and Officers of State, with an average of eight. See, for example, *A.P.S.*, IV, 194, 261, 280, 365–6, 413, 466–7, 526–7, 594–5; V, 9; Rait, *Parliaments*, pp. 7–8; Terry, *Parliament 1603–1707*, pp. 103–20. In 1606 there was a debate whether new Lords of Articles should be elected at the start of each session of Parliament or, as was the case, at the beginning of each Parliament, see *A.P.S.*, IV, 279–280.

[15] *A.P.S.*, V, 9. According to the Covenanters in 1640, the retiring away from the chamber was introduced along with the bishops in the Parliament of 1617, see below. But it is hard to tell from *A.P.S.* since on some occasions the registers recorded that 'Eodem die domini electi ad articulos',

upon the announcement of the membership of the Articles, the remainder of the Estates dispersed and left the Committee to deliberate and frame legislation. Following the Articles' deliberations, the whole Parliament was re-convened and passed all of the legislation in a single day—as was the custom.[16]

As an institution then, the Scottish Parliament was neither over-sophisticated nor could it be described as a forum for continuous debate in the unicameral chamber, since on convening it passed that function to the Lords of the Articles. Its spasmodic and short meetings in the sixteenth and seventeenth centuries militated against the constitutional and procedural development of Parliament. Yet even with these flaws it was one of the few national institutions, in a society dominated by provincial magnates and the Crown, capable of bringing together the political nation under one roof. After the departure of King James VI and I in 1603 and the subsequent dispersal of the Scottish court, the status of Parliament as a national institution was correspondingly enhanced.

4

Charles I has passed into history as a monarch with a devotion to episcopacy and a detestation of Parliaments. In England, from 1629 to 1640, he famously ruled without Parliament and ended up fighting against the Long Parliament (which the Scottish Covenanters forced him to call in November 1640) for the next eight years. In Scotland he called a Coronation Parliament in 1633, after eight years of delays and excuses, and forced through his own legislative programme whilst punishing even the most innocuous opposition.[17] Six years later, when the Covenanters' resistance to his civil and ecclesiastical policy enjoyed the support of most of the country, Charles allowed a Parliament to assemble only to avoid the complete breakdown of his authority—and to allow him time to raise forces in England and Ireland for an ambitious, and ultimately futile, assault on his Scottish kingdom.[18] As in Scotland, the English Parliament became the hub of resistance to the King during the 1640s. In both instances the political nation chose Parliament as the forum for opposition to the King and the institution through which settlement was to be validated—although both institutions would have to be reformed first in strikingly similar ways.[19]

That the Covenanters intended to use the Scottish Parliament as the platform for their resistance to the absentee rule of Charles I explains why changes to

---

[15] *(contd.) A.P.S.*, IV, 467 (1612), 526 (1617), 594 (1621). At other times the Registers state only 'Domini electi ad articulos' *A.P.S.*, III, 4 (1567), 195 (1581), 290 (1584). However, in 1592 it was stated 'the haill estaittis of parliament cheisit [. . .] derwttn to be lordis of the articles', *A.P.S.*, III, 530, and in 1604 'the q'lk day the haill estaittis of parliamet [sic] cheisit the lordis underwrittin to be upoun the articlis', *A.P.S.*, IV, 260. In 1639, the Earl of Argyll questioned the method of election away from the chamber, *A.P.S.*, V, 252–3.

[16] *A.P.S.*, IV, 467, 527, 595; *A.P.S.*, V, 11.

[17] MacInnes, *Covenanting Movement*, pp. 86–89; P. Donald, *An Uncounselled King: Charles I and the Scottish Troubles, 1637–1641* (Cambridge, 1990), pp. 29–32.

[18] J.J. Scally, 'The Political Career of James, Third Marquis and First Duke of Hamilton (1606–1649) to 1643' (University of Cambridge Ph.D., 1992), pp. 214–262.

[19] The most important of the reforms to the Scottish Parliament—Triennial Parliaments, parliamentary approval of the appointment of officers of state—quickly became demands in the English Parliament, cf. C. Russell, *The Causes of the English Civil War* (Oxford, 1990), pp. 27–8.

Parliament were so high on their agenda. The initial aim was to transfer the personnel of the Tables, the unofficial and illegal, executive of the Covenanters, into a reformed Parliament.[20] The 1633 Parliament had demonstrated that it, through the operation of the Lords of the Articles, was a mere rubber stamp for royal legislation. The Covenanters recognised that bishops were the agents of the despised religious changes and, just as importantly, had aspirations in civil spheres which encroached upon the nobility's traditional interests.[21] Finally, it was essential to separate the civil and ecclesiastical functions of the state with Parliament and Privy Council on one side and General Assembly and ecclesiastical courts on the other.[22]

Since episcopacy had been abolished at the Glasgow Assembly in 1638 (re-confirmed in the Edinburgh Assembly in August 1639), there was an immediate problem of a missing estate in the Parliament of August-November 1639.[23] As it turned out, the barons, as Commissioners of the Shires, eased themselves into the former episcopal estate, and so lay interest benefited at the expense of clerics. Nonetheless, it was also resolved temporarily, and after considerable protest, to allow John, first Earl of Traquair, Lord Treasurer and the King's Commissioner in Parliament, in the name of the Crown, to assume the role that the bishops had had in the election of the Committee of the Articles.[24] Such a measure was only allowed in this session, as the majority, led by Argyll, believed that each Estate should be allowed to choose their own representatives on the Articles.[25] Traquair's problems, however, were exacerbated by the want of the Parliamentary Registers which undoubtedly favoured the innovators.[26] Moreover, the central role of the Earl of Argyll in orchestrating the elections to the Articles was underlined by the King's Commissioner in his report back to court.[27]

Yet it was not until the next session of Parliament the following year that far reaching constitutional change was introduced by the hitherto cautious Cove-nanters, under the guidance of the Earls of Argyll, Rothes, Montrose, Eglinton, Cassillis, Lothian and Lords Lindsay, Balmerino and Burleigh. This time Parliament met from 2 to 11 June in defiance of the Crown's proclamation to extend the previous prorogation and with no King's Commissioner present.[28] Throughout the session it was iterated that the King had failed to appear personally or to send a Commissioner whilst at the same time mobilising his other two kingdoms (England and Ireland) to invade Scotland, an action tantamount, in effect, to

[20] For the composition and political role of the Tables, see MacInnes, *Covenanting Movement*, pp. 166–8; Stevenson, *Government under the Covenanters*, pp. xv–xvi; J.K. Hewison, *The Covenanters* (2 vols., Glasgow, 1913), I, 256, 264.

[21] Scally, 'Hamilton', pp. 209–10.

[22] The division is clearly stated in *A.P.S.*, V, 260. See also, Scally, 'Hamilton', pp. 214–97.

[23] *A.P.S.*, V, 251–8.

[24] *Ibid.*, pp. 252–3; Traquair MSS. (Maxwell-Stewart, Traquair House, Innerleithen), 28/iii/41 (21 Aug. 1639); 43 *passim*.

[25] Traquair MSS., 28/iii/41 (21 Aug. 1639)

[26] *Ibid.*

[27] *Ibid.*, Traquair to Charles I, 30 Aug. 1639.

[28] Parliament had reluctantly agreed to a prorogation in the last session, and when the King attempted to prorogue Parliament again they decided to sit on the day appointed, 2 June 1640. See *A.P.S.*, V, 258–259; Traquair MSS., 28/iii/43 (1–5 Nov. 1639).

abandoning his duties to his native kingdom.[29] So the threat of impending invasion and the alienation of the supreme magistrate ushered in radical constitutional change in Parliament. Immediately on convening, and 'by his Maties speciall indictione and authoritie', a president of Parliament was elected to replace the King's Commissioner. The next priority was to underline that the new composition of the three estates represented 'a compleit and perfyte Parliament':[30]

> And ordeanes all Parliamentis heireftir to be constitute and to consist onlie in all tyme comeing of the Noblemen Barronis and Burgess as the memberis and thrie estatis of Parliament And reschindis and annullis all former laws and actis of Parliament mad[e] in favouris of whatsoever Beshopis Archbeshopis Abbotis Pryoris or other prelatis or churchmen whatsoevir for thair ryding sitting or vo[i]ceing in Parliament.

After prohibiting 'all personis whatsomevir to call in questione the authoritie of this present Parliament . . . under pain of treason,' a raft of some 60 acts were introduced that formed the core of the constitutional revolution.[31] All acts of the Glasgow and Edinburgh Assemblies were ratified including subscription of the National Covenant as a test for civil and ecclesiastical office. A Triennial Act ensured that a Parliament would be called at least every three years. Proxies were disallowed and noblemen who did not own land in Scotland were no longer allowed to sit.

As for the overmighty Committee of Articles, it was stated on 6 June that 'all subsequent parliamentis may according to the importance of effaires for the tyme either choose or not choose severall Committies for Articles as they shall thinke expedient'. It was emphasised that the Committees, if chosen, were to prepare articles which they received from the Estates, and then return them to the chamber, where they would be debated and the estates would 'ordeene suche of the saidis articles as they find to desserve consideration to be formed and past as articles to be voyted in plaine p[ar]liament.' Finally, and most importantly, it was stressed:[32]

> That the rest of the estates by and besyde these of the severall Comitties of the Articles shall be holdine continowally to sit for receiving advysing and discussing of all articles propositions overtures and materes [that] shall be presented to them fro[m] the begining of the Parlia[men]t to the cloosure therof.

So with the Articles cut down to size, legislative power shifted into the chamber and Parliament became a debating, consultative and legislative body.[33] The demise

---

[29] *A.P.S.*, V, 259, 261.

[30] *Ibid.* p. 260. The two main acts that the Covenanters rescinded were: Act, 15 Ja. VI c. 235, concerning the Kirk, particularly prelates representing the third estate; Act, 18 Ja. VI c. 2, for the restitution of the estate of bishops.

[31] *A.P.S.*, V, 258–300. Of the 60 items of legislation, about 50 were public acts that formed the core of the constitutional revolution. Thirty nine of the most important of these were published. The public acts printed in the reign of Charles I are bound together in a volume in the National Library of Scotland, shelfmark Nha.L92 (1–8).

[32] *A.P.S.*, V, 279.

[33] Parliament exercised greater power during the incompetent and absentee reign of David II (1329–1371), and took on the executive role, see *A.P.S.*, I, 15, 73–6.

of the old Lords of the Articles spawned a committee system in which various committees, rather than one all-powerful Committee of Articles,[34] considered items and dutifully reported back to the chamber.[35] A Committee of Estates was also invested with full parliamentary power and usually sat in the interval between Parliaments, at least during the three kingdom crisis.[36]

In 1640 the Covenanters justified their constitutional agenda in *A True Representation of the Proceedings of the Kingdom of Scotland* in which it was stated that 'Parliament is the only lawfull mean to remeid[y] our evils, remove distractions, and settle a solide and perfect peace.'[37] Most of the Covenanter fire was aimed at the bishops who had 'usurped to be the Kirk, and did in name of the Kirk represent the third estate', and it was argued that at the Glasgow Assembly in 1638 'both' of these functions were 'renounced and condemned' by the Kirk.[38] It was also claimed that bishops were responsible for the recent excesses of the Lords of the Articles. Historically the Articles, since King David II (1329–1371), had not always been used but when they were:[39]

> the nomination and election of them, was ever with the common consent and advice of the whole Parliament, till the Parliament in *anno* 1617. That the Bishops took upon them to remove out of plaine Parliament, to the Inner-house, and choysed some out of the Noblemen, & the Noblemen them, and they two choysed the Commissioners to be on articles of Shires and Burroughs, which as it was against the first institution, & form of election of al preceeding articles, introduced by & with prelats: So do it fall & ought to be removed with them.

The Articles, it was argued, were never intended to have 'a boundlesse and illimited power' and were designed to be 'onely preparative, and no wayes determinative'.[40]

The changes of 1639–40 transformed parliamentary procedure but were largely prepared beforehand by the Covenanter leaders and received a fairly easy passage in the invasion-threatened 11 day session of 1640.[41]

---

[34] It became a regular feature that at the beginning of a session a powerful committee (variously called, *inter alia*, the Committee for 'Dispatches', or 'for Burdens and Pressures' or 'Dangers, Remedies and Duties') composed of leading party *élites* would be established to consider key issues, then report back to Parliament, cf. *A.P.S.*, VI, i, 287, 477–8; VI, ii, 10, 13, and below.

[35] The Scottish parliamentary committees of the period, and much more besides, are listed and thoroughly analysed in Young, 'The Scottish Parliament, 1639–1661', *passim*. Dr Young's work on the Scottish Parliament is to be published by John Donald in 1996.

[36] The Committee of Estates was often further divided with some members staying in Edinburgh, some travelling with the Covenanting Army, and other members chosen as Commissioners to attend the English Parliament in London.

[37] *A True Representation of the Proceedings of the Kingdom of Scotland since the Late Pacification: By the Estates of the Kingdome* ([Edinburgh], 1640), p. 13.

[38] *Ibid.*, p. 11.

[39] *Ibid.*, p. 20.

[40] *Ibid.*, p. 21.

[41] At the beginning of the session in June 1640 a Committee of the Articles in the old style was chosen with four of each estate, it was not until a week into the session and after 'diverse questions [had] arisen' that the Covenanters fully reformed the Articles, see *A.P.S.*, V, 262, 278–279.

5

By the parliamentary session of 1641 (15 July–17 November), however, the Covenanters were less united and focused than they had been in previous sessions. The repellent Prayer Book had been withdrawn, bishops were gone and the threat of war had receded. A Parliament sat at Westminster, the Scottish and English armies were on the point of disbandment, the peace treaty of London was being brought from England to be signed in Parliament and the King had decided to attend the session in Edinburgh.[42] In addition, James, fifth Earl of Montrose's Cumbernauld Band of August 1640—an anti-Argyll polemic rather than a coherent political agenda—signalled a split in the Covenanter ranks when it was revealed in November 1640.[43] It was apparently a reaction to the alleged treason spoken by the Earl of Argyll, the leader of the Covenanting Movement, in June 1640, in which he confirmed that a king could be deposed if found guilty of certain crimes.[44] The Band proved to be a damp squib, but it did lead to the formation of another party headed by Montrose at the end of the year (with Lord Napier, Sir George Stirling of Keir and Sir Archibald Stewart of Blackhall) who established links at court with the Earl of Traquair, now exiled Lord Treasurer, and James, fourth Duke of Lennox, gentleman of the King's Bedchamber and the King's cousin, and offered to serve Charles in Scotland if religion and liberties were secured by the King in Parliament.[45] It was also rumoured that Montrose intended to accuse (presumably of treason) the Marquess of Hamilton, the King's Court adviser on Scottish affairs,[46] and the Earl of Argyll, 'in the face of Parliament'.[47]

Charles therefore had the bones of a royalist, or anti-Campbell/Hamilton, party prior to his trip to Scotland, a group with connexions at court, a charismatic, though politically naive, leader in Montrose, and a moderate, and able, polemicist in Lord Napier.[48] Still, some of their potential was lost from June onwards following the forced retirement of Traquair from court and the imprisonment of the Montrose group in Edinburgh.[49] On the other side, Hamilton's proximity

[42] C. Russell, *The Fall of the British Monarchies 1637–1642* (Oxford, 1991), pp. 303–29; Donald, *Uncounselled King*, pp. 259–319; Scally, 'Hamilton', pp. 298–323.

[43] It was signed by 17 lords including Marischal, Montrose, Wigton, Kinghorne, Home, Athol, Mar, Perth, Seaforth, Almond and Johnstone, as well as Carnegy, Master of Lour, see M. Napier, *Memorials of Montrose and His Times* (2 vols., Maitland Club, Edinburgh, 1848–51), I, 254–5.

[44] Tollemache MSS. (Sir Lyonel Tollemache, Buckminster Park, nr. Grantham, Lincs.), 3748 (depostion of Walter Stewart, 5 June 1641); Traquair MSS., 28/iii/20, information against Argyll and Rothes [n.d]; Scottish R.O., GD 406/1/1382 Loudoun to Hamilton, 13 July 1641.

[45] Tollemache MSS., 3748, deposition of Walter Stewart, 5 June 1641. See also, Russell, *Fall of the British Monarchies*, pp. 311–15; Donald, *Uncounselled King*, pp. 292–5; Stevenson, *Scottish Revolution*, pp. 224–7.

[46] Hamilton had been drifting away from the King since the summer of 1639, and his deepening friendship with Argyll over the spring/summer of 1641 was another visible sign of this, see Scally, 'Hamilton', pp. 263–307.

[47] Baillie, *Letters and Journals*, I, 391. Montrose, by focusing his fury on the two most able politicians of the 1640s, seems at least this once to have caught the measure of the King's dilemma.

[48] For Napier, see Stevenson, *Scottish Revolution*, pp. 225–7; and *idem*, 'The "Letter on Sovereign Power" and the Influence of Jean Bodin on Political Thought in Scotland', *Scottish Historical Review*, LXI (1982), 25–43.

[49] Stevenson, *Scottish Revolution*, p. 228.

to the Scottish Crown—next in line after the royal Stewarts—added a further dimension to the Argyll/Hamilton friendship, fuelled over the summer visit not only by the memory of Argyll's talk of deposing the King but by negotiations for a marriage between Argyll's son and Hamilton's eldest daughter in the second half of the year.[50]

The political situation in Scotland was therefore highly combustible, quite apart from the difficult parliamentary negotiations over the Scottish settlement that was ostensibly the purpose of the royal visit.[51] Charles's main aim when he arrived in Edinburgh on 14 August was to settle Scotland, dissolve the Parliament and return to England and do the same. Instead, when he left on 17 November, the Covenanters under Argyll and Hamilton had virtually been handed control of the country and the Irish rebellion, which began on 22 October, gave the English Parliament a new *raison d'être*.

The full Parliament had been sitting at Edinburgh since 15 July preparing business for the King's arrival.[52] On 19 July, in the final phase of reform which had begun in 1639, new orders for the Parliament were introduced. In 1632 preparations had commenced to construct a new building to house Parliament and the Convention of Estates, Court of Session and Privy Council. Although the building was first occupied in August 1639, it was not finally completed until 1640–41.[53] The new Hall of Parliament, which was to be the official meeting place of the Estates until 1707, was 120 feet long, 50 feet wide, and 40 feet high, with a hammerbeam roof of Danish oak by John Scott.[54] Stimulated more by the acquisition of a new building than by revolutionary fervour, it was decided to consider new orders for conduct, protocol and attendance in Parliament.[55] The interior walls of the new chamber were 'to be hung and the claith of state put up'. Each member was allocated a seat which was left vacant in their absence, fines were imposed for non-attendance,[56] 24 hours was allowed for each estate to consider propositions, prayers were to be said at the beginning and end of each day, all dialogue was to be directed through the President, and swords only

---

[50] H.M.C., *Hamilton, MSS.*, p. 55, (item 117), contract of marriage [n.d]; National Register of Archives (Scotland), No. 1209, Argyll Muniments, p. 31 (bundle 61), antenuptial contract of marriage, 10 Jan., 22 Apr. 1642.

[51] Russell, *Fall of the British Monarchies*, Chapter 8, *passim*. See also, Stevenson, *Scottish Revolution*, pp. 233–42; Donald, *Uncounselled King*, pp. 299–319; S.R. Gardiner, *History of England, 1603–42* (10 vols. 1883–4), X, 3–80.

[52] The Parliament had been prorogued a number of times, see *The Diary of Sir Thomas Hope of Craighall, 1634–45*, ed. T. Thomson (Bannatyne Club, Edinburgh, 1843), p. 148; Scottish R.O., GD 406/1/1386, Loudoun and Dunfermline to Charles I, 16 July 1641. Apart from framing the orders of the House, most of the time was spent preparing evidence against the Incendiaries (Traquair, Sir John Hay, Sir Robert Spottiswood, Walter Balcanqual and the Bishop of Ross) and the Montrose group or the Plotters (Montrose, Napier, Keir and Blackhall), cf. Traquair MSS., 37/18, 11/47.

[53] R.K. Hannay and G.P.H. Watson, 'The Building of the Parliament House', *Book of the Old Edinburgh Club*, XIII, (1924), 1–78, esp. pp. 76–7. Sir Thomas Hope recorded in his diary that the session beginning in Aug. 1639 sat in the new Parliament House, Thomson (ed.), *Diary of Sir Thomas Hope*, p. 105.

[54] J. Gifford *et al*, *Edinburgh* (1984), pp. 119–23; Hannay and Watson, 'The Building of the Parliament House', pp. 1–6, 17–58.

[55] *A.P.S.*, V, 313–14.

[56] Fines for non-attendance per day reflected the social position of each estate: noblemen, 18 shillings, barons, 12 shillings, and burgesses, 6 shillings, see *ibid.*, 314.

were to be worn by Members in the chamber. Thus the acquisition of a new building provided another opportunity to enhance the status of Parliament and to further formalise its procedures.

Charles came to Parliament at 11 *a.m.* on 17 August with due ceremony: Hamilton bore the crown, Argyll the sceptre and the Earl of Sutherland the sword.[57] The Treaty of London was ratified nine days later, but the other vexed issues of the Incendiaries, the Montrose group and the appointment of officers of state dragged on to the beginning of October.[58] Charles eventually agreed to appoint officers of state, judges and councillors with the advice and approval of Parliament on 16 September which signalled the start of a bruising contest largely with Charles nominating candidates and the Earl of Argyll's circle (Cassillis, Balmerino, Burleigh, Lindsay, Loudoun, Glencairn and Wariston), in alliance with Hamilton, rejecting them; and marked by particularly acrimonious exchanges over the appointment of a Chancellor and Treasurer.[59] As Robert Baillie succinctly put it, 'upon these jarres whole moneths were mispent'.[60]

Argyll and Hamilton constituted the most powerful force in the parliamentary negotiations, especially since Montrose languished in the castle.[61] If Argyll's growing dominance and alleged talk of deposing the King in 1640 had split the Covenanter Movement, Hamilton's alliance with Argyll in 1641 enraged royalists in Scotland. This was reflected in the vengeful atmosphere against the two noblemen that developed towards late September.[62] From this familiar miasma around the King came the conspiracy to remove Hamilton and Argyll known as the Incident.[63] The plot was essentially a *coup d'état*, probably sanctioned by the King, to remove the dominant Argyll/Hamilton axis from Parliament and replace it with a ragbag of royalist anti-Campbell opportunists headed by the Earls of

[57] Nat. Lib. Scotland, Adv. MS. 33.7.7., p. 44.

[58] *A.P.S.*, V, 342–344; Russell, *Fall of the British Monarchies*, pp. 321–2; Stevenson, *Scottish Revolution*, p. 235.

[59] The Covenanter nominees were Argyll for Chancellor and Loudoun for Treasurer. Charles put forward Morton for Chancellor and Loudoun for Treasurer, but Argyll vigorously opposed Morton even though he was his father-in-law. Then Charles proposed Loudoun as Chancellor and Almond as Treasurer, but Almond was rejected. Loudoun was eventually appointed Chancellor at the end of September.

[60] Baillie, *Letters and Journals*, I, 391. Appointment of officers of state was a very important issue, see Scottish R.O., GD 406/1/1396, [Privy Council] to Charles I, 24 July 1641.

[61] Bodl. Lib., MS. Carte I, ff. 456–66, esp. ff. 465–6, Sir Patrick Wemyss to Ormond, [early Oct.] 1641; Scottish R.O., GD 406/1/1430, Henry Percy to Hamilton, 20 Sept. [1641]; *The Nicholas Papers: Correspondence of Sir Edward Nicholas, 1641–1652*, ed. G.F. Warner (4 vols., Camden Soc., new ser. XL, L, LVII, 3rd ser. XXXI, 1886–1920), I, 12–13, Vane to Nicholas, 17 Aug. 1641; Earl of Clarendon, *History of the Rebellion and Civil Wars in England*, ed. W.D. Macray (6 vols., Oxford, 1888) [hereafter Clarendon, *History of the Rebellion*], I, 389 n.; Stevenson, *Scottish Revolution*, p. 237; Donald, *Uncounselled King*, pp. 310–11.

[62] On 29 Sept. a drunken Lord Ker, son of the Earl of Roxburgh, had sent the Earl of Crawford with a message challenging Hamilton to a duel, see Baillie, *Letters and Journals*, I, 391; H.M.C., *Salisbury MSS.*, XXII, 368; Bodl. Lib., MS. Carte I, ff. 465–66, Sir Patrick Wemyss to Ormond, [early Oct.] 1641; H.M.C., *4th Report*, p. 167, Will Murray's deposition, 25 Oct. 1641; Clarendon, *History of the Rebellion*, I, 389 n.

[63] For a full examination of the Incident, see Scally, 'Hamilton', pp. 307–14; and Charles' affection for plots see C. Russell, 'The First Army Plot of 1641', *Unrevolutionary England, 1603–1642* (1990), pp. 281–302.

Montrose and Crawford, Will Murray of the Bedchamber, some officers from the recently disbanded Scottish army, and an outer circle, or alternative parliamentary party, containing the Earls of Home, Roxburghe, Airth, Mar, Lords Gray, Ogilvy, Kilpont (or Kinpont), Ker, Almond and, lastly, William Drummond.[64] It was also an attempt to overawe the Parliament by a show of force dressed up as a legal process.[65] And significantly it was Parliament, ably controlled in the absence of Argyll and Hamilton by the Chancellor John Campbell, Lord Loudoun, the President of Parliament Lord Balmerino, the Earl of Lauderdale (a Hamiltonian), Lord Lindsay (Hamilton's brother-in-law), and Archibald Johnston of Wariston, who took it as a severe infringement of parliamentary privilege that some of its Members had to flee for their lives from the capital.[66] Equally it was only under the protection of Parliament that Argyll, Hamilton and the Earl of Lanark, Secretary for Scotland (and Hamilton's brother), agreed to return to Edinburgh.[67] By gambling so much on the plot, its failure meant the loss of much of the King's credibility and power in Scotland.[68] Unwittingly, by engaging in a trial of strength with his newly reformed Scottish Parliament, Charles had greatly enhanced its status as an effective buffer against a bullying Crown. As so often happened, Charles' actions produced an effect that was far worse than the situation that had caused him to act in the first place—now Parliament controlled the executive and the judiciary. Parliament was dissolved on 16 November and next day Charles departed from Edinburgh leaving the government of Scotland to the Argyll party of the Covenanters (Loudoun, Balmerino, Cassillis, Eglinton, Burleigh, Crawford-Lindsay, Lothian, Glencairn and Wariston) for the next six years—it would not be until 1647 that a party, ironically led by Hamilton, would take control of Parliament in the King's interest.

6

The only hiccup in the Argyll Covenanters, unhampered control of the reformed Parliament and Convention of Estates between 1641 and 1646 was the limp attempt by a faction led by Hamilton (Lanark, Lauderdale, Southesk, Roxburgh, Annandale, Callendar and Dunfermline) in the summer of 1643 to spoil the negotiations between the Scottish and English Parliaments for the Solemn League

[64] H.M.C., *4th Report*, pp. 163–70, esp. p. 167.

[65] The day after the plot was revealed, Charles went to Parliament escorted by an armed force amongst whom were many of the men who had been implicated in the conspiracy, see Scottish R.O., GD 406/1/1440, relation of the Incident by Earl of Lanark.

[66] *A.P.S.*, V, 373–375, 378; Scottish.R.O., GD 406/1/1542/1–2, draft addresses to Parliament; GD 406/M1/284, [copies] Order of Parliament, President of Parliament (Balmerino) to Hamilton, Argyll and Lanark, Charles I to Hamilton, Argyll and Lanark, 1 Nov. 1641; GD 406/1/1562, Lauderdale to Hamilton, 1 Nov. 1641; GD 406/1/1564, Charles I to Hamilton, Argyll and Lanark, 1 Nov. 1641; GD 406/1/1449, Loudoun to Hamilton, 1 Nov. 1641. For Baillie's account of the Incident see, *Letters and Journals*, I, 391–395. For Montrose's supplication to Parliament see, Scottish R.O., GD 406/M1/284.

[67] *A.P.S.*, V, 373–5, 378.

[68] Charles tried something similar in England in January of the following year with his attempt to arrest some of his adversaries in the English Parliament on a charge of high treason, see *L.J.*, IV, 500–1; Gardiner, *England*, X, 135–142; Russell, *Fall of the British Monarchies*, pp. 447–53; A.J. Fletcher, *The Outbreak of the English Civil War* (1981), pp. 180–4.

and Covenant—a military treaty to ensure the English Parliament defeated Charles in England and a coalition for mainland religious uniformity, Presbyterian of course, to satisfy the Scots.[69] The split between Argyll and Hamilton that led to the latter heading a rival faction against Argyll's dominant party was occasioned by the single issue of whether the Scots should intervene in the Civil War in England, and it was this clash that dominated the period from late 1642 down to the meeting of the Convention of Estates on 22 June 1643.[70] Argyll's supporters eventually gained the initiative through skilful exploitation of fears of papists in arms in England, the consequent threat to domestic religion and liberty and the omnipresent dangers in Ireland.[71] On the other hand, Hamilton's delicate, perhaps over-cautious, policy of Scottish non-alignment in the English Civil War, peppered by assurances that the gains of 1638–41 were safe in Charles's hands, was dealt a serious blow in early June by revelations of Catholic plots to effect a royalist rising in Scotland.[72] To many, it was further proof that the papist, with a letter of approval from the King, was on the march in the three kingdoms. Consequently, Hamilton's and Lanark's vocal support for the King's many assurances that religion and liberties were secure rang hollow on the eve of the Convention of Estates.[73]

With the Anti-Solemn Leaguers softened up beforehand, the Convention of Estates was a less even contest than it might have been.[74] Yet it was still the case, as it had been since at least the beginning of the year, that members had initially to fall in behind either Hamilton or Argyll. At the first meeting, the King's letter was read out restricting the Convention to discussions of how to maintain the Scots army in Ireland and how to get repayment of the Brotherly Assistance from the English Parliament. Above all, the Convention was not to 'medle with the affaires of England'.[75] The profile of the Convention was clearly shown on 24 June by the membership of the committee to draw up an act of constitution defining the Convention's powers.[76] In short the committee would decide whether the Convention should obey the King's restrictions or not. The membership of

---

[69] Scally, 'Hamilton', pp. 328–38.

[70] *Ibid.*, pp. 329–31; *The Register of the Privy Council of Scotland, 1625–1660, 2nd Series* (8 vols., Edinburgh 1899–1908) [hereafter *R.P.C.S., 2nd Ser.*], *1638–43*, pp. 359–404; Scottish R. O., GD 406/1/1692/1–3; Traquair MSS., 14/26; Baillie, *Letters and Journals*, II, 57–64. Before the Convention met, without the King's permission, Hamilton and Argyll had slogged it out in the Privy Council.

[71] Burnet, *Lives of the Dukes of Hamilton*, p. 280, Councillors and Conservators to Charles I, 2 May 1643; *R.P.C.S. 2nd Ser., 1638–43*, pp. 429–434.

[72] The Earl of Antrim, the Catholic Earl of Nithsdale and Lord Aboyne, the Earl of Huntly's son, were the main protagonists though Henrietta Maria, Huntly and Montrose were also involved, *R.P.C.S. 2nd Ser., 1638–43*, pp. 436–8; Baillie, *Letters and Journals*, II, 72–75; Stevenson, *Scottish Revolution*, pp. 270–5. For a full account of Antrim's career see, J.H. Ohlmeyer, *Civil War and Restoration in the Three Stuart Kingdoms: The Career of Randall MacDonnell, Marquis of Antrim, 1609–83* (Cambridge, 1993).

[73] Just before the Convention, the English Parliament requested that the Earls of Morton, Roxburgh, Annandale, Kinnoul, Lanark and Carnwath be charged as Incendiaries. See *R.P.C.S. 2nd Ser., 1638–43*, pp. 450–2; Baillie, *Letters and Journals*, II, 77–8.

[74] The Covenanters' request that the King call a Parliament was refused, and the First Triennial Parliament was not due to assemble until June 1644, see Scally, 'Hamilton', pp. 330–1.

[75] Baillie, *Letters and Journals*, II, 76–77; Traquair MSS., 14/26, 'Relation Concerning sume passagis of business in Scotland'.

[76] Stevenson, *Scottish Revolution*, pp. 276–8.

the committee showed that Hamilton had most of the nobility behind him, but Argyll carried more support in the other two estates, the barons and the burgesses.[77] Thus, on 26 June, the committee concluded that the Convention had power 'to treate, consult and determine in all matters that shall be proposed unto them'.[78] This effectively handed control of the Convention to Argyll and from that day Hamilton never returned to the Chamber.[79] Yet this meant that the King did not have his most effective politician in the House, leaving his potential supporters leaderless. By trying to restrict the Convention's remit so absolutely Hamilton, and Charles, had foolishly manoeuvred themselves into a corner and out of the Parliament House. The Convention of Estates sat on without Hamilton and the other royalists who had chosen not to participate. In early August, the long-awaited Commissioners from the English Parliament arrived requesting 'mutuall defence against the papists and prelaticall factioun and their adherents in both kingdoms'.[80] In just over a week, the Solemn League and Covenant was drawn up,[81] and in January 1644 another Covenanted army marched into England, as it had done in 1640, to tilt the balance, once more, away from the King.[82]

Meanwhile, Charles's imprisonment of Hamilton in England at the end of 1643 on allegations of treason brought by the Montrose group ensured that any parliamentary faction capable of mobilising moderate Covenanter opinion in favour of the King would be leaderless.[83] Instead Charles opted for the extra-parliamentary guerrilla tactics of Montrose, which enjoyed initial spectacular successes before inevitable defeat at Philiphaugh in September 1645.[84] Until the King's arrival at Newcastle in May 1646 under the 'protection' of the Scottish army, and Hamilton's release from prison in April, parliamentary politics in Scotland was dominated by Argyll's party. Given that, the first five sessions of the first Triennial Parliament (4 June 1644—4 February 1646) were largely occupied with prosecuting the war in England, quelling the rebellion in Ireland and organising the campaigns against Montrose in Scotland.[85]

---

[77] *A.P.S.*, VI, i, 5–6; Stevenson, *Scottish Revolution*, p. 277. The committee was made up of eight from each estate and the nobles voted for Hamilton, Argyll, Morton, Roxburgh, Lauderdale, Southesk, Lanark, Callendar and Balmerino.

[78] *A.P.S.*, VI, i, 6.

[79] Baillie, *Letters and Journals*, II, 77.

[80] The English commissioners were the Earl of Rutland, Sir William Armyn, Sir Henry Vane the younger, Thomas Hatcher and Henry Darley, see *A.P.S.*, VI, i, 23–4. They were accompanied by two English ministers, Stephen Marshall and Philip Nye.

[81] *Ibid.*, pp. 6–23, 23–43. The Covenant is at pp. 41–3. Both sides got what they wanted; the English their military alliance and the Scots their religious coalition.

[82] *Ibid.* pp. 43–59; Traquair MSS., 14/26, 'Relation Concerning sume passagis of business in Scotland'. For Baillie's version, see *Letters and Journals*, II, 76–101. For a detailed narrative, cf. Stevenson, *Scottish Revolution*, pp. 284–91; G. Donaldson, *Scotland: James V-James VII* (Edinburgh, 1987), pp. 329–33.

[83] Scally, 'Hamilton', pp. 334, 340. Montrose, Nithsdale, Aboyne, in alliance with Queen Henrietta Maria, were the authors of Hamilton's fall.

[84] Montrose was eventually defeated by David Leslie at Philiphaugh in Sept. 1645. Before being defeated Montrose, uncharacteristically, in his capacity as Lieutenant Governor of Scotland had summoned a Parliament on 20 Oct. 1645, see Donaldson, *Scotland*, p. 334.

[85] *A.P.S.*, VI, i, 95–611.

7

The sixth session of the First Triennial Parliament which assembled at Edinburgh on 3 November 1646 signalled the beginning of a sea-change in Parliament. The thorny problem of what to do with an uncovenanted King who had been defeated in England and was now at Newcastle with the Scottish army was the key political issue, and this was counterpointed by the steady collapse of the military and religious alliance between the Parliaments of England and Scotland. Although unwilling to sign the Covenant or accept the Newcastle Propositions, Charles generated considerable support in Scotland by throwing himself on the mercy of his native subjects, and, moreover, as the survival of Secretary Lanark's letter book shows, dispensing numerous gifts to a great number of the parliamentary *élite* assembled in Edinburgh, many of whom travelled south to kiss the King's hand.[86]

Significant too, was the arrival of the Duke of Hamilton back onto the political scene, for he was a totem of moderate Covenanter opinion which had lacked a leader since 1643 against Argyll, Cassillis, Balmerino, Wariston and the other committed Solemn Leaguers. Not only that, the duke could, in the changed political circumstances of 1646–48, rely on a potent inner circle of family collaborators including Secretary Lanark, Lord Treasurer Crawford-Lindsay, the Earls of Glencairn and Haddington, the Laird of Bargany, Sir John Hamilton of Orbiston, Justice Clerk, Sir James Lockhart of Lee, and Sir John Hamilton of Beil. Yet for all that, Hamilton was reluctant to champion the King's case in Parliament. He had already been imprisoned in 1643 for failing to hold an untenable position for the Crown, and was unwilling to do so again. To secure Hamilton's support in Parliament Charles had to accept the Covenant, otherwise the King's position in Scotland was futile.[87] It was a political necessity, not a religious one, that Charles accepted the Covenant. Not only Hamilton, but other Covenanters such as Crawford-Lindsay, Loudoun, Lauderdale, Lanark and Glencairn believed this too. From his experiences between 1638 and 1642 Hamilton also knew that Charles only made concessions when he was pressed extremely hard to do so.[88] When one applies these factors to the Hamilton party's position between 1646 and the signing of the Engagement in December 1647, then their policy becomes more coherent. Neither royalists nor hard-line Covenanters, and true to the traditions and ambiguities of the National Covenant, they are better described as the Hamilton party or the Hamilton faction.[89]

[86] Tollemache MSS., 3750, ff. 5v–40r. Charles's bounty caused consternation in the Committee of Estates who tried to limit it to those recommended by Parliament, see Scottish R.O., GD 406/1/1965, 18 May 1646. For Charles's answer, see *ibid.*, 2027.

[87] The correspondence between Hamilton in Edinburgh and Sir Robert Moray at Newcastle shows that both men felt the King's position in Scotland was hopeless unless he accepted the Covenant and Presbyterianism in some form, see, for example, Scottish R.O., GD 406/1/2099, 2102, 2105, 2106, 2108; *The Hamilton Papers*, ed. S.R. Gardiner (Camden Soc., new ser. XXVII, 1880), pp. 106–47.

[88] Scally, 'Hamilton', pp. 214–98.

[89] In 1646 Charles I distinguished '4 factions' in Scotland, 'Mountroses, the Neutralls, the Hamiltons, and the Campbells', see *Charles I in 1646: Letters of King Charles I to Queen Henrietta Maria*, ed. J. Bruce (Camden Soc., old ser. LXIII, 1856), pp. 48–9.

The sea-change in the Parliament of 3 November 1646 was reflected in the membership of the main parliamentary committee, the committee for the burdens and pressures of the kingdom in which the Hamilton party balanced the Argyll party.[90] The two main issues of the moment were discussed by the committee: what to do with the King and with the Scots army in England. However, with the King refusing to concede ground at Newcastle and dabbling in his usual intrigues, Hamilton's party were both unwilling and unable to press a royalist case without the required concessions from Charles.[91] It was in this spirit of despondency that Hamilton and his supporters viewed the surrender of the King to the English Commissioners at the beginning of 1647 on payment of £200,000, half of the agreed sum owed to the Scots by the English Parliament.[92] Even worse, Charles was handed over before the Parliament received an answer to their request that any decision on the King's future should be decided by the two kingdoms.[93]

A sentimental attachment to the King of Scotland, and a sense of shame that they had sold him to a pack of sectaries in England, was enough to alter the complexion of Parliament in Hamilton's favour.[94] On 11 March it was decided to send the Earl of Lauderdale, a Hamiltonian, to England with new instructions for himself and for the Commissioners in London which illustrated a softening of the Scottish Parliament's stance not only towards the King, but to former incendiaries such as the Earl of Traquair, and supporters of the Earl of Montrose like Lord Ogilvy.[95] In particular, the instructions stated that Charles might only have to accept the Covenant as a law, but not subscribe it himself.[96] In this mood the Parliament was dissolved on 27 March 1647, after appointing a Committee of Estates to sit in the interval before the first session of the Second Triennial Parliament due to assemble in March 1648.[97]

[90] This committee was a variation on the Committee of Dispatches which considered the most pressing issues confronting Parliament. There were ten from each Estate on the committee. The nobles were split thus with Hamilton, Lanark, Glencairn, Roxburgh, Tullibardine, and possibly Findlater; and on the other side Argyll, Marshall, Cassillis and Balmerino, cf. *A.P.S.*, VI, i, 616. The Earl of Loudoun, Chancellor, and the Earl of Crawford-Lindsay, President of Parliament, were voted supernumeries and both were slowly moving towards Hamilton's party.

[91] Scottish R.O., GD 406/1/2102, 2106, 2108, 2109. Charles' public position can be recovered from the Moray/Hamilton correspondence cited above, whilst his covert thoughts are evident in his correspondence with the Queen, see Bruce (ed.), *Charles I in 1646*, passim, but esp. pp. 24–5, 27.

[92] Guthry's claim, even if it is true, that Fletcher of Innerpeffer, one of the Shire Commissioners, had twice in Nov. 1646 offered the support of the barons should Hamilton declare for the King must be viewed in the light of Hamilton's views on Charles's intransigence and, moreover, Guthry's dislike of Hamilton which went back at least to 1638, see Guthry, *Memoirs*, pp. 234–6. Guthry did concede that Hamilton and Lanark, with the Earls of Kinghorne and Tullibardine, Lords Spynie and Elibank, as well as eight Commissioners from the barons and burghs, voted against leaving the King at Newcastle, *ibid.*, p. 237. The agreed sum to be paid was £400,000, half was to be paid before the Scots army withdrew, see D. Stevenson, *Revolution and Counter-Revolution in Scotland*, 1644–1651 (1977), p. 73.

[93] *A.P.S.*, VI, i, 659.

[94] However, Argyll had managed to force through the disbandment of the Army that had been in England, leaving only a New Model force under David Leslie to clear the Highlands of rebels, see Stevenson, *Revolution and Counter-Revolution*, pp. 82–3.

[95] *A.P.S.*, VI, i, 764–766.

[96] Instruction 2, 'that his Matie may sweare and subscryve the solemne League and covenant at least give his consent that it may be confirmed as a law'. *A.P.S.*, VI, i, 764.

[97] *Ibid.*, pp. 766–8, 856.

The membership of the Committee of Estates illustrated once again that the balance of power was still on a knife edge, divided between Argyll and Hamilton.[98] Two issues separated the protagonists during the lifetime of the Committee: first how to respond to the deteriorating situation in England, especially after the King was seized by the English New Model army on 4 June, and secondly, what to do with the Scots army under Argyll which was campaigning in the West. On the first issue, Hamilton's supporters publicly encouraged the belief that the King was in imminent danger from the English sectarian army whilst privately hoping that Charles's deteriorating situation in England would force him to make the appropriate concessions to the Scots that would allow them to invade on his behalf. On the other side, Argyll's party at heart felt the King's unreliability disqualified him from being offered military assistance in England. The second issue, that of the Scottish army, was a critical element to both political factions. The restructuring of the Scottish army that left Newcastle at the beginning of 1647 had favoured Argyll since the commanders were loyal to him. Hamilton, therefore, throughout most of the year of the Committee of Estates (March 1647—March 1648) pressed for the army to be disbanded, and until that was achieved argued against aiding the King. Hamilton nearly achieved his aim on 8 September, but at another 'frequent' meeting of the Committee on 15 October Argyll managed by a single vote to have the army kept intact until the meeting of the Parliament in March.[99]

Meanwhile, on 17 and 18 August, following the return of Argyll from campaigning in the west, the Committee of Estates framed new instructions for the Commissioners in London, including a request that the King be allowed to go to the capital to receive further propositions. In addition, and most importantly, two more commissioners, the Earls of Lanark and Loudoun, were to go south.[100] The two were representatives of both leading parties: Lanark for his brother Hamilton, and Loudoun for his kinsman Argyll. Yet on balance this was a victory for Hamilton, since Loudoun was neither as hard-line as Argyll, nor was he as opposed to aiding the King. Even more significant, however, Loudoun was to concern himself with matters relating to the English Parliament while Lanark was to concentrate on matters relating to the King.[101] Evidence also suggests that the

[98] The committee consisted of 60 from the three estates (21 nobles, 19 barons and 20 burgesses) with about ten supernumeraries including Lord General Leven, Chancellor Loudoun, the Lord Treasurer and President of Parliament Crawford-Lindsay as well as the Scottish Commissioners in England, see Scottish R.O., PA 11/5, ff. 3r–5v. Curiously, Argyll is not included in the list of nobles, but took the oath after the powers of the committee was read out, and appears in the subsequent attendance lists, see, PA 11/5, ff. 5v, 7r–21v. The Hamiltons apparently believed they had more than half of the committee on their side, see Fotheringham (ed.), *Diplomatic Correspondence of Jean De Montereul*, II, 70–1.

[99] Scottish R.O., PA 11/5, ff. 92r–v, 93r–4v, 112r, 118v, 119r–20r (15 Oct.), 131v–4r. A frequent meeting of the committee was one in which most of the members attended, certainly one where heads of the main political factions were present.

[100] *Ibid.*, ff. 59v–60v, 61r, 71v–72v, 74v–75r, 75v. The Independents in the House of Commons objected to Lanark's appointment as a commissioner, but he was defended by Sir Henry Vane the elder, Hamilton's old friend, see Scottish R.O., GD 406/1/2254, Lauderdale to Lanark, 14 Sept. [1647].

[101] Scottish R.O., PA 11/5, f. 76r, Committee of Estates to Commissioners in London, 21 Aug. 1647; *ibid.*, ff. 77v, 97r, 107r, 109r–v.

Hamiltons were already involved in secret negotiations with the King through Lauderdale and Robin Leslie, a servant who had been in Hamilton's circle since at least 1630.[102]

What all this eventually led to, amidst a flurry of peace proposals from the English army and the English Parliament, intensified by rumours that plans were aloft 'to destroy his Maties person', was the signing of the Engagement on 26 December 1647 between the Scottish Commissioners and the King.[103] The Engagement stated that Charles would establish Presbyterian church government in England for a trial period of three years, the Solemn League and Covenant would be confirmed in the English Parliament but universal subscription would not be pressed, and finally moves would be made for economic union and, if possible, 'a complete union of the kingdoms' according to the designs of James VI and I.[104] News of the Engagement was initially very well received in the Committee of Estates and after a detailed report by Loudoun and Lauderdale on 10 February the Commissioners' proceedings were approved.[105] However, the Commission of the Kirk was split over the deal, but eventually came out against the Engagement when it became apparent that Hamilton, not Argyll, was the driving force behind it.[106]

The final contest between Hamilton and Argyll, the two main political figures in Scottish politics throughout the decade from 1639, took place in the first session of the second Triennial Parliament, the last full session of a Parliament in the reign of Charles I. The profile of the so-called Engagement Parliament which sat down on 2 March 1648 is best described by Argyll's supporter, Robert Baillie, in his wry summary:[107]

> Never so many noblemen present in any of our Parliaments; near fyftie Earls and Lords. Among whom were found about eight or nyne for our way; Argyle, Eglintone, Cassillis, Louthian, Arbuthnot, Torpichen, Rosse, Balmerino, Cowper, Burleigh, and sometimes the Chancellour and Balcarras. All the rest, with more than the halfe of the barrons, and almost the halfe of the burgesses, especiallie the greater tounes, Edinburgh, Perth, Dundee, Aberdeen, St. Andrews, Linlithgow, ran in a string after Duke Hamilton's vote.

As had become the custom since the demise of the Lords of the Articles, a committee was established to consider the principal issues that concerned the

---

[102] Scottish R.O., GD 406/1/2246, Robin Leslie to [Lanark], 25 July [1647]; 91, Will Murray to Hamilton, 5 Mar. 1627/8.

[103] *Ibid.*, 9773, [drafts of letters] Lanark to Charles I, 22 Nov. to 13 Dec. 1647. These letters show that Lanark was inching towards an agreement, yet concerning the Covenant he reminded Charles that he was wrong to believe that 'Scotland would be engaged at an easier rate'. See also, Scottish R.O., PA 11/5, ff.107v–8r.

[104] S.R. Gardiner, *Constitutional Documents, 1625–1660* (Oxford, 1899), pp. 347–53, esp. p. 351.

[105] Scottish R.O., PA 11/5, ff. 199v (21 Jan. 1648), 209v–10v, 212v.

[106] *Ibid.*, f. 216r (25 Feb. 1648); Scottish R.O., GD 406/1/2377; Baillie, *Letters and Journals*, III, 34–35; Guthry, *Memoirs*, pp. 257–9, 260; Stevenson, *Revolution and Counter-Revolution*, pp. 102–4.

[107] Baillie, *Letters and Journals*, III, 35. Fifty-six nobles are recorded in the sederunt for 2 Mar., see *A.P.S.*, VI, ii, 3–4. Argyll's party, normally so adept at mobilising the barons of the shires, appears to have suffered as a result of 'double-elections' whereby of the two barons sent, one supported Hamilton, the other Argyll, see Guthry, *Memoirs*, p. 259.

Parliament, appropriately named in this instance the 'Committee for Dangeris, Remedies and Dewties'.[108] The committee's remit was to discuss the Engagement agreed with the King and how it should be put into effect, though this was couched in more emotive language of 'the dangeris iminent to Religion The Covenant The Kingis Matie Monarchicall government and the thrie kingdomes'.[109] However what was new, and echoed back to the overarching role of the old Lords of the Articles, was the granting of new powers to the committee on 17 March to operate unilateraly in matters concerning the safety of the kingdom.[110] In an atmosphere of increasing violence which had led to a series of duels involving, most notably, Argyll and Crawford-Lindsay, and Eglinton and Glencairn, Argyll immediately protested at the committee's new powers and when his protest was denied he walked out of Parliament with about 47 of his supporters, including the Earls of Cassillis, Eglinton, Lothian, Lords Balmerino, Burleigh, Coupar, Arbuthnot and Torphichen, as well as the Lairds of Wariston, Scotiscraig and Humbie and George Porterfield, Burgess of Glasgow, and John Short, burgess of Stirling.[111]

Although Argyll and the others were called back and took their seats, the support for the Engagement was now overwhelming and Parliament occupied itself with choosing commanders and mobilising the country for an invasion, whilst simultaneously canvassing assistance from sympathizers in Ireland and England.[112] The Engagement Parliament was finally dissolved on 11 June, and, as had been the custom for most of the 1640s, a Committee of Estates was appointed to sit in the interval before the convening of the second session of the second Triennial Parliament. By the time Parliament sat down again on 4 January 1649, Hamilton's army had been ignominiously defeated at Preston, and Argyll, with the assistance of Cromwell, had taken control of Parliament just in time to preside over the chaos caused by the execution in London of King Charles I of Scotland on 30 January.[113]

Never in the history of the Scottish Parliament has there been a series of roller-coaster events such as those in the reign of Charles I. Seven years late, he presided over his Coronation Parliament in 1633 with a rod of iron, only to have it turned against him by the Parliament of 1639–41 which initiated a constitutional transformation that allowed it to govern Scotland with an agenda fashioned first by Argyll's political party, then by Hamilton's party in 1647–48. In the crucial period between 1639 and 1641 Parliament, housed in a magnificent new building, became a consultative and legislative body freed from the control of the all-powerful Lords of the Articles. As an institution Parliament was robust enough

---

[108] *A.P.S.*, VI, ii, 10.

[109] *Ibid.* There were six of each Estate on the Committee plus Loudoun as supernumerary; Argyll and Wariston were members but were hopelessly outnumbered by the supporters of Hamilton and Callander.

[110] Initially this concerned the immediate securing of Berwick and Carlisle, see *A.P.S.*, VI, ii, 13.

[111] Guthry, *Memoirs*, pp. 262–4; Baillie, *Letters and Journals*, III, 37–8; *A.P.S.*, VI, ii, 13.

[112] *A.P.S.*, VI, ii, 23–124; Scottish R.O., PA 11/6, ff. 1–47; Baillie, *Letters and Journals*, III, 37–55; Guthry, *Memoirs*, pp. 263–301.

[113] *A.P.S.*, VI, ii, 124–316.

to act as an effective buffer against an aggressive Crown in 1641, as well as mobilising the country for war between 1643 and 1646, and in 1648. Perhaps the triumph of the Covenanting period was the creation of a Parliament capable of doing this.

In terms of personnel, Parliament also experienced considerable change. The clerical estate was outlawed in 1639, and the estate was occupied by the barons of the shires. In the period 1639–51 the barons played an important, though not the leading, role in Parliament. Together with the burgess estate, the barons largely accepted the hierarchical nature of Scottish politics in Parliament, a pattern in which the nobility were the natural leaders of political parties and factions. Although the political landscape in Parliament had altered dramatically during the reign of Charles I, the nature of political relationships had not changed correspondingly. For the decade immediately following Charles's death it would temporarily be a different story.

Traces of Party Politics in Early Eighteenth-Century Scottish Elections*

DAVID HAYTON

The Queen's University of Belfast

In general the political history of eighteenth-century Scotland has attracted little academic investment, but even within this depressed area of historiography the study of parliamentary elections stands out as an unemployment black spot. The standard text on electoral procedure remains William Ferguson's 1957 Ph.D. thesis: indeed, Dr Ferguson is the only historian to have seriously investigated the topic.[1] For elections themselves, beyond the (usually truncated) constituency reports presented in the 1715–1790 sections of the *History of Parliament*,[2] research has been confined to a handful of case studies—Dr Ferguson's thesis again, with its pioneering work on Cromarty, Ronald Sunter's doctoral dissertation on Stirlingshire, and the further accounts of individual constituencies contained in his *Patronage and Politics in Scotland 1707–1832*.[3] In recent years interest has been shown in the emergence of popular politics in some of the better documented burghs,[4] but in comparison with the intense scrutiny to which the 'unreformed electoral system' in England has been subjected, and the lively debate which that

* It is a great pleasure to acknowledge the enormous debt I owe to the staffs of the National Library of Scotland, the National Register of Archives (Scotland), and the Scottish Record Office, for their expert guidance and unfailing courtesy. I am particularly grateful to Jane Hill of the N.R.A., for smoothing my path into many a private archive; and to David Brown, Tristram Clarke, and John Shaw, at Register House, for doing their best to improve my lamentable ignorance of Scottish history. I must also thank Mr David Wilkinson of the History of Parliament Trust for pointing out errors in an earlier draft. For permission to inspect and quote from their manuscripts, I am grateful to the Dukes of Atholl, Buccleuch, Hamilton, and Roxburghe, the Earls of Annandale and Mansfield, Lord Home of the Hirsel, and Sir David Ogilvy.

[1] W. Ferguson, 'Electoral Law and Procedure in Eighteenth- and Early Nineteenth-Century Scotland' (University of Glasgow Ph.D., 1957). See *idem*, 'The Electoral System in the Scottish Counties before 1832', *Miscellany II*, ed. D. Sellar (Stair Society, XXXV, Edinburgh, 1984), pp. 261–94.

[2] R.R. Sedgwick, *The House of Commons, 1715–1754* [hereafter *H.P., 1715–54*] (2 vols., 1970), I, 381–404 (most Scottish constituency reports by J.M. Simpson); Sir Lewis Namier and J. Brooke, *The House of Commons, 1754–1790* [hereafter *H.P., 1754–90*] (3 vols., 1964), I, 469–512 (most Scottish constituency reports authored by Lady Haden-Guest). By contrast, the articles in R.G. Thorne, *The House of Commons, 1790–1820* (5 vols., 1986), II, 512–623, the vast majority written by D.R. Fisher or Thorne himself, are admirably thorough and detailed.

[3] R.M. Sunter, 'Stirlingshire Politics, 1707–1832' (University of Edinburgh Ph.D., 1971); *idem*, *Patronage and Politics in Scotland 1707–1832* (Edinburgh, [1986]).

[4] A.J. Murdoch, 'Politics and the People in the Burgh of Dumfries, 1758–1760', *Scottish Historical Review*, LXX (1991), 151–71; R.A. Houston, 'Popular Politics in the Reign of George II: The Edinburgh Cordiners', *ibid.* LXXII (1993), 167–89.

scrutiny has engendered, the sum total of interest in Scottish elections still rates as barely a glance.[5]

The reason for this neglect cannot lie in any lack of raw materials, for the Scottish political classes of the eighteenth century (especially those active in its first decades) have left behind them a mountain of documentation. Instead, we must look to the prevailing perceptions of the artificiality of Scottish political culture in this period, and the irrelevance of parliamentary representation to wider historical questions concerning the structure and development of Scottish society.[6] With some justification, critical observers will point to the quintessentially elitist nature of the unreformed electoral system in Scotland, dominated as it was by arrogant magnates, obsequious lairds, and self-perpetuating, and self-interested, urban oligarchies. A narrow franchise, pervasive corruption, and the over-mighty power of proprietorial interest, appear to have been the main features of an arid political landscape, where votes were determined by habits of deference, promises of advantage, or a reciprocal exchange of benefits. In short, this was politics without issues; or in the words of the Earl of Ilay, himself perhaps the most skilful practitioner of the political arts in his generation in Scotland, 'a perpetual war and game' between the magnates.[7] For glamour and excitement one looks instead to the exploits of Highland Jacobites; for intellectual refreshment to the salons and university lecture-halls of the Scottish enlightenment. Small wonder then that most eighteenth-century specialists prefer the romance of military adventure, or the invigorating discipline of moral philosophy, to what appears as the irredeemable pettiness of everyday political realities in eighteenth-century Scotland, and are happy to leave the pathology of Scottish parliamentary history to a minority of scholars temperamentally disposed to relish the exhumation of long-forgotten intrigues.

There is some element of caricature in this depiction of eighteenth-century elections in Scotland, but it is not very far from the truth. As John Brooke remarked, in what is still the best short account of the unreformed electoral system in Scotland—a section of his introductory survey to the 1754–1790 *History of Parliament* volumes—'county elections in Scotland in no way resembled those in

---

[5] See especially G. Holmes, 'The Electorate and the National Will in the First Age of Party', in his *Politics, Religion and Society in England, 1679–1742* (1986), 1–33; N. Landau, 'Independence, Deference, and Voter Participation: The Behaviour of the Electorate in Early Eighteenth-Century Kent', *Historical Journal*, XXII (1979), 561–84; F. O'Gorman, 'Electoral Deference in Unreformed England, 1760–1832', *Journal of Modern History*, LVI (1984), 391–429; idem, *Voters, Patrons and Parties: The Unreformed Electorate of Hanoverian England, 1734–1832* (Oxford, 1989); J.A. Phillips, *Electoral Behavior in Unreformed England: Plumpers, Splitters, and Straights* (Princeton, N.J., 1982); idem, *The Great Reform Bill in the Boroughs: English Electoral Behaviour 1818–1841* (Oxford, 1992); W.A. Speck, *Tory and Whig: The Struggle in the Constituencies 1701–1715* (1970); idem, 'The Electorate in the First Age of Party', in *Britain in the First Age of Party: Essays Presented to Geoffrey Holmes*, ed. C. Jones (1987), pp. 45–62. A full bibliography would be many times longer.

[6] 'Future historians must relate the tiny political nation of early eighteenth-century Scotland and their electoral high-jinks to the broader development of Scottish society . . . The minutiae of patronage and intrigue seem sometimes to have happened in a vacuum': J.M. Simpson, 'Who Steered the Gravy Train, 1707–1766?', in *Scotland in the Age of Improvement: Essays in Scottish History in the Eighteenth Century*, ed. N.T. Phillipson and R. Mitchison (Edinburgh, 1970), p. 48.

[7] Quoted in W. Ferguson, *Scotland 1689 to the Present* (Edinburgh, 1968), p. 138.

England, but were more akin to the struggles in an English rotten borough',
where 'public opinion could not express itself'; while Scottish burgh Members
showed 'a contempt for the electorate which . . . would hardly have been used
by an English electoral manager for any but the most abject of rotten boroughs'.[8]
And even though Professor Sunter's careful reconstructions demonstrate that
electoral patrons could not always take for granted the votes of their constituents
in either shire or burgh seats, and, unlike English electoral managers in rotten
boroughs, might occasionally have to work quite hard to retain support, it was
vested interest rather than public opinion that they were obliged to consult.
Successful candidates appealed to the electorate because of their skill as lobbyists
or their influence as patronage-brokers, not through oratory or the defence of
principle.

Reference to Jacobitism suggests one explanation for the colourless parliamentary scene in Hanoverian Scotland; namely that the life-blood of politics in the
preceding century had been drained away into extra-parliamentary agitation,
conspiracy and rebellion. The disputes over religion which had made the seventeenth century an age of violent confrontation in Scottish politics were no longer
a part of conventional political life. After the Hanoverian succession Scottish
parliamentary politics was a game in which only Whigs, or 'Revolution men',
could play. Non-juring Episcopalians, and *a fortiori*, Catholics, were barred. This
is not to say, of course, that religion was the only subject capable of arousing the
political passions of eighteenth-century Scotsmen: the Shawfield riots of 1725,
and the Porteous riots of 1736, demonstrate that material grievances and slights
to national pride could still inflame popular opinion, and agitate Scottish politicians
and Members of Parliament, but these were issues (for all but the most resolute
anti-Unionists) specific to time and place: the enthusiasms and political alignments
to which they gave rise were transitory, while divisions over religion had a more
permanent quality, producing distinct and opposed political parties, both at the
centre, at Edinburgh and Westminster, and in the localities.

In his thesis Dr Ferguson offered an alternative explanation for the torpor of
the eighteenth-century political system in Scotland, by focusing on the effects of
the Act of Union.[9] Indeed, he presented the Union as the *fons et origo* of Scottish
parliamentary corruption. This is not simply an expression of nationalist prejudice.
The argument rests on two premises: first that by sharply restricting the numbers
of parliamentary seats available to local political interests in Scotland, to one per
county (instead of anything up to four) and one per district of burghs, the new
electoral arrangements encouraged unprecedented competition for seats; secondly,
that the assumption of sole jurisdiction over Scottish electoral causes by the
Commons at Westminster encouraged the unscrupulous to resort to corrupt
methods of maximising support, notably the multiplication of freeholds in counties
and the temporary conveying of lands in trust, in the confident expectation that
friends and allies at Westminster would ignore evidence and deliver judgment

---

[8] *H.P., 1754–90*, I, 40, 46.
[9] The argument is briefly restated in his *Scotland 1689 to the Present*, pp. 135–6.

on a partisan basis. Before the Union, Dr Ferguson argued, the more flexible Scottish electoral system had been able to accommodate rival interests. Put crudely, there were enough shire commissionerships to go round. After 1707, with each county reduced to one Member, magnates who had formerly shared out the representation among themselves were forced into conflict with each other. And whereas previous disputes over the qualification of individual voters had been appealed to the Scottish Parliament or in Parliament's absence to the Court of Session, which came to judgment after a proper hearing of the evidence, under the united Parliament no such judicial reviewing mechanism was provided, and these delicate and complex questions were decided by the cynical exercise of political muscle in the House of Commons, that 'most corrupt court in Christendom', as English M.P.s themselves regarded it.[10]

The argument that the Union had poisoned the waters of Scottish politics would certainly have been recognised by contemporaries, for the first general election to the new Parliament of Great Britain, in 1708, witnessed some scandalous examples of electoral malpractice. In Dumfriesshire, for example, where Lord Annandale's heir, James, Lord Johnston, stood against Grierson of Lag, a client of the Scottish Secretary of State, the Duke of Queensberry, Annandale fulminated: 'there never was such irregular and illegal practices as has been by his grace and the other pretended ministry of this part of the kingdom'.[11] Not only had Queensberry's agents 'gripped by warrant' and 'threatened with imprisonment' several of Lord Johnston's voters; they had also recruited a troop of new electors of their own through the division and conveyancing of freeholds.[12] It was a similar story in Lanarkshire. There the Duke of Hamilton's brother, Lord Archibald, faced opposition in his family's traditional stronghold from James, Lord Carmichael, son of the courtier Lord Hyndford. 'There are such violations and encroachments on our constitution as were never attempted before', ranted the Duke,

> To make votes . . . they have been endeavouring the bringing in eleven new barons [freeholders], several of them inferior servants and dragoons in the Lord Carmichael's regiment, who were to be purchasers of land they knew nothing of, nor had paid nothing for, but their names used even without the knowledge of some of them; and if this trick had taken effect it was redeemable for less than 20s., the freeholds to be redelivered after the elections are over.

In these circumstances the eventual result was gratifying: 'my brother Lord Archibald carried his election . . . after all the malicious, unfair dealing that ever

[10] See W.A. Speck, ' "The Most Corrupt Council in Christendom": Decisions on Controverted Elections, 1702–42', in *Party and Management in Parliament, 1660–1784*, ed. C. Jones (Leicester. 1984), pp. 107–21. The quotation is from the parliamentary diarist Sir Richard Cocks: Bodl., MS. Eng. hist. b. 210, f. 5. My edition of this diary is in the press.

[11] Sir W. Fraser, *The Annandale Family Book of the Johnstones, Earls and Marquesses of Annandale* (2 vols., Edinburgh, 1894), II, 240.

[12] Annandale MSS. (the Earl of Annandale, Raehills, nr. Lockerbie, Dumfriesshire), bundle 411, William Johnston to [Lord Johnston], [1708]. See also B.L., Add. MS. 61628, ff. 120–1; Scottish R.O., GD 220/5/802/11 (Montrose papers), Mungo Graham to Montrose, 26 June 1708; H.M.C., *Hope-Johnstone MSS.*, p. 123. I wish particularly to thank Lord and Lady Annandale for their hospitality at Raehills, and Mr Duncan Adamson for facilitating my study of the muniments there.

was in any county'.[13] Other *causes célèbres* were the clash between the Duke of Argyll and Lord Mar in tiny Clackmannanshire, which resulted in a brisk exchange of accusations in the Edinburgh newspapers (a 'pen and ink scuffle' much enjoyed by the spectating Daniel Defoe);[14] a struggle between the Dukes of Atholl and Montrose in Perthshire, which as in Dumfriesshire featured arrests of electoral agents as well as the manufacture of new votes;[15] a sharp encounter in Stirlingshire which more than doubled the electorate at one swoop;[16] and even a contest in Moray, in which Sir Harry Innes of that ilk was frustrated by a suspiciously late influx of new freeholders in favour of his opponent (in his own, somewhat cryptic expression, he had been 'overthrown by great women's influence').[17] Of course, what we have here could be no more than orchestrated howls of complaint from rejected candidates, but the universality of the concern expressed—including at least one contemporary pamphlet which detailed the various abuses practised in the election[18]—and the tone in which even successful candidates commented on the subterfuges of their opponents, seem to indicate a genuine sense that something unpleasant had entered Scottish politics. And this apprehension of a loss of innocence was neither confined to county elections nor was peculiar to the immediate aftermath of Union, when many of those who had expressed qualms about the treaty might be expected to bewail its effects. Four years later the Earl of Sutherland's heir, Lord Strathnaver, was warned of 'a thing whispered about . . . which will endanger the ruining the great interest such ancient families as your lordship has in Scotland if not crushed in the bud, which is purchasing the votes of burghs for money'.[19]

Thus far the circumstantial evidence seems to lend support to Dr Ferguson's contention that the Union constituted a turning point in the corruption, or commercialisation, of the Scottish electoral system. However, a closer look at the political scene before 1707 might prompt a reconsideration of one of the premises of his case, the notion that representation in the Scottish Parliament had been more accessible, and that leading magnates and proprietors had not needed to compete with one another to secure what they considered their due. Simply

[13] B.L., Add. MS. 61628, ff. 98, 100.

[14] Scottish R.O., GD 124/15/754/1, 7, 18, 23 (Mar and Kellie papers), Lord Mar to Lord Grange, 6 Jan., 19 Feb., 16 Apr., 4 May 1708; GD 124/15/768/5, Grange to Mar, 28 Feb. 1708; GD 124/15/762/9, George Erskine to Grange, 25 Mar. [1708]; GD 124/15/868/1, Mar to Lord Stair, 20 June 1708; SC 64/63/24 (Alloa sheriff court recs.), Clackmannanshire electoral court mins. 16 June 1708; Lincolnshire Archives Office, Yarborough MSS. 16/7/1, Defoe to Lord Treasurer Godolphin, 29 June 1708.

[15] B.L., Add. MS. 61631, f. 54; Add. MS. 9102, f. 74; C.J., XVI, 227.

[16] Scottish R.O., SC 67/60/10 (Stirling sheriff court recs.), list of enrolments, 2 June 1708; GD 220/5/154/2, Lord Linlithgow to Montrose, 1708; GD 124/10/831/12, Mar to Sir David Nairne, 8 June 1708.

[17] C.J., XVI, 15; Scottish R.O., GD 205/36/6 (Ogilvy of Inverquharity papers), Innes to William Bennet, 26 June 1708.

[18] In the *Edinburgh Courant*, 23–26 July 1708, Patrick Moncreiff of Reidie, the recently elected Member for Fife, disclaimed authorship of an *Account of the Divisions in Scotland, and of the Measures Taken about the Elections of Members for the Ensuing Parliament*. Searches in Scottish and other libraries, and the E.S.T.C., have failed to locate a surviving copy of this pamphlet.

[19] National Library of Scotland, Dep. 313/532 (Sutherland papers), Robert Munro to [Strathnaver], 20 Dec. 1712.

because three or four places were available on a county's parliamentary commission did not mean that rival interests would quietly share out those places among themselves. In the general election of 1702 county after county was hotly contested: all four places on the Lanarkshire commission were disputed; all three in Ayrshire, where Queensberry and Argyll each put up a slate of candidates; all three in Orkney. Burghs were similarly affected; and not merely Edinburgh itself and the larger towns but smaller corporations, of the size and relative insignificance of Arbroath, Culross and Dornoch.[20] But it was in the counties that the storm raged most fiercely. The eight voters of Clackmannanshire found their favours the subject of a 'great struggle'; while in Wigtownshire the electoral court endured an all-night sitting, from 1.30 in the afternoon through till nine the following morning.[21] Even Kincardineshire, one of the most passive of counties after the Union, saw a contested election, when the Court party set up the lord of session Lord Phesdo against Sir Thomas Burnet.[22] In general 'the elections for the ensuing Parliament has engrossed all business these several weeks', the Countess of Roxburghe was informed, 'never were there greater heats, intriguing, and caballing'.[23]

What is particularly striking about this election is the degree to which the tiny Scottish electorate seems to have been politicised. Prolonged attacks on the ministry by opposition factions, delivered both within and beyond the Parliament House, which capitalised on libertarian and patriotic sentiment and exploited such emotive issues as the Darien disaster and the continuance of a standing army after the peace of Ryswick, had culminated in 1702 in the secession of 74 'Country party' Members from the old Convention Parliament, when it reassembled after the accession of Anne. On the inevitable dissolution that followed this mass withdrawal, the opposition alliance went on to fight a strenuous election campaign, in which no stop was left unpulled.[24] A courtier was warned of their diligence:

[20] The controverted elections recorded in *Acts of the Parliament of Scotland* (12 vols., 1844–75 [hereafter *A.P.S.*]) were in Ayrshire, Berwickshire, Caithness, Clackmannanshire, Dumfriesshire, Dunbartonshire, Fife, Haddingtonshire (East Lothian), Lanarkshire, Linlithgowshire (West Lothian), Orkney, Renfrewshire, Arbroath, Dornoch, Haddington, and Kirkcaldy (XI, 33, 38–40, 43–5, 48, 62, 64–5, 75). A list of returns in the Yester papers (Nat. Lib. Scotland, MS. 14498, ff. 82–3) additionally notes contests for Kincardineshire, Roxburghshire, Culross, Edinburgh, and Montrose. There is also evidence of contests in Aberdeenshire (Aberdeen University Library, Duff House [Montcoffer] MSS., 3175/Z174, 'A list of the barons and for whom they voted . . . 1702', 'Memorandum against Stonywood, 1702'); Midlothian (*Letters of George Lockhart of Carnwath 1698–1732*, ed. D. Szechi [Scottish History Society, 5th ser., II, 1989], pp. 2–3); Cupar (Scottish R.O., GD 406/1/4962 [Hamilton papers], Rothes to the Duke of Hamilton, 8 Oct. 1702); and Perth, where the townsmen were 'in great heats' (Atholl MSS. [by permission of the Duke of Atholl, from his collection at Blair Castle, Blair Atholl, Perthshire], 45/II/206–8, [Lady Tullibardine] to Lord Tullibardine, 29, 30 Sept. 1702, George Robertson to [Oliphant] of Balgonie 30 Sept. 1702). On the Ayrshire election, and the involvement of Argyll and Queensberry, see Scottish R.O., GD 406/1/4921, John Brisbane to Hamilton, 6 July 1702.

[21] Scottish R.O., GD 406/1/4953, Daniel Hamilton to the Duke of Hamilton, 24 Oct. 1702; GD 18/5246/1/13 (Clerk of Penicuik papers). Lord Galloway to Sir John Clerk, 3 Nov. 1702.

[22] Atholl MSS., 45/II/169, Duke of Hamilton to [Lord Tullibardine], 20 Aug. 1702; Scottish R.O., SC 5/70/10 (Stonehaven sheriff court recs.), Kincardineshire poll 1702.

[23] Roxburghe MSS. (the Duke of Roxburghe, Floors Castle, Kelso, Roxburghshire), bundle 726, William Bennet to [Lady Roxburghe], 8 Oct. 1702.

[24] P.W.J. Riley, *King William and the Scottish Politicians* (Edinburgh. 1979), pp. 135–62; *idem*, 'The Formation of the Scottish Ministry of 1703', *Scottish Historical Review*, XLIV (1965), 112–34; *idem*,

'every elector is writ or spoke to and cajoled, and consultations how to influence over all the shires in the kingdom'.[25] And at electoral courts up and down the country freeholders exercised the Scottish custom (which had recently reappeared in England too) of 'instructing' their representatives, this time in what amounted in many cases to an extensive agenda for political reform.[26] In Roxburghshire the commissioners were instructed not only to inquire into the tragedy of the Caledonia settlement, to scrutinise public accounts, and to 'narrowly sift into the full design' of the proposed Anglo-Scottish union, but to 'endeavour' the passage of measures for triennial elections, the exclusion of placemen from Parliament, the prevention of a standing army and confirmation of the right of the Scottish estates to give their consent separately to declarations of war.[27] Similarly, in neighbouring Berwickshire, the freeholders called for annual elections to Parliament, 'a duly regulat[ed] national force instead of a standing army', and 'the securing of the civil and religious rights of the subject', while their counterparts in Perthshire spoke strong words on the issue of Darien and on the damaging effects of war taxation as well as demanding the full observance of the Claim of Right.[28]

This evidence of widespread political awareness among Scottish county voters (admittedly at an exceptional juncture of affairs—a crisis in the Scottish economy and grave uncertainty about the settling of union and succession) points to the direction I wish to follow in this essay. It suggests that we ought to be asking not only why the Scottish representative system suddenly became so susceptible to abuse in the early eighteenth century (always assuming that electoral corruption *was* a new phenomenon north of the Tweed), but also why a relatively sophisticated electorate, which had demonstrated its receptivity to rhetoric, should within a generation have become so much more deferential and pragmatic. If we are concerned with the arrival of political corruption in Scotland, then we may indeed focus on the Union as the avenue of infection; but if the emphasis falls instead on the demise of 'issue politics' in relation to Scottish parliamentary history, then there are alternative turning points to be considered. We may well find ourselves back with Jacobitism, contemplating the decline in the power of religion as a divisive force in parliamentary politics.

[24] *(contd.)* The Union of England and Scotland: A Study in Anglo-Scottish Politics of the Eighteenth Century (Manchester, 1978), pp. 32 *et seq.* Riley's account of these developments pays very little attention to the 1702 election itself.

[25] Buccleuch MSS. (the Duke of Buccleuch, Drumlanrig House, Thornhill, Dumfriesshire), bundle 1151 [William Morison?] to [-], 28 Aug. 1702.

[26] For the survival in the Scottish representative system of the medieval idea of 'attorneyship', see Ferguson, 'Electoral Law and Procedure', Chapter 1; and for some later eighteenth-century examples of politically oriented 'instructions', P. Kelly, 'Constituents' Instructions to Members of Parliament in the Eighteenth Century', in Jones (ed.), *Party and Management in Parliament*, pp. 178–9.

[27] Scottish R.O., GD 6/1061/6 (Biel papers), 'Some heads by way of instructions . . . 1702'. The background to this episode is described in Roxburghe MSS., bundle 726, William Bennet to [Lady Roxburghe], 8 Oct. 1702.

[28] Duns Library, Local History Collection, folio 9, folder 36, Berwickshire electoral court mins., 22 Oct. 1702; Atholl MSS., bundle 683, 'Instructions for those who are to be elected Members of Parliament' [1702]. For another example, from Aberdeenshire, see Aberdeen Univ. Lib., Duff House (Montcoffer) MSS., 3175/Z174, 'Queries proposed anent electing comm[issione]rs . . . 1702'.

Union, as a significant factor, cannot be left out of the discussion. But I would judge its impact differently to Dr Ferguson, who regards the implementation of the Act of Union as having sealed off Scottish M.P.s from public discussion of political issues. In the last Parliament of Scotland, he claims, there had indeed been 'embryonic parties', and 'popular opinion' had influenced parliamentary decisions; but after 1707 the masses 'dropped out of politics', and 'parties' rapidly declined into little more than personally or territorially based connexions.[29] This is to jump from sequence to causation. Furthermore, a strong case can be made on the other side, to show that in some respects Union actually provided a highly favourable medium in which 'embryonic' political parties could grow. For the political world in which Scottish representatives now found themselves having to operate was dominated by perpetual warfare between two great political parties. Englishmen (and Welshmen) interpreted their own parliamentary behaviour in party terms, and wasted no time in applying Whig and Tory labels to their new colleagues from North Britain.[30] The very fact of participating in a parliamentary system where party affiliation was one of the first characteristics applied to an individual naturally induced Scotsmen to classify themselves in the same way. Scottish parliamentary representatives began to integrate themselves into English party structures, and through their integration the political culture of Scotland took on some of the characteristics of the 'divided society' of Augustan England. By the time of Queen Anne's death, recognisable 'Whig' and 'Tory' interests had appeared in Scotland. What cut short their development was the Hanoverian succession, and the widespread involvement of leading Scottish 'Tories' in the Fifteen. Jacobitism had always been closer to the centre of cavalier or 'Tory' identity in Scotland than in England, and Scottish Tories were politically emasculated by the public exposure of their legitimist scruples. But between 1707 and 1715 the 'embryonic parties' of pre-Union Scotland had come a long way towards maturity, a process which we can trace in the localities as well as at Westminster; in electoral courts as well as in the House of Commons.[31]

Of course we have to be careful in assuming that English attitudes and practices could be transplanted directly. In its social structure, its intellectual and constitutional traditions, and in the prevailing conventions of its political life, Scotland differed markedly from England and Wales. For one thing the parliamentary electorate was much smaller. The 100 or so voters in Midlothian represented the largest figure for any county,[32] by some distance, and the number of councillors prescribed in a burgh sett would seldom exceed a dozen. Moreover the nature of Scottish landed society, and the complex requirements of the Scottish franchise,

---

[29] Ferguson, *Scotland 1689 to the Present*, p. 137.

[30] See for example, B.L., Add. MS. 70421, Dyer's newsletter, 11 Nov. 1710, which interpreted the recent Scottish election results in English terms, noting the return of 'some High', and 'some Low' M.P.s.

[31] This argument was first adumbrated in P.W.J. Riley, 'The Structure of Scottish Politics and the Union of 1707', in *The Union of 1707: Its Impact on Scotland*, ed. T.I. Rae (Glasgow, 1974), pp. 13–17.

[32] Szechi (ed.), *Letters of George Lockhart*, pp. 69–71; Lauderdale MSS. (in the possession of the Earl of Lauderdale), 2/19, list of Midlothian freeholders (election forecast), 1713.

meant that in the shires only the more substantial lairds would be involved in electing M.P.s.[33] This was a face-to-face political society, where personal relationships mattered a great deal: candidates could canvass every voter individually, and breaking a promise or otherwise defaulting on a prior obligation constituted a serious impropriety. There was also a legalistic element in the elections themselves. A county's electoral court was precisely that, and most of its time was spent in determining whether each individual voter was properly qualified, with objections and counter-objections carefully recorded. Despite occasional disturbances, the atmosphere was redolent of the courtroom rather than the hustings. Each of these factors—a small, socially exclusive electorate, close familiarity between candidates and electors, and the juridical nature of the electoral process—made for a political system in which the influence of great landed proprietors was much more powerful than it was in English counties.

However, there is no need to be too determinist. Small electorates, as contemporary English borough patrons were only too well aware, were not always malleable, and in Scottish counties the social and economic standing of the lesser barons might encourage a certain independence of mind; what Lord Galloway, speaking of the voters of Kirkcudbright Stewartry, resented as their 'insolent carriage'.[34] In the remote northern shire of Caithness, for example, the absentee magnate, Lord Breadalbane, found his wishes ignored by the disputatious freeholders: 'I know none within the shire . . . we can influence to vote as we would have them', his son reported, 'I fear the barons have not that deference to us, that our letters would have any weight with them, nor no fit person there to instruct in managing anything . . . our jurisdiction is laughed at there as it is managed.'[35] Nor were conventions always honoured in strict observance. In the run-up to the Berwickshire election of 1710 the Earl of Lauderdale showed how it was possible neatly to circumvent the formal requirements of good manners. Approached by Lord Home to write to two freeholders on behalf of a candidate, he 'answered . . . that I believed the gentlemen were pre-engaged'. But when Lord Polwarth, the son of Home's local rival, Lord Marchmont, made a similar request in favour of another nominee Lauderdale felt free to offer an endorsement, though he took care to 'signify to my Lord Polwarth that I would not have it known that I wrote to them since the receipt of my Lord Home's letter'.[36] Lastly, the inquisitorial process in the electoral court often served in practice as an irritant: minutes show time and again a long-drawn-out series of challenges to individuals' voting rights which would inevitably have raised antagonisms and hardened lines

[33] Put at its simplest a landed proprietor could vote in a Scottish county election if he possessed freehold land worth 40s. p.a. of 'old extent' (the medieval valuation) or possessed a 'superiority' (land held immediately of the Crown) worth £400 Scots. The exception was in Sutherland, where there were no 'superiorities', and vassals of the Earl of Sutherland voted instead.

[34] Annandale MSS., bdle. 826, Galloway to [Annandale], 26 June 1708.

[35] Scottish R.O., GD 112/39/243/36 (Breadalbane papers), Lord Glenorchy to Breadalbane, 26 Aug. 1710. On the peculiar difficulties faced by the Breadalbanes in Caithness, where they were deeply unpopular, see J.T. Calder, *Sketch of the Civil and Traditional History of Caithness, from the Tenth Century* (Glasgow, 1861). pp. 166–8. The earl was not helped by his own financial difficulties and the vast distance of Caithness from his seat in the Perthshire Highlands.

[36] Scottish R.O., GD 248/800/3 (Seafield papers), Lauderdale to [Seafield], 5 Oct. 1710.

of division. It is interesting to observe that correspondence about elections in Scotland in this period contains little of that pious concern for preserving (at least a nominal) consensus among the 'county community' which was still to be found in the utterances of the more old-fashioned of eighteenth-century English squires, clinging to an ideal of unity in an age of conflict.[37] Ruminating Scotsmen were more likely to extol the civic virtue of the independent freeholder: as the Banffshire laird James Ogilvy rather primly informed Lord Findlater, in reply to a bread-and-butter request for his vote, 'I think all the [e]state of barons are so much concerned in the freedom of their elections, and so tied up both by conscience and honour, that both as electors and when elected nothing of friendship, fear, or interest should bias them'.[38]

The realities of the Scottish electoral system can perhaps be seen most clearly in the behaviour of the smaller constituencies. Post-Union elections in burgh districts were by definition relatively 'open'. Even where individual town councils were controlled by patrons, as Inveraray was by Argyll, Lanark by Hamilton, or Sanquhar by Queensberry, it was difficult to be sure of carrying the entire district by proprietorial influence alone. In the Dumfries district in 1708 for example, Queensberry's nomination of the commissioner for Sanquhar was overmatched by Annandale's interest in Annan and Lochmaben, while 'the towns of Dumfries and Kirkcudbright judge themselves free and independent'.[39] Counties, being unitary constituencies, were *ipso facto* easier to 'close'; and some were entirely in the hands of the dominant local magnate: in Argyllshire, to cite probably the most obvious example, where always at least half the voters attending the election were Campbells and where the Duke of Argyll did not need to make a single new voter between 1707 and 1715 to maintain his iron grip;[40] in the scattered parcels of the barony of Cromarty, with a mere five voters, over whom the Earl of Cromarty presided untroubled until his death in 1714;[41] or in Sutherland, whose dozen or so lesser barons were all vassals of the Earl of Sutherland.[42] But few even of the underpopulated Scottish counties were so enthralled as not to require careful management, or so supine as not to suffer the slightest twitch of restlessness. As we have seen, Clackmannanshire witnessed a bitter conflict in

---

[37] On this theme, see M.A. Kishlansky, *Parliamentary Selection: Social and Political Choice in Early Modern England* (Cambridge, 1986).

[38] Scottish R.O., GD 248/566/85/25. Ogilvy to Findlater, [?1713].

[39] Annandale MSS., bundle 602, John Hutton to [Annandale], 22 Apr. 1708.

[40] Scottish R.O., SC 54/21/1 (Inveraray sheriff court recs.), pp. 1–14, Argyllshire electoral court mins., 1708–13.

[41] Ferguson 'Electoral Law and Procedure', Chapter 3; Sir W. Fraser, *The Earls of Cromartie: Their Kindred, Country and Correspondence* (2 vols., Edinburgh, 1876), II, 158, 458–61; Scottish R.O., SC 24/20/1/8, 13 (Cromarty sheriff court recs.), Cromartyshire electoral court mins., 1702, 1703.

[42] *A.P.S.*, V. 62–3, 384–5; *Original Papers: Containing the Secret History of Great Britain, from the Restoration to the Accession of the House of Hannover . . .*, ed. J. Macpherson (2 vols., 1775), II, 18; Scottish R.O., GD 124/14/3/25, list of Sutherland freeholders, 1709. Interestingly, though, even here the election of one of the two commissioners in 1702 was controverted (*A.P.S.*, XI 11), and prior to the 1713 election Sutherland's son, Lord Strathnaver, who was managing the family interest, took care to obtain the approval of the Breadalbanes for his nomination of his father-in-law William Morison of Prestongrange: Scottish R.O., GD 112/39/243/36, Lord Glenorchy to Breadalbane, 26 Aug. 1710.

1708 between candidates sponsored by Argyll and Mar, admittedly a battle fought largely by stage armies of 'faggot' or 'fictitious' voters who had been created for the occasion; and two years later in Kinross-shire the local lairds mounted a determined and ultimately effective resistance (decided by a Commons' judgment) to the prospect of having the Duke of Montrose's factor, Mungo Graham, foisted upon them.

Kinross is in many ways the most interesting of these examples, since here we can find traces of what may well be 'party' feeling (in a Whig-and-Tory sense). The party affiliations of the *dramatis personae* could scarcely have been clearer: on the one side stood Montrose and his local agents—the nominee, Graham, and the principal manager for the election, Montrose's son-in-law Sir John Bruce of Kinross House—all publicly identified with the Whig and 'Revolution' cause; on the other was the candidate of 'all our Kinross-shire lairds', Sir John Malcolm of Lochore in Fife, son of a nonjuror, brother of a staunch Jacobite, and himself the beneficiary of the counsel and assistance of the Tory Lord Mar.[43] At Westminster this election was seen as a simple choice between representatives of the two political parties, and English (and Scottish) Members divided accordingly.[44] The evidence from the constituency itself would not allow such a clear-cut description, but there are some significant details to be noted, such as Malcolm's allegation that one of the unqualified voters admitted to poll for his opponent was 'a Presbyterian minister . . . whose freehold did not consist of the the the tenth part required by law'.[45]

In order to understand how 'Whig' and 'Tory' parties came to emerge in Scotland we must return briefly to the Glorious Revolution and its aftermath. A rigorously presbyterian church settlement not only meant the immediate removal of episcopacy in 1689 but in due course the exclusion of a substantial minority of parish ministers and university teachers who were unable to accept the Revolution in church and state.[46] This Episcopalian remnant, concentrated in (but by no means confined to) the north-east, stood as the conscience of the 'cavalier' element in the Scottish political nation: noblemen and lairds who under Charles

[43] Scottish R.O., GD 124/15/978/8, Lord Colvill (of Ochiltree) to Lord Grange, 13 Oct. 1710; *The Case of the Controverted Election for the Shire of Kinross* [1711] (Lincoln's Inn Library, MP 100/145); *The Case of the Election of Kinross in Answer to the Petition* [1711] (B.L., Dept. of Printed Bks., 816.m.4 [61]). For an indication that Malcolm's Jacobite brother James had had a 'share' in the election, see Scottish Catholic Archives, Blairs College MSS., BL2/168/3, James Carnegy to the Scots College, 20 Jan. 1711 (a reference I owe to the kindness of Professor Daniel Szechi).

[44] Scottish R.O., GD 220/5/808/17–18, Mungo Graham to Montrose, 10, 13 Feb. 1711. The Glasgow M.P. Thomas Smith, himself a staunch Presbyterian and Whig, reported, 'the greatest part of our Scots Members were for him [Graham], but the Tories were obliged . . . to oblige their friends of our country. Those [Scottish M.P.s] against him were . . . of that kidney, who indeed have never spared one Whig in their votes since they came hither. So that however these gentlemen are inclined in our elections, their English friends will always be [?determined] by them': Nat. Lib. Scotland, Advocates' MSS., Wodrow Letters Quarto V, f. 128, letter of Smith, 10 Feb. 1710–11, transcribed by Robert Wodrow for private circulation.

[45] *C.J.*, XVI, 419.

[46] On the ecclesiastical settlement in Scotland, see A.L. Drummond and J. Bulloch, *The Scottish Church, 1688–1843* (Edinburgh, 1973); A.I Dunlop, *William Carstares and the Kirk as by Law Established* (Edinburgh, 1964); and, especially, T.N. Clarke, 'The Scottish Episcopalians, 1688–1720' (University of Edinburgh Ph.D., 1987), Chapters 1–2.

II and James VII and II had acted as the instruments of royalist reaction in Scotland, and who, under the new political order, were likewise excluded, or had excluded themselves, from public life. It was the 'cavaliers' who did their best to protect Episcopalian clergy from ejection after 1689, and in the last resort provided household chaplaincies and tutorships for those whose incumbencies they could not preserve.

At first the essential differences between 'Episcopalians' and 'Presbyterians' were constitutional rather than theological.[47] Except for its prelatic superstructure, the pre-Revolution Church of Scotland had been broadly acceptable to Presbyterians, with only a handful of Episcopalian zealots pressing for liturgical innovation. In the same way, the discipline and worship of the Kirk after 1689 would seem to have been acceptable to many Episcopalians. The sticking point was the Revolution itself. Principled Episcopalians regarded monarchy and prelacy as alike divinely ordained, and it was their refusal to break oaths of allegiance to the legitimate Stewart King which was the cause of clerical deprivations. In political terms the immediate effect was to marginalise the Episcopalian and cavalier interest. Whether nonjurors were inevitably committed Jacobites is far from certain, but most would have been at least sympathetic to the Jacobite cause, and in any case their enemies wasted no time in smearing them as disloyal. In order to retain influence, and a place in the great game of politics, the most important magnates on the Episcopalian side, the Duke of Queensberry and the Marquess of Atholl, promptly took the oaths and tried to portray themselves and their families as staunch to the Revolution.[48] The cavaliers were thus left without strong leadership, the only prominent politicians who did show some interest in mobilising Episcopalian opinion being highly ambiguous figures: Viscount Tarbat, later 1st Earl of Cromarty, a man whose perpetual deviousness deprived him of political ballast; and the Duke of Hamilton, whose own presbyterian upbringing had imparted something of a Whiggish colouring in Scottish politics, and whose blatant opportunism discouraged trust.[49]

In William's reign power in Scotland was confined to those magnates and politicians who were, or who assumed the pose of, 'Revolution men'. But, as Dr Riley has demonstrated, the multiplicity of factions made for chronic instability. Magnates with the *amour propre* of Atholl, Queensberry, Hamilton, and the Duke of Argyll could not work together for long in harmony; nor could any of them successfully govern Scotland on their own.[50] In 1702 the latest pause in the merry-go-round found Queensberry at the head of a fragile and battered Court party, presiding over a coalition of different interests with in opposition a similarly broad alliance, calling itself the Country party, under the general leadership of

---

[47] Here I follow the argument in Clarke, 'Scottish Episcopalians', Chapter 1. See also B. Lenman, 'The Scottish Episcopal Clergy and the Ideology of Jacobitism', in *Ideology and Conspiracy: Aspects of Jacobitism, 1689–1759*, ed. E. Cruickshanks (Edinburgh, 1982), pp. 39–41.

[48] P.W.J.Riley, *King William and the Scottish Politicians* (Edinburgh, 1979), pp. 12–13.

[49] Hamilton's brother wrote to him from London in January 1702: 'I hear [the Earl of Sunderland] is not well pleased with you. What, will you be a Tory in England and a Whig in Scotland?' (Scottish R.O., GD 406/1/7441, Orkney to Hamilton, 8 Jan. 1701–2).

[50] This is in essence the thesis propounded in Riley, *King William and the Scottish Politicians*.

Hamilton, and including a contingent of cavaliers. Between the accession of Queen Anne and the Union these groupings divided and re-formed again several times. First Queensberry was forced by English ministers into a shotgun marriage with Tarbat, Atholl and the 'cavaliers', which ended in divorce after one traumatic parliamentary session; then in 1704 came another unsuccessful ministerial exper-iment, to replace Queensberry with a splinter group from the 'Country party' opposition, the so-called 'new party' or '*Squadrone Volante*' (flying squadron). Finally an uneasy combination of Queensberry's followers, Argyll's, and the *Squadrone* came together to carry the treaty of union.[51]

The kaleidoscopic appearance of Scottish high politics in this period disguises two important long-term developments. The first was the emergence of the *Squadrone*, an unusual collectivity comprising a number of smaller connexions—those of Marchmont, Tweeddale, Roxburghe, Rothes, and Montrose—which in the case of Marchmont and Tweeddale were distinguished by a 'presbyterian' religious tinge, and a record of commitment to principles of civil liberty and parliamentary independence. Already partly 'Whiggish' in complexion, and re-garded as 'republican' by some on the cavalier side,[52] the *Squadrone* contracted a tactical alliance with the English Whig Junto, which, the longer it continued, served to reinforce ever more strongly their partisan orientation. Parallel with the appearance of a Scottish Whig interest was the re-emergence of the cavaliers as a political force. The accession of Anne, daughter of James VII and II and herself a staunch Anglican, persuaded former nonjurors to take the oaths and return to active politics. They did so still under the nominal leadership of Hamilton, in default of an alternative magnate, but preserved a separate identity through such organisations as the pseudo-Jacobite 'Mitchell's Club'.[53] Thus when Queensberry referred, in his correspondence with Westminster, to the 'cavalier' and 'presbyterian' parties as the Scylla and Charybdis between which his own course had to be charted, he was not simply, as Dr Riley argues, resorting to customary cant in order to hide the complex truth from innocent Englishmen, but was describing an increasingly significant reality.[54]

At the time of the Union there were four important power blocs in Scottish politics: Queensberry's Court party; the Argyllites; the *Squadrone*; and Hamilton's connexion, which incorporated the revived cavalier interest. Except for Argyll, who was in a weak position, having alienated even members of his own clan by his tergiversation and rampant egoism,[55] each group had established alliances, or at the very least a correspondence, with factions in English politics: Queensberry with Lord Treasurer Godolphin, the *Squadrone* with the Whig Junto, and the cavaliers, naturally enough, with the English Tories. In the years following the

[51] The process can be followed closely in P.W.J. Riley. *The Union of England and Scotland: A Study in Anglo-Scottish Politics of the Eighteenth Century* (Manchester, 1978).

[52] The adjective was Lord Breadalbane's: Scottish R.O., GD 26/13/151/3 (Leven and Melville papers), Breadalbane to Leven, 14 June 1708.

[53] Riley, *Union*, p. 48.

[54] Buccleuch MSS., bdle 1202, Queensberry to [Godolphin], 1 Sept. 1703: Riley, *Union*, pp. 61–3.

[55] D. Hayton, 'Constitutional Experiments and Political Expediency, 1689–1725', in *Conquest to Union: Fashioning a British State, 1485–1725*, eds. S.G. Ellis and S. Barber, 1995), p. 302.

Union these associations became firmer, and in the Parliament of 1708–10, with Argyll effectively sidelined, the Scottish Members conformed to the pattern of English politics: Queensberry's party and the *Squadrone* supported the Court, in the same uneasy alliance as obtained between Godolphin and the Junto; while Hamilton led the cavaliers, and his own personal adherents, in opposition. The ministerial revolution of 1710 produced a further simplification. At first the political changes in Scotland were kept to a minimum. The new chief minister, Robert Harley, came into power anxious to keep the allegiance of as many members of the old 'Court party' as he could; so far as was consonant with his own prior commitments to both Argyll and Hamilton, and with the prejudices of the English Tories on whom his administration ultimately relied. But within a year the coherence of Queensberry's connexion had been destroyed by the duke's death, many of his former followers (with the important exception of the Earl of Findlater) drifting into opposition alongside the *Squadrone*; and in 1713 Argyll broke with Harley on personal grounds, and sought to re-invent himself as a Whig. The ministry's Scottish policy thus lost its claim to even-handedness or moderation: and just as in his relations with the English parties, Harley's political management of Scotland had become dependent on the Tories.[56]

By 1710 the Scottish cavaliers were indeed calling themselves 'Tories', or at the very least 'Episcopal Tories'.[57] In the general election of that year they secured a strong representation in the Commons, winning about a third of the Scottish seats, and also made inroads into the Court and *Squadrone* domination of the representative peers. These significant gains emancipated them from Hamilton's ascendancy. Even before his fatal duel in December 1712 the duke had been by-passed by a new generation of Scottish Tories. In the Lords the running was now being made by peers like Balmerino, Eglinton, Kilsyth and Linlithgow, less personally imposing (in terms of wealth, property or influence) but more vociferously anti-Whig; while in the House of Commons the Scottish Tory interest was led by what one modern historian has called a 'steering committee' of five back-benchers: the noted anti-Unionist George Lockhart of Carnwath, Sir Alexander Areskine (or Erskine, the Lord Lyon), the young advocate John Carnegy, James Murray (son and heir of Viscount Stormont), and the county Member for Aberdeen, Sir Alexander Cumming.[58] Such men acted together not from family or personal attachment (in Cumming's case there were previous ties of clientage to Argyll)[59] but from common principles, in particular a devotion to the Episcopalian cause. In the Commons their main objectives seem to have been to

[56] The fullest discussion of developments in Scottish politics after 1710 is to be found in P.W.J. Riley, *The English Ministers and Scotland 1707–1727* (1964), Chapters 11–15. See also G. Holmes, *British Politics in the Age of Anne* (1967), pp. 242–5.

[57] D. Szechi, 'Some Insights on the Scottish MPs and Peers Returned in the 1710 Election', *Scottish Historical Review*, LX (1981), 61–75.

[58] D. Szechi, *Jacobitism and Tory Politics 1710–14* (Edinburgh, 1984), pp. 85–7, 99–102; *The Lockhart Papers*, ed. A. Aufrere (2 vols., 1817), I, 338–9, 423, 444–52.

[59] [J. Maidment,] *The Argyle Papers* (1834), pp. 93–5, 97–8, 101–2, 120; J. M'Cormick, *State-Papers and Letters Addressed to William Carstares . . .* (Edinburgh, 1774), p. 704. The connexion had been resumed by 1714: Aberdeen Univ. Lib., Duff House (Montcoffer) MSS., 3175/2382, Kreienberg to Cumming, 14 Nov. 1714.

protect individual ministers, like the celebrated James Greenshields, and to make progress towards a full toleration for Episcopalians.[60] To this end they quickly entered into full co-operation with English Tory back-benchers of similar prejudices. As early as March 1711 a presbyterian M.P. reported: 'I am told we have a party of our Scots Members that are in concert with the October Club, and some of the members of the Convocation, to bring about a revolution in the Church of Scotland.'[61]

The mutual identification of Scottish cavaliers and English Tories in Parliament coincided with the acquisition by Scottish Episcopalians of a more distinctively 'High Church' character. Encouraged by High Churchmen in England, Episcopalian clergy and congregations began to practise an Anglican liturgy. By 1709 'the English service' was said to be 'in great vogue' in Edinburgh, and in places as far apart as Elgin, Perth, and Craill in Fife, ministers were prosecuted for making use of the Book of Common Prayer.[62] Thinking in unionist terms, the deprived clergy and their meeting house congregations began to regard themselves as integral members of the Church of England. County and burgh addresses on the occasion of the Scottish Toleration and Patronages Acts of 1712 expressed gratitude for the Queen's favour to 'the sons of the Church of England in these parts' (Craill, Stirling), to 'those of the episcopal persuasion and communion of the Church of England here in Scotland' (Forfar), or simply to 'the Church' (by which the council of Arbroath did not mean the established Church of Scotland, but the Church of England).[63] In this way the parliamentary fusion between Scottish cavaliers and English Tories was given a local expression, and the more successful the alliance became at Westminster, the more firmly did Episcopalian interests in the localities push the identification home. With typical bravura, the 'gentry, clergy, and others of the Episcopal persuasion in the shire of Banff', protested in their address to the Queen against[64]

---

[60] This formulation consciously by-passes the issue of Jacobitism in a Scottish parliamentary context. For many (perhaps most) Scottish Tories, however, constitutional and ecclesiastical issues were interwoven. As an example it may be worth quoting a back-bench Scottish Tory, George Mackenzie of Inchcoulter (M.P. Inverness Burghs 1710–13), who in November 1710 looked forward to his election to Parliament in these terms: 'if I have a voice in settling the monarchy and church interest I'll have what I most desire' (Nat. Lib. Scotland, MS. 1343 [Delvine papers], f. 106, Mackenzie to John Mackenzie of Delvine, 3 Nov. 1710).

[61] Nat. Lib. Scotland, Advocates' MSS., Wodrow Letters Quarto V, f. 172, letter of [Thomas Smith, MP Glasgow Burghs], 17 Mar. 1710–11, transcribed for private circulation. See also D. Szechi, 'The Politics of "Persecution": Scots Episcopalian Toleration and the Harley Ministry, 1710–12', in *Toleration and Persecution: Studies in Church History XXI*, ed. W.J. Sheils (Oxford, 1984), 275–87.

[62] Clarke, 'Scottish Episcopalians', pp. 186–7, 189–90, 322–4; Nat. Lib. Scotland, Advocates' MSS., Wodrow Letters Quarto II, f. 128, J[ohn] Maxwell to Robert Wodrow, 7 Nov. 1709.

[63] *Scots Courant*, 23–25 July, 5–8 Sept., 15–17 Oct., 26–28 Nov. 1712. The Whig John Forbes of Culloden used the phrase 'High Church' to describe an address from Inverness-shire in December 1714: *Culloden Papers . . .* (1815), p. 33. This was of course a time-honoured ploy by which Scottish Episcopalians had sought to engage the sympathies of High Churchmen in England: see Sir George Mackenzie (the future Earl of Cromarty) to Lord Nottingham, July/Aug. 1690, printed in H.M.C., *Finch MSS.*, II, 392–3.

[64] Scottish R.O., CH 12/12/1853 (Episcopal Church of Scotland papers), copy of Banffshire address [1712?].

the lamentable state and condition of those of your Majesty's most dutiful subjects in this part of North Britain who adhere to the doctrine and worship of the Church of England, in opposition to all antimonarchical and seditious principles and practices, and that this our misery is occasioned by fanatical fury and tyrannical usurpation of the Presbyterian party over our persons and consciences . . .

An inevitable consequence of the identification of Scottish factions with English parties, and the simultaneous alignment of Scottish Episcopalianism and English High Churchmanship, was that political and religious divisions in Scotland came to be described in English 'party' terms. The Scottish political nation began to repeat the slogans and debate the issues which animated English politics. In the spring of 1710 Scottish 'Tories' rejoiced over the outcome of the trial of Dr Sacheverell. An agent of the Duke of Hamilton wrote from Edinburgh in March: 'Many people here are very well pleased with the turn that Dr Sacheverell's affair is like to take in his favour; and I assure your grace the hot prosecution of that affair has rendered the Whigs and our Squadrone most despicable'.[65] Once again the loyal addresses which rained down upon Queen Anne's court after 1711 provide a revealing insight into the language of post-Union politics: those devised by local 'Whigs' concentrated on the maintenance of the Hanoverian Succession and of the Kirk establishment; those promoted by 'Tories' spoke not only to the tribulations of Episcopalian ministers but to the advantages of the peace of Utrecht and the ending of a 'destructive' continental war, and emphasised as strongly as possible 'loyalty' to the traditional ideal of monarchy, sometimes even shading off into Jacobite ambiguity. Factions in Stirlingshire in 1713 produced rival addresses, which contemporaries described as 'Whig' and 'Tory', and which differed fundamentally in their attitudes to the Church, the peace, and the Protestant Succession.[66]

Increasingly Scotsmen (and women) came to use party labels in their electoral correspondence. One forecast for a Linlithgowshire election, possibly as early as 1708, marked voters as 'W' or 'T'.[67] More explicitly, in 1710, the cavalier Lord Stormont confessed his fear of the recent advance of 'the Whig set' in municipal elections in the burgh of Perth, while in the run-up to the general election of that year the veteran *Squadrone* M.P. George Baillie described the councils of Haddington and Jedburgh as 'both somewhat Tory'.[68] Three years later we can find references to 'the great change the To[rie]s have made . . . of late' in the government of the town of Inverness, and in Linlithgowshire again, presbyterian

[65] Scottish R.O., GD 406/1/5622, John Hamilton to Duke of Hamilton, 16 Mar. 1710.

[66] *Flying Post*, 4–7, 7–9 Apr. 1713.

[67] Scottish R.O., GD 30/2216/1 (Shairp of Houstoun papers), list of Linlithgowshire freeholders [1708].

[68] Mansfield MSS. (the Earl of Mansfield, Scone Palace, Perthshire), bundle 1248, Stormont to Alexander Barclay, 2 Oct. [1710]; Scottish R.O., GD 158/1257/4 (Hume of Marchmont papers), Baillie to [?Lord Polwarth], 28 Oct. 1710. In 1702 Lady Tullibardine had written that the council of Perth 'was said to be in three parties', 'the Highland party', 'the Presbyterians', and, presumably, the followers of the Duke of Atholl: Atholl MSS., 45/II/195, Lady Tullibardine to Lord Tullibardine, 24 Sept. [1702].

lamentations that divisions among 'the Whigs' threatened to allow the return of the High Tory John Houstoun.[69] And shortly after the Hanoverian Succession the Earl of Mar wrote to his follower Sir John Erskine, to remind him of the necessity of supporting the candidacy of the sitting Member Sir Hugh Paterson in the forthcoming election for Stirlingshire, adding, 'I hope the Tories will stick together and go in a lump whenever it may be'.[70]

At the local level the division between Tory and Whig in Scotland resolved itself into an opposition of Episcopalian to Presbyterian.[71] Ecclesiastical and political conflicts were indistinguishable. Thus the cavalier Lord Home's patronage of Episcopalian ministers, and his resistance to a Presbyterian challenge to his right of presentation in his own parish,[72] were of a piece with his strenuous endeavours to overturn the power of Lord Polwarth in Berwickshire politics. Having obtained a grant of the sheriffdom of the county from the new Tory ministry in 1710, he opposed 'all he could' the re-election of Polwarth's candidate for the county, in favour of his own nominee.[73] Naturally, the Polwarth interest responded in kind. Home's despairing description of the canvassing conveys the atmosphere of bitter family rivalry and sectarian animosity which prevailed. 'Since I left Ed[inburgh]', he told Lord Mar's brother,[74]

> the lairds of Wedderburn, Crossrig, Burncastle, and Berryhaugh, are frighted from the course they had frankly undertaken and were firmly resolved to follow out. The first is threatened by Sir Patrick Hume, his father-in-law, with ruin; the second is managed by Sir David Dalrymple; the third by whom I don't yet know; and the fourth is restrained by Sir Alex[ande]r Inglis sore against his inclinations, as by letter under his hand. Wedderburn has three or four voters who promised to go along with him and who would undoubtedly serve our interest if left to themselves, but Sir Patrick's threatenings are against him and all that concur with him. This proceeds from Sir Patrick directly, but a great man is the cause thereof. We daily meet with more and more discouragements. Some of our barons pretend the Kirk is in hazard, others are cajoled, a third sort are threatened, a fourth stand off because of oaths, and a fifth pretend to be such politicians as not to declare themselves till the day of election.

[69] Scottish R.O., GD 124/15/1112/1, George Mackenzie to Lord Grange, 28 Dec. 1713; Nat. Lib. Scotland, Advocates' MSS., Wodrow Letters Quarto VII, f. 177. J. Hart to [?Robert Wodrow], 29 Aug. 1713. In the end the Whigs managed to unite against Houstoun and defeat him at the electoral court. According to the Presbyterian minister Robert Wodrow, the contest was very much a party affair, Houstoun being 'set up upon the Tory side', and his opponent Sir James Carmichael, 'on the other': R. Wodrow, *Analecta: Or, Materials for a History of Remarkable Providences* (Maitland Club, LX, 4 vols., Glasgow, 1842–3), II. 246.

[70] Nat. Lib. Scotland., MS. 5072 (Erskine Murray papers), f. 24, Mar to Erskine, 7 Sept. 1714.

[71] The sectarian nature of political divisions did not, however, preclude all fluidity in allegiance: Sir William Scot of Thirlestane reported in 1713 that he had been 'spoke to to set up in opposition to John Pringle in our shire [Selkirk] at this time, by one once a Tory now I think turned angry Whig': Scottish R.O., GD 124/15/1105, Scott to Lord Grange, 23 Aug. 1713.

[72] Clarke, 'Scottish Episcopalians', pp. 69–70; Douglas-Home MSS. (Lord Home, The Hirsel, Coldstream, Berwickshire), box 22, folder 2, J. Gordon to Lord Home, 7 Feb. 1713.

[73] Scottish R.O., GD 158/967, pp. 43–4, Polwarth to Lord Ross, 23 Sept. 1710; *ibid.*, pp. 48–9, same to Duke of Hamilton, 27 Sept. 1710 (original in GD 406/1/5643).

[74] Scottish R.O., GD 124/15/1017, Home to Lord Grange, 28 Oct. 1710.

Political conflict between Tory and Whig parties blazed most intensely in those regions in which Episcopalian patrons, congregations and ministers survived in substantial numbers: in and around Edinburgh, in Fife, in Perthshire, and the counties of the north-east. The capital itself had long been a magnet for deprived and nonjuring clergy, and at one point, in 1708, as many as 17 Episcopalian ministers from city and suburbs had been summoned to appear before the magistrates for using the Book of Common Prayer in their services. (It was from one such magisterial crackdown that the celebrated test case of James Greenshields had arisen.)[75] Elections in the burgh constituency were unaffected, since control of the council was held firmly in the hands of the Presbyterian commercial *élite*, but the large Midlothian electorate included a substantial cavalier element, and was susceptible to appeals to religious prejudice. George Lockhart, the first representative sent by the county to the Parliament of Great Britain, was a resolute opponent of the Union and a barely concealed Jacobite: he was in consequence 'greatly beloved in the shire', and retained his seat until the Hanoverian Succession because of his popularity with 'a majority of the gentlemen'.[76] In others, of course, his political stance produced a violent reaction: staunch Presbyterians like old Sir John Clerk of Penicuik, who told Lockhart to his face before the 1708 election 'that I would never be for him whilst he was a high-flyer; that I was in concert already with a very honest Revolution party.'[77] Opposing candidates duly emphasised their Presbyterian and 'Revolution' credentials. In 1713 the former Solicitor-General for Scotland, Sir David Dalrymple, a quondam Queensberryite who had been driven into opposition, proclaimed that in proposing to stand for Midlothian 'my chief motive is to serve the Revolution interest'.[78] Placing his confidence in the prevailing 'sentiments of the freeholders', he canvassed presbyterian voters through one of their ministers, to whom he introduced himself by saying, 'I hope I need not tell you on what interest I set up, or what interest chiefly will stand in opposition to me'. He was especially concerned that pious Presbyterians who baulked at taking the oaths should swallow their scruples and qualify themselves:[79]

> to these I would say . . . it would be surprising to see Jacobites swear against their consciences, and at the same time see men betray that interest they are ready to maintain with their lives and estates, by leaving the representation of the country in the hands of men ill-affected, or at best indifferent (I wish I could say so much of my competitor) at so nice a time . . .

But it was in the north-east that the most serious and sustained conflict occurred between the Established Church and Episcopalian nonconformists. In

[75] Clarke, 'Scottish Episcopalians', p. 190; Szechi, 'Politics of "Persecution" ', pp. 280–1.

[76] Scottish R.O., GD 124/15/804/1, James Smith to Mar, 9 Mar. 1708; Szechi (ed.), *Lockhart Letters*, pp. 42–3.

[77] Scottish R.O., GD 18/2092/2, Sir John Clerk's 'moral journals', 9 Feb. 1708. Lockhart's tactful reply was that '[we] were all of that party', so that, as Sir John recorded, 'we ended fairly'.

[78] Scottish R.O., GD 18/3149/2, Dalrymple to Sir John Clerk, 2 Mar. 1713.

[79] Nat. Lib. Scotland, MS. 25276/43 (Newhailes papers), Dalrymple to the minister of [Kirknewton?], n.d. [1713], same to Sir Alexander Cumming, 9 Apr. 1713.

1710–14 relations between Episcopalian congregations and local presbyteries reached new depths, with a series of legal disputes, public demonstrations and even incidents of physical violence. Episcopalian ministers were prevented from preaching, and even forcibly removed from their parishes, while on the other side, sympathetic noblemen and gentry made a public show of attending Episcopalian services; mobs 'rabbled' ministers whom the Presbyterian authorities sought to intrude into supposedly 'vacant' congregations; and in one notorious episode the magistrates of Montrose burned a proclamation from the presbytery of Angus and the Mearns ordering a fast to avert God's judgment on innovations in worship.[80] In the far northern counties of Ross and Cromarty religious differences were exacerbated by a clash of cultures, as Lowland Presbyterianism advanced into the Catholic and Episcopalian Highlands, with the result that landed society became polarised.[81] A campaign by the presbytery of Cromarty and Dingwall to plant 'vacant' parishes met stiff opposition. Newly appointed ministers found that, at the very least, church keys would be withheld from them. At other times they would be physically obstructed by the local tenantry, or be arrested and imprisoned by the laird. One timorous appointee arrived in his new parish of Kilmuir Wester accompanied by the county sheriff and a guard of two dozen armed men.[82] 'The opposition that the gospel did and does meet with in the western parts of this shire', complained the minister of Tarbat, 'is such, as the like can scarcely be instanced in any church that hath a civil sanction.'[83] The commission of the peace split into Presbyterian and Episcopalian factions, each claiming exclusive authority and denying the legitimacy of the sessions held by their opponents. Their judicial power was abused for sectarian ends: the Presbyterian justices of Easter Ross evidently exploited royal proclamations against immorality and for the enforcement of sabbath observance in order to intimidate the Highlanders of the west with wholesale prosecutions.[84] At parliamentary elections the freeholders divided along precisely the same lines, Presbyterian Rosses and Munroes, from the east of the county, confronting Episcopalian Mackenzies, whose clan base was in the west, while individuals who had been prominent in ecclesiastical controversies (like Sir John Mackenzie of Coul, organiser of the lock-out of a Presbyterian minister at

---

[80] Clarke, 'Scottish Episcopalians', pp. 277–81, 283, 285, 293–4, 354, 357–8, 360.

[81] A point originally made in Ferguson, 'Electoral Law and Procedure', p. 132, where Cromarty is described as 'the tip of that wedge of lowland culture which, firmly based on Aberdeenshire, has for centuries been driven into the north-east Highlands'.

[82] Clarke, 'Scottish Episcopalians', pp. 262, 286, 351–2, 544. The incident at Kilmuir Wester is described in Scottish R.O., GD 305 addit./bundle xiv (Cromartie papers), George Mackenzie to [Cromarty], 21 Sept. 1711. See in general J. Noble, *Religious Life in Ross*, ed. J. Kennedy Cameron and D. Maclean (Inverness and Edinburgh, 1909).

[83] Scottish R.O., GD 305 addit./bundle xiii, David Ross to [Cromarty], 28 Mar. 1709.

[84] B.L., Add. MSS. 61629, ff. 116–17; 61631, ff. 183–6; 61632, ff. 3–4, 42–4; Fraser, *Earls of Cromartie*, II, 73, 89–90, 99–103; Scottish R.O., GD 305/1/159/7–8, 25–28, 121, 141 (Cromartie papers); GD 305/1/160/92–3; GD 305/1/164/80, 253; GD 305/1/168/23–5, 30, 89; GD 305 addit./bundle 13, Alexander Mackenzie (sheriff depute) to Cromarty, 29 Aug. 1709; GD 305 addit./bundle 15, [Lord Royston] to [Cromarty], [1709]; GD 305 addit./bundle 38, [-] to [Cromarty], 'date of the justices' meeting' [1709], Mackenzie of Allangrange to [same], 26 May [?1710].

Gairloch) were also among the most active agitators in the electoral court.[85]

But even in areas where there was no substantial Episcopalian presence, and the presbytery's monopoly remained unchallenged, religious issues could still play a part in determining elections. Ordinary Presbyterian voters were fearful of what a strong Tory interest might do at court and in Parliament, and assumed that the ultimate outcome of Tory machinations would be a Jacobite counter- revolution. In Lanarkshire, despite the influence of the Duke of Hamilton, 'the commons' were considered to be 'generally Whiggish', and when Sir James Hamilton of Rosehall found himself opposed in 1713 by the wealthy Glasgow merchant, Daniel Campbell of Shawfield. he was advised that if he would only 'declare himself for the established government in church and state' he should not have to fear any 'competitor'.[86] Fortunately for him, the ecclesiastical preferences of the Hamiltons were sufficiently broad (the dowager duchess, who still directed the family interest, being staunch to the Kirk) that his candidacy did not repel Presbyterian voters; and despite the best efforts of a number of ministers on Campbell's behalf he was returned comfortably, and with widespread support from 'the country people'.[87] Even in Ayrshire, whose overwhelmingly Presbyterian complexion precluded any electoral intervention in 1713 from the local Tory magnate, the Earl of Eglinton, the unanimous electors could not resist a statement of partisan loyalty as they made their choice: the minutes of the electoral court record not only the unopposed re-election of John Montgomerie but a formal statement approving Montgomerie's conduct in the previous Parliament, 'and particularly . . . his care and support of the Presbyterian church as by law established.'[88]

Lanarkshire was only one of many constituencies in which ministers of religion played a significant role in canvassing voters, thereby both implicitly acknowledging, and at the same time actively promoting, the notion that parliamentary elections had taken on a religious as well as a political aspect. The influence wielded by the church had long been recognised by those involved in local politics, for when Lord Hyndford had challenged the Hamiltons in Lanarkshire in 1708 he had 'made strong applications to the ministers to bring over the bishop's vassals in the nether ward to his son's interest'.[89] As party animosities deepened, so the involvement of the clergy in elections became more extensive. It was almost routine for Tory candidates, like John Houstoun in Linlithgowshire in 1713, to complain of the activities of local Presbyterian ministers on behalf of

[85] Scottish R.O., GD 129/box 29/116/46A (Balnagown Castle papers), 'Information for the laird of Balnagown against George Mackenzie of Inchcoulter', 20 June 1705; GD 129/box 29/106/14, electoral court mins., 26 June 1708; GD 129/box30/116, poll, 1708; GD 129/box 7/11/40, electoral court mins., 29 Sept. 1710; GD 129/box29/106/15, electoral court mins., 22 Oct. 1713; GD 305/1/168/21, electoral court mins., 3 Mar. 1710.

[86] Macpherson (ed.), *Original Papers*, II, 11; Hamilton MSS. (the Duke of Hamilton, Lennoxlove, Haddington, East Lothian), C3/16, Pencaitland to Duchess of Hamilton, 3 Sept. 1713.

[87] Nat. Lib. Scotland, Advocates' MSS., Wodrow Letters Quarto VII, f. 181, R. Wylie to [Wodrow], 9 Sept. 1713; *ibid.*, f. 189, J. Crosse to same, 3 Oct. 1713; *Scots Courant*, 2–5 Oct. 1713.

[88] Scottish R.O., SC6/78/11 (Ayr sheriff court recs.), Ayrshire electoral court mins., 2 [Oct.] 1713.

[89] Szechi (ed.) *Lockhart Letters*, p. 38.

their Whig opponents.[90] But the boot could appear on either foot. In 1710 the Hon. James Murray, son and heir to the cavalier Lord Stormont, in attempting to upset the Duke of Queensberry's interest in Dumfriesshire, was faced with a concerted campaign of political preaching and personal canvassing by local Presbyterian ministers for Queensberry's candidate.[91] Three years later, when Murray was obliged to look elsewhere for a seat, and was invited to contest the northern burgh district of Elgin, it was his opponents' turn to protest against clerical interference, this time from the Episcopalian side. In the burgh of Elgin itself, it was reported, 'none was so violent for Mr Murray as the meeting-house minister'.[92]

Just as in England, the impact on Scottish political life of a great conflict of 'parties', identified with questions of principle rather than with individuals, was to disrupt pre-existing patterns of allegiance: friendships, family connexions, personal loyalties to patron or landlord. Perhaps the most striking case was the rift in the immediate family of the 1st Duke of Atholl, which resulted in an unusual contest for the representation of Perthshire in the general election of 1713. Atholl's brother, Lord James Murray, who was the outgoing Member, refused to make way for the duke's younger son, also Lord James, and forced the issue to a contest, in which he was successful. The division within the Atholl household carried over into the Fifteen, from which the duke and the dutiful Lord James the younger recoiled, while Atholl's eldest son, Lord Tullibardine, and two other brothers 'came out' with the Jacobites. (On this occasion Lord James the elder maintained a discreet silence.) By cynics the family's variegated loyalties have been interpreted as calculated policy: the Janus-faced Atholl ensuring the survival of his house whatever the outcome of the crisis over the succession.[93] But a close reading of the duke's correspondence shows that there were genuine differences of opinion and allegiance, and that it was probably Atholl himself who was out of step. His two wives had successively influenced him towards their own brand of stiff Presbyterianism. The first, a sister to the Duke of Hamilton, invited ministers to preach at Blair Castle to whom even her husband's factors flatly refused to listen; the second, a daughter of Lord Ross, evidently dissuaded Atholl in 1713 from lending his protection to a local meeting house, a betrayal of his cavalier heritage which antagonised many local Episcopalians.[94] If we add to these tensions over religious observance a persistent needling grievance over perceived inadequacies in the financial provision enjoyed by his brother and sons, it is easy to see why Atholl's relationships should have been so fraught; and certainly his own complaints about them seem heartfelt.[95]

The troubles of the Murray clan represent an extreme example of the divisive potential of party differences. Ties of kinship and marriage did prove stronger than

---

[90] *C.J.*, XVII, 484.

[91] Mansfield MSS., bundle 1248, Stormont to Alexander Barclay, 3 Sept. 1710.

[92] Scottish R.O., GD 248/561/49/30, W. Lorimer to Findlater, 26 Sept. 1713.

[93] Riley, *King William and the Scottish Politicians*, pp. 12–13.

[94] Atholl MSS., box 45, bundle 3, nos. 146–7, 162, Duchess of Atholl to the duke, 5, 7 Nov., 4 Dec. 1703; bundle 5, no. 11, same to Duchess of Hamilton, 15 Jan. 1705; 45/11/48, Lord Gray to [Atholl], 12 Nov. 1713; 45/11/65, John Douglas to same, 18 Feb. 1714; B. Lenman, *The Jacobite Risings in Britain 1689–1746* (1980), pp. 49–50, 62–4, 146.

[95] E.g. Hamilton MSS., C3/1719. Atholl to Duchess of Hamilton, 13 Feb. 1716. See also Lenman, *Jacobite Risings*, p.146.

political sympathy in other families, as in Inverness-shire in 1710 when one of the McIntoshes explained his failure to vote for the Tory and future Jacobite rebel Alexander Mackenzie of Fraserdale by reference to his own precarious domestic finances: 'the influence of a Whig bedfellow is hard to resist', agreed Mackenzie, 'especially when seconded by a father-in-law entirely master of his [McIntosh] business'.[96] The significance of Atholl's difficulties in Perthshire is not that partisan considerations were *always* the most important factor, but that they *could* overcome entrenched material interests and customary obligations. Even when the patron's wishes were enforced, the equation between clientage and obedience was not always a simple one. The failure of James Murray in 1710 to persuade his Queens-berryite opponent in Dumfriesshire, William Grierson, to withdraw, on the grounds that both candidates were champions of the Episcopalian and Tory cause (Grierson was the son of the notorious 'Auld Lag', hammerer of the Covenanters in the 'Killing Times', and was later to be 'out' himself in the Fifteen) may be less important than the fact that Murray considered the stratagem worth trying.[97]

If we concentrate our attention on constituencies in which party loyalties seem to have predominated, to the extent that the established electoral interests of powerful magnates were overturned, an interesting pattern emerges. In each case what we see is the appearance of a 'popular interest' of lesser lairds able to defy aristocratic influence; usually (but not inevitably) Episcopalian gentlemen throwing off the domination of a Presbyterian magnate, like 'the minor barons' who elected George Lockhart in Midlothian in 1708 against the express opposition of the 'greater' (admittedly after a split in the Court/Squadrone vote), or the Kinross-shire lairds who two years later rejected Mungo Graham.[98] Sometimes the power of a 'popular' interest can only be inferred from the event, as in Stirlingshire in 1710, when an inevitable victory for the Tory Paterson, reversing sharply the result of the previous poll, was expected well in advance because of the changing tide of national party politics.[99] Elsewhere there is direct evidence. Lord James Murray's campaign against his nephew in Perthshire in 1713 was backed by a few of the larger landowners in the county—the Jacobite Lord Nairne acted as the 'manager' of his canvassing, with several other wealthy lairds (though not the Tory Lord Breadalbane, who canvassed and voted for Lord James the younger)— but his main strength lay in the support of 'the gentlemen', mostly freeholders from the western, Highland, part of the county.[100] This Tory success takes on

[96] Nat. Lib. Scotland, MS. 1342 (Delvine papers), f. 31, Alexander Mackenzie to [John Mackenzie of Delvine], 3 Apr. 1713.

[97] Ewart Library, Dumfries, Grierson MSS., 14D/Group B9/3, William Alves to William Grierson, 2 Aug. 1710. For Grierson's Jacobitism, see *ibid.*, 14D/Group B9/4, Anthony Cracherode to Grierson, 24 May 1716; *The Secret History of Newgate* (1717), pp. 15–17, 20, 25, 42–8; [P. Rae,], *The History of the Late Rebellion* (1718), p. 325.

[98] Scottish R.O., GD18/2092/2, Sir John Clerk's 'moral journals', 1 June 1708.

[99] Scottish R.O., GD 124/10/985/2, Col. John Erskine to Lord Grange, 17 Aug. 1710.

[100] Nat. Lib. Scotland, MS. 1403 (Delvine papers), Lord James Murray to John Mackenzie of Delvine, 30 June 1713; MS. 1415 (Delvine papers), Lady Anne Murray to same, 21 Sept. 1713; Scottish R.O., GD 112/39/270/25, Breadalbane to Colin [Campbell], 1713. Many of the 'gentlemen' who opposed Atholl at the election were probably among the signatories to a High Tory address circulated in the county in Nov. 1713 without the duke's knowledge or approval (Atholl MSS., 45/11/48, Lord Gray to [Atholl], 12 Nov. 1713).

even greater significance when compared to previous elections for the county, for it was not only the proprietorial influence of Atholl which had been over-thrown, but also that of his traditional rival in the county, the Duke of Montrose. Before 1713 elections in Perthshire had been fought out by the two magnates: now Montrose's faction had not even bothered to put up a candidate, and Atholl had been rebuffed.[101] A similar situation developed in Fife, where elections had been traditionally fought over by Lords Leven and Rothes. There had, however, always been a third force, an independent cavalier element, generally referred to in the correspondence of the two Presbyterian peers as 'the Jacobites', or 'the disaffected'.[102] In 1704 Leven had managed to secure their support by promising to 'join with them in choosing whom they please if a new Parliament should be called, provided they would oppose my Lord Rothes'; and in 1708 he did so again, using his influence with government to offer protection to suspected Jacobites in return for their assistance.[103] But at the next election the cavalier lairds voted for one of their own kind, the Lord Lyon, Sir Alexander Areskine, and not even a reconciliation between the Queensberryite Leven and his Squadrone rival Rothes could prevent Areskine's return.[104] For the remainder of the Queen's reign Leven and Rothes were in full retreat: in 1712 a Tory address of congratulation on the peace was signed by over 150 Fife freeholders, and the following year, although Rothes once again proposed a Presbyterian alliance against the common enemy, Areskine was elected unanimously.[105] And according to one Whig commentator, the only reason that the Tories were beaten in 1715 was because Areskine's *Squadrone* opponent insisted that all lesser barons be required to qualify themselves by taking the oaths.[106]

The power of 'Whig' and 'Tory' (or 'Presbyterian' and 'Episcopalian') ani-mosities to generate sharp divisions, and sometimes violent conflict, within the political nation—to divide brother from brother, landlord from tenant, and patron from client—suggests that what was emerging in the aftermath of the Union was an incipient 'party' system in Scottish electoral politics, on the lines of the well-established 'party' system in England. One final comparative test remains: to see whether voting patterns among the electorate were as clearly defined as in England. How firmly were electoral allegiances set? How far did voters 'swing' between parties? How substantial was the 'floating vote'? Because of the nature

---

[101] Scottish R.O., GD 406/1/7926, Atholl to Duchess of Hamilton, 18 June 1708; GD 112/39/269/19, Charles Tais to Breadalbane, 26 Sept. 1713.

[102] Nat. Lib. Scotland, MS. 14415 (Yester papers), ff. 121–2, Rothes to [Tweeddale]. 25 Mar. 1706.

[103] Nat. Lib. Scotland, MS. 14415, ff. 67–8, 194, Rothes to [Tweeddale], 19 Oct. 1704, 14 Dec. [1709]; MS. 7021 (Yester papers), f. 130, Yester to Tweeddale, 1 Apr. 1708; Scottish R.O., GD 220/5/159/4–5, Rothes to Montrose, 30 Mar. 1708, 'Saturday six at night' [1708].

[104] Riley, *English Ministers and Scotland*, p. 151; Scottish R.O., GD 124/15/975/10, Mar to Lord Grange, 27 July 1710. Areskine himself admitted to receiving only one Presbyterian vote: Scottish R.O., GD 124/15/1011/3, to Lord Grange, 1710.

[105] *London Gazette*, 2–5 Aug. 1712; Nat. Lib. Scotland, Advocates' MSS., Wodrow Letters Quarto VII, f. 177, J. Hart to [?Wodrow], 29 Aug. 1713; P.R.O., C219/114; *Scots Courant*, 25–28 Sept. 1713.

[106] Scottish R.O., GD 27/3/24/4 (Kennedy of Dalquharran papers), Mungo Graham to Cornelius Kennedy, 12 Feb. 1715.

of Scottish elections, and of the documentary evidence they produced, these are probably the hardest questions to answer. Where county polls survive in sufficient numbers to allow comparison across time, the number of freeholders is often too small for statistical significance; and of course consistency of voting in itself proves nothing about motive, possibly indicating no more than the strength of a dependent relationship.

None the less, some of the evidence is suggestive. In Haddingtonshire John Cockburn of Ormiston, representing the *Squadrone*, was returned at all three elections between 1708 and 1713: in 1708 he defeated William Nisbet of Dirleton, who was eventually to throw in his lot with the Tories, by 20 votes to 17;[107] in 1710 there was no opposition; and in 1713 he held off a challenge from another Tory, James Hamilton, by the more substantial margin of 23–15. In the unopposed election of 1710, 24 freeholders were present, of whom 15 had voted for Cockburn in 1708 and only four for Nisbet. The 1713 election showed a further continuity: of Cockburn's voters 14 had voted for him in 1708 and been present in 1710, three had not voted in 1708 but had attended in 1710, while only two had voted for Nisbet; of Hamilton's, six had voted for Nisbet in 1708 and absented themselves two years later (including Nisbet himself), and only a single freeholder had supported Cockburn in that first election. No one had voted for Cockburn in 1708, acclaimed his return in 1710, and then voted for Hamilton.[108] Another remarkable example of consistency was provided by the electors of Roxburghshire, where no less than 17 of Sir William Bennet's 23 voters in the 1710 general election had previously voted for the combined ticket of Bennet and Sir Patrick Scot in 1702, and 20 out of 33 freeholders voting for Sir Gilbert Eliott of Stobs in 1710 had plumped for him eight years earlier: only one elector, Sir Walter Riddell, had changed sides.[109]

Elsewhere, results which may appear statistically to represent swings in electoral preference often reveal themselves on closer inspection as the product of a turnover in the electorate, with those voting in more than one election proving to be immutable in their allegiance. In Ross-shire, in some respects a model of a 'divided society', there is a full record of voting from 1708, when the Mackenzies' candidate, Hugh Rose, narrowly defeated the Master of Ross in a strenuous contest, an incomplete set of minutes from a by-election in January 1710 at which General the Hon. Charles Rosse turned the tables on Sir James Mackenzie of Royston, and an attendance list from 1713, when only the Rosses and their allies turned up in order to re-elect the general.[110] Between 1708 and 1710 there do not seem to have been any shifts in voting allegiance, the difference being made by the qualification of more new voters on the Ross than on the Mackenzie side. Of those who attended the electoral court in 1713 only the former candidate, Hugh Rose, and his father, had previously voted for the Mackenzie interest; they

[107] Roxburghe MSS., bundle 784, Roxburghe to [his mother], 1 Dec. [?1712].
[108] Scottish R.O., SC 40/68/3, Haddington sheriff court recs., pp. 5–15, Haddingtonshire electoral court mins., 1708–13.
[109] Scottish R.O., GD 6/1062/b2, poll for Roxburghshire 1702; GD 6/1063/b, poll 1710.
[110] See above, n. 85.

had in the meantime been enrolled among General Rosse's supporters. Of those who stayed away, only one had voted for the Master of Ross in 1708, Charles Ross of Eye, who had recently been engaged as a factor for a prominent associate of the Mackenzies.[111] Another reversal of fortune occurred in Stirlingshire between 1708 and 1710: at the first election Henry Cunningham defeated Sir Hugh Paterson 18–13, but in 1710, with the same candidates, Paterson secured a remarkable triumph by 23–9. In fact only three of Cunningham's voters in 1708 had crossed over, including Sir John Erskine, who had changed his patron from Montrose to Mar: eight had remained loyal, seven were absent. All of Paterson's original supporters voted for him again, the difference being made by seven new voters.[112]

I would not try to argue on the basis of these examples that Scottish parliamentary elections in the early eighteenth century were a cockpit, where battles were fought out between fully-fledged Whig and Tory parties, and that what we have become accustomed to regard as a political system and a political culture dominated by deferential relationships and quasi-commercial transactions, was in fact a scene of heated debate over great questions of principle. For one thing, I have deliberately selected evidence to demonstrate the vitality of a certain type of issue in the brief period 1708–15,[113] and have left unrecorded the many instances in which elections, even in the larger counties, were decided by the application of the customary means of magnate influence. Nor must we forget that 'party' colours, and 'party' rhetoric could cloak more traditional forms of political rivalry: in Ross-shire, which I have hitherto held up as an example of rampant sectarian animosity, the two factions were clan- and magnate-oriented, and political conflict originated with the ambition of the 12th Lord Ross (whose Presbyterian credentials did not pass the scrutiny of every observer) to intrude himself into the territory of the Earl of Cromarty, and grab control of the county representation by manufacturing freeholds from his own and his kinsmen's estates.[114] Ross-shire also shows us a second trap for the unwary historical sightseer, namely the chameleon-like ability of many Scottish politicians to assume political camouflage according to habitat. Charles Rosse, the 'Whig' Member returned in 1710 and 1713, in fact behaved very much like a Tory at Westminster, and has been suspected by one modern historian of Jacobite tendencies.[115] It suited some players in this complicated game to make themselves appear as Whigs to some audiences and Tories to others: in 1713 Lord Ilay, writing to a prominent English Whig, was anxious to represent his brother Argyll's 'creature' John Middleton, recently returned for Aberdeen Burghs, as a staunch 'Hanoverian',

[111] W. MacGill, *Old Ross=Shire and Scotland* . . . (2 vols., Inverness, 1909–11), I, 132.

[112] Scottish R.O., SC 67/60/1, Stirling sheriff ct. recs., pp. 1–14, Stirlingshire electoral ct. mins., 2 June 1708, 17 Oct. 1710; Sunter, 'Stirlingshire Politics', pp. 19–20.

[113] I have also ignored, for present purposes, the extent to which Tory interests articulated, and no doubt in doing so consciously exploited, patriotic opposition to the Union.

[114] MacGill, *Old Ross=Shire*, I, 263–4; Fraser, *Earls of Cromartie*, II, 50; *More Culloden Papers*, ed. D. Warrender (5 vols., Inverness, 1932–5), II, 22–3; Nat. Lib. Scotland, MS. 1391 (Delvine papers), ff. 290, Sir Robert Munro to John Mackenzie, 21 Oct. 1708.

[115] Holmes, *British Politics*, p. 28; Szechi, *Jacobitism and Tory Politics*, pp. 107, 133, 183, 201.

and tactfully omitted to mention that Middleton was a kinsman of the exiled Jacobite, Lord Middleton, himself the son of the principal of King's College, and a man with many 'Tory' political contacts which he did not hesitate to make use of.[116] Equally misleadingly, Lord Dupplin sought to stir up English Tory resentment at William Grierson, the Queensberryite candidate for Dumfries-shire in 1710 by calling him a 'republican', while he was in fact a Jacobite.[117] Sometimes an M.P. may genuinely have espoused different interests in different places: one of the candidates for the Aberdeen district in 1710, James Scott of Logie, depended on Presbyterian support in two of the constituent burghs, Brechin and Inverbervie, but was himself an Episcopalian, with qualms about swearing the abjuration, and in his own town of Montrose, a citadel of 'high-flying' Toryism, took a leading part in the notorious public burning in 1712 of the synodical fast proclamation.[118]

However, neither the survival of traditional manifestations of aristocratic political power, nor the mischievous and self-serving use of political labels, nor even the occasional dislocation of local and national politics in Scotland, should lead us to underestimate the power of 'party' allegiances in the years before 1715. Differences over religion were clearly a powerful force in Scottish political life in the early eighteenth century, and seem actually to have gained in strength after the Union. Given the right circumstances, in favourable locations, political parties did begin to develop, even in the electoral system which their own constitutional traditions and the terms of the Treaty of Union had bequeathed to the Scots. That the growth of this two-party system should have been cut short was in large measure the outcome of the events that followed the death of Queen Anne, which turned many Tories in Scotland towards armed Jacobite rebellion. Those historians seeking an explanation of the nature of Scottish political development in the first half of the eighteenth century would therefore be well advised to consider the long-term effects of the Fifteen, in addition to the impact of Union, and perhaps explore the later history of the emergent Tory interest in Scotland, as it suffered and contracted in the cold climate of the Hanoverian regime.

[116] Hertfordshire R.O., Panshanger MSS., D/EP F54, Ilay to Lord Cowper, 1 Oct. [1713]; *H.P., 1715–54*, II, 257; Aufrere (ed.), *Lockhart Papers*, I, 395, 397; Scottish R.O., GD 248/561/49/4, James Allardice to [-], 10 Apr. 1713; GD 124/15/1129/6, Mar to Lord Grange, 7 Aug. 1714; Aberdeen Univ. Lib., Duff House (Montcoffer) MSS., 3175/F51/4, Lord Arbuthnott to Sir Alexander Cumming, 1 Feb. 1719.

[117] H.M.C., *Portland MSS.*, IV, 564.

[118] D. Fraser, *Montrose (before 1706)* (Montrose, 1967), pp. 122–4; D. Black, *The History of Brechin to 1864* (Edinburgh, 1867), pp. 122–3; Wodrow, *Analecta*, I, 320; *The Case of William Livingston. Esq: Petitioner, Against James Scot, Esq: Sitting-Member . . .* (1710); Nat. Lib. Scotland, MS. 20772 (Fleming of Wigton papers), f. 63, Lord Southesk to the Earl Marischall, [1716]; Advocates' MSS., Wodrow Letters Quarto VII, ff. 166–7, Alexander Archer to [Wodrow], 11 June 1713; Wodrow Letters Quarto VIII, ff. 174–5, James Traill to Alexander Archer, 10 Sept. 1714; Clarke, 'Scottish Episcopalians', p. 354; H.M.C., *Portland MSS.*, X, 280–1; *Flying Post*, 7–9 Oct. 1712. I am obliged to Mr D.J. Munro of the Institute of Historical Research, University of London, for advice on the history of Montrose.

'Nothing but Strugalls and Coruption': The Commons' Elections for Scotland in 1774*

DAVID J. BROWN

Scottish Record Office

Im told great strugalls is thoroug[h] all poor Scotland, & nothing prevaills but coruption.[1]

The dowager Countess of Eglinton's lament on the general election of 1774 points to the unusually active nature of the politics of the time. That year saw contests in 16 of the 45 Scottish county and burgh seats and political activity that stopped short of an open contest in several other constituencies. This compares with the elections of 1754 (four contests), 1761 (eight), and 1768 (13).[2] One observer remarked that there had not been so much electoral activity in Scotland since Sir Robert Walpole's time.[3] Why was this?

One reason was that the general election had not been expected until 1775 and was sprung by government as a surprise. That surprise added desperation and confusion to the activities of many local politicians contemplating the ruin of plans set to a longer timetable. The effects of this early dissolution of Parliament were as marked in Scotland as they were elsewhere in Britain.

Perhaps a more important reason was that for much of the eighteenth century Scotland had been 'managed' by a succession of men who had been secretaries of state in all but name. The most prominent—or notorious—had been John and Archibald, 2nd and 3rd Dukes of Argyll, who had taken and held the leading position in Scottish politics, acting successively as managers between 1725 and 1761. They in their turn were succeeded by James Stuart Mackenzie, who managed Scotland first for his brother Lord Bute and then, after Bute's removal, for the Grenville ministry. Grenville dispensed with Mackenzie's services in 1765. Thereafter, Scottish politicians were left largely to their own devices, soliciting for patronage and electoral support directly from the government offices in

---

* I am grateful to Dr John Brims, Dr William Ferguson, Miss Aileen Lightbody, Dr Alexander Murdoch and Dr Graham Townend, for their comments on an earlier draft of this paper.

[1] Scottish R.O., GD24/1/384/15 (Moray of Abercairney), Countess of Eglinton to James Moray, 9 Feb. 1774.

[2] The figures for 1754, 1761 and 1768 come from *The History of Parliament: The Commons, 1754–1790*, eds. Sir L. Namier and J. Brooke (3 vols., 1964) [hereafter cited as *HP 1754–90*], I. Scottish seats contested in 1774 were Ayrshire, Clackmannanshire, Dunbartonshire, Midlothian, Kirkcudbrightshire, Lanarkshire, Nairnshire, Stirlingshire, Edinburgh and the burgh groups of Dysart, Elgin, Haddington, Linlithgow, Stirling, Tain, and Wigtown.

[3] Scottish R.O., GD267/22/7 (Home of Wedderburn papers), George Home to Patrick Home, 14 Mar. 1774.

London. There are now several studies of Scottish politics in the years 1707–1765 and whatever the strength and relative influence with government enjoyed by each manager, historians are agreed that it was a prime function of the job to broker local alliances in the Scottish constituencies to ensure the election of as many government supporters as possible and to minimise local contests and dissent.[4] One of the first fruits of the end of management was the mayhem that ensued at the general election of 1768 and which was so much commented on by contemporaries. Similarly, the 1774 election passed with only limited and unsystematic interference from London and to this opportunity for unrest was added all the bad blood that had accumulated from the struggles of six years previously.

To this potential for trouble arising from the earlier elections must be added the incendiary effect in the counties of a recent change in the interpretation of Scottish electoral law. The county franchise had been defined by legislation of the Scottish Parliament in 1681, and by 1774 there were three possible qualifications by which a county freeholder might be enfranchised. The most common of these was the right to a vote derived from the possession of the superiority of property valued at £400 Scots in the county land tax ('cess') books. Since the right derived from the superiority rather than the actual land itself, it was feasible for a major proprietor to have his lawyers separate the properties and superiorities on his estate so that he could retain his land while parcelling out £400 superiorities to enfranchise his supporters. Scots politicians had long been aware of the possibilities for making 'nominal' votes in this way and the legislature and the Court of Session had regularly found themselves trying to curtail such activity. In law it had come to be held that the improper nature of such votes derived from the fact that the voters holding them were intended to vote at the behest of the individual who had transferred the superiorities. Since a vote founded on a mere superiority was essentially legal, however, everything hinged on the need to prove this intention. There was considerable vote creation in the prelude to the 1768 election and subsequent events contrived to weaken the restraints that the Court of Session could exercise. In two cases arising from the shires of Forfar and Cromarty, the Court had instituted a series of questions ('special interrogatories') to be put to individuals claiming enrolment. Taken under oath, these could unambiguously identify individuals with nominal qualifications and so facilitate the rejection of their claims. The Court intended that the device should subsequently be made available to Head Courts in their local deliberations. Unfortunately an appeal followed to the House of Lords and produced a judgement in 1770 from Lord Mansfield finding such interrogatories to be *ultra vires*.[5] This was the signal to the nobles and other large landowners to create as many votes as they could, and in county after county considerable numbers were made. This significantly raised the temperature of local politics not only in the feuds between

---

[4] See in particular J.S. Shaw, *The Management of Scottish Society, 1707–1764*, (Edinburgh, 1983) and A.J. Murdoch, *The People Above*, (Edinburgh, 1980).

[5] For Scottish election law, see W. Ferguson, 'The Electoral System in the Scottish Counties Before 1832', in *Miscellany Two*, (Stair Society, XXXV, Edinburgh, 1984), pp. 261–94.

rivals but also in the bitter resentment felt by those freeholders who possessed genuine qualifications and who saw the importance of their votes diminished by the hordes of newcomers.

The consequences both of the absence of management and of the explosion in vote creation will become evident in what follows. The main intention of this article, however, is to link them to two other influences at work in Scotland in 1774. Murdoch and Dwyer have recently pointed to the political tensions that arose from the 1760s onwards as new men with colonial or mercantile fortunes started to carve footholds in Scottish constituencies.[6] There is also striking evidence that some of the political unrest arose from the first electoral forays of Henry Dundas, Solicitor General for Scotland since 1766 and later to become its most famous manager.

With hindsight it is clear that the election in Midlothian was the most important. The sitting M.P., Sir Alexander Gilmour, had been a supporter of the Duke of Newcastle and was not without influence at Westminster. He held the county only through the influence of the family of the Lord President of the Court of Session, Robert Dundas of Arniston, and by 1770 it was clear that the President's half brother Henry aspired to the seat.[7] In September of that year Gilmour had a cordial meeting with his putative rival at which Dundas made plain his intention to sit for Midlothian. Gilmour was in debt and needed the protection afforded by being in Parliament. If another seat cast up, it was agreed that in certain circumstances Dundas might accept it rather than force Gilmour from Midlothian. If there was only the Midlothian seat, Dundas would not be opposed by Gilmour.[8] In October 1771 Gilmour, apparently reneging, informed the Arnistons that he was beginning a canvass. Henry Dundas at once commenced his own and rode the county in ten days, securing over 40 promises of votes to Gilmour's ten with the rest undeclared. This should have been decisive and Gilmour was said to have given up,[9] but in fact he fought on for almost three years.

From the start Dundas had been afraid that Gilmour or his friends would paint him as anti-government. He asked Sir Gilbert Elliot, the Roxburghshire M.P., to guard against misrepresentations 'above', and apparently received assurances of similar help from Stuart Mackenzie, the former manager and now Privy Seal. Dundas also wrote a clear declaration of his support to the Prime Minister, Lord North.[10]

---

[6] See J. Dwyer and A. Murdoch, 'Paradigms and Politics; Manners, Morals and the Rise of Henry Dundas', in *New Perspectives on the Politics and Culture of Early Modern Scotland*, eds. J. Dwyer, A. Murdoch and R. Mason (Edinburgh, 1982), pp. 215–6.

[7] For Gilmour, see *HP, 1754–90*, II, 501–3.

[8] Scottish R.O., RH4/15/5 (Dundas of Arniston papers), letterbook 6, no. 107, Henry Dundas to Robert Dundas, Lord President, 27 Sep. 1770, printed in GWT Omond, *The Arniston Memoirs, 1571–1838*, (Edinburgh, 1887), pp. 183–4.

[9] Scottish R.O., GD235/8/4/13–14 (papers of Bonar, Mackenzie and Kermack, W.S.), Christian Dundas to Lady Ann Gordon, 4 Nov. [1771]; GD267/22/7, George Home to Patrick Home, 11 Dec. 1771.

[10] N[ational] L[ibrary of] S[cotland], MS. 11018, ff. 9–10 (Minto papers), Dundas to Sir Gilbert Elliot, 17 Oct. [1771]; Scottish R.O., GD 235/8/4/13–14, cited in note 9; N.L.S., MS. 16, f. 39 (Melville papers), Dundas to North, 2 Nov. 1771 (copy).

The dominance of the Dundases in Midlothian had been partly by default, for the interest of the Buccleuchs, perhaps the principal noble family there, had long been dormant. This had ended with the succession of the young 3rd duke, Henry, in 1767. From their first meeting in that year the duke and Dundas had become friends[11] and when Gilmour's representatives approached Buccleuch for support, 'saying he might gain what ascendant in the county he pleas'd and intirely take it out of the Arniston family', his reply was dusty.[12] Dundas now turned their friendship into something far stronger. In November, writing an account of his successful canvass, he desired to meet the duke,[13]

> to hint to you how far you should not step a little more forward in the political scene of this country, where you have so much residence & property. I can assure you I hint not only my own ideas, but of many very good friends of yours with whom of late I have had many conversations on this subject. Your age, your property, the independance of your seat in Parliament, & the footing you will daily gain more & more in the affections of the country, do most certainly open scenes to your view, which I hope you will not overlook.

Buccleuch's youth and character, his residence in Scotland at a time when many landowners were absentees, his education by Adam Smith, his involvement in agricultural innovations and his first steps against government interference in the election of Scottish representative peers, all made him a source of fascination. The *literati* of Edinburgh would come to see and lionise him as the model of an enlightened, improving nobleman with the best interests of his country at heart.[14] Dundas seems to have joined in these sentiments, and he had every interest in an alliance with such a man.

Buccleuch's response to Dundas's letter must have been positive, for within months there was clear evidence in neighbouring East Lothian of the existence of a partnership that would come to dominate Scots politics for the next 40 years. In 1768 that county, long held by a concert between the Fletchers of Saltoun and the Dalrymples, had been captured by Lord President Dundas for his relative Sir George Suttie.[15] In the spring of 1772 Dr Alexander Carlyle, minister of Inveresk parish, describing Buccleuch as 'the Genl. Patron of rising merit in this country', solicited his support for the candidacy of Colonel John Fletcher of Saltoun, son of the 3rd Duke of Argyll's old friend, Lord Milton. Carlyle knew that Buccleuch's sympathies would lie with the Dundases and their candidate but, as he warned a Buccleuch ally, they were not popular in East Lothian:[16]

---

[11] For the meeting see Eugene [Hugo Arnot] *A Letter to the Lord Advocate of Scotland* (Edinburgh, 1777), p. 6.

[12] Scottish R.O., GD 235/8/4/13–14, cited in note 9.

[13] Signet Library, Edinburgh, Melville papers, Dundas to Buccleuch, 30 Nov. 1771 (copy). Quoted with the kind permission of the Society of the Writers to the Signet.

[14] Murdoch and Dwyer, 'Paradigms' pp. 212–3, 236.

[15] *HP, 1754–90*, I, 483–4.

[16] N.L.S., MS. 23765, ff. 10–11, 146–8 (Carlyle-Bell papers), [copy/draft] letters of Carlyle to Buccleuch and [Thomas Bowlby], undated but *post* 24 May 1772.

It is proper that the Dundass's should belong to the Duke of Buccleugh. But nothing can be so improper as the inverse proposition . . . If he goes along with them in East Lothian . . . he will be consider'd as the property of the Dundass's, which I do assure you will be a fatal blow to his interest in this country.

Since Buccleuch had little property and no votes in East Lothian, Carlyle may well have been hoping for his intervention with the Dundases. This was unrealistic. Neither Carlyle nor Adam Smith could persuade the duke to support Fletcher, and after a delay he declared for Suttie.[17]. The manner in which Buccleuch was perceived to be guided by the Dundases, an inversion of the normal eighteenth century pattern where the noble politician would expect to lead his gentry adherents, was significant and was noted by contemporaries, as Carlyle had warned.[18]

Carlyle wrote of the East Lothian gentry who had let Suttie win in 1768: 'They have seen that folly & will probably now be united'.[19] They were not, and by mid-1773 they had three candidates. Fletcher had dropped out but Suttie stood again. He was opposed by William Nisbet of Dirleton backed by the Dalrymples of North Berwick, Kinloch of Gilmerton and two judges of the Court of Session, Lord Hailes (a Dalrymple) and Lord Coalston. Captain James Stuart, son to Lord Blantyre, entered the lists in April 1773[20] with the support of Hay of Drummelzier and the Marquess of Tweeddale. It was a close contest, but in late 1773 the Treasury Secretary John Robinson was told that Suttie was secure.[21] The announcement of the general election caught the contestants out, with nobody having a decisive lead. The Nisbet and Stuart camps met at Gilmerton after the Michaelmas Head Court of October 1774 and discussed uniting behind one candidate to beat Suttie. Stuart could transfer only two votes and Nisbet privately told Sir Hew Dalrymple that Buccleuch and Dundas had already offered him a deal. In return for his support at the forthcoming election, Suttie would resign in three or four years and help Nisbet to succeed him. Dalrymple disapproved since it would need the approval of Nisbet's supporters and the parties adjourned to a later meeting. Before that could take place, however, an angry Dalrymple learned that Nisbet had gone to see Dundas at Dalkeith House to accept the bargain and in effect to commit his allies to it. Dalrymple was not mollified by a letter from Coalston, who, while admitting Nisbet's 'rash and inconsiderate step', pointed out that their party was in a minority and that a compromise with Suttie was the most palatable of the various choices on offer.[22] Neither he nor

---

[17] N.L.S., MS. 23764, f. 61, Fletcher to Carlyle, 16 Aug. 1772.

[18] See Anon., *To the D. of B.* by *One of Your Best Friends* (Edinburgh, October 1777).

[19] N.L.S., MS. 23765, ff. 146–8.

[20] Scottish R.O., GD206/2/286 (Hall of Dunglass papers), Hon. Alexander Stuart to Sir John Hall of Dunglass, 8 Apr. 1773.

[21] *The Parliamentary Papers of John Robinson*, ed. W.T. Laprade (Camden Society, 3rd series, XXXIII, 1922), p. 8. Many of Robinson's Scottish predictions were inaccurate.

[22] Scottish R.O., GD 110/947/9, 19 (Dalrymple-Hamilton of North Berwick papers), Sir Hew Dalrymple to [Lord Hailes], 22 Oct. 1774 (copy and draft); GD 110/952/11, Lord Coalston to [Dalrymple], 20 Oct. 1774.

Stuart, whose conduct he respected, attended the election at which Coalston, Hailes, Kinloch and the rest of the Dalrymples joined to re-elect Suttie. The Dundases kept their bargain and Suttie resigned his seat in 1777, allowing Nisbet an unopposed election.[23]

Beyond the Lothians, Dundas and Buccleuch proceeded to interest themselves in a string of local struggles. Perhaps the most controversial was that for Ayrshire. The county was atypical both in having a large electorate (128 in 1774, of whom 107 voted) and in having a pattern of landownership which not only included a number of peers—common enough in other counties—but also a significant number of substantial country gentlemen. The resentment of these lesser landowners at the political ambitions of their noble neighbours was on full display.

In 1768 the Earl of Eglinton had supported his brother Archibald Montgomerie only to see him defeated by the Earl of Cassillis's brother David Kennedy, who was supported by the Earls of Loudoun, Glencairn, and Dumfries together with Sir Adam Fergusson of Kilkerran, Lord Auchinleck (James Boswell's father, and a Court of Session Judge) and other gentry. From 1770 Sir Adam was planning to sit for the county himself.[24] It is not clear when his friend Henry Dundas stepped in to join him, but the county itself took fire in early 1773 when Loudoun, Eglinton and Cassillis changed their previous positions and formed a 'triple alliance'. This 'strange coallition', apparently brokered by a local laird and Eglinton supporter, John Hamilton of Bargany, aimed to re-elect David Kennedy and, more ambitiously, to control the county representation for 21 years. This was too much for the undeclared and independent freeholders many of whom fell in behind Fergusson in a struggle against noble domination.[25]

The struggle first manifested itself in vote creation. The Ayrshire freeholders' Head Court of 6 October 1772 ended with a total roll of 92 voters. That of 5 October 1773 saw the removal of six deceased voters and the addition of 20, bringing the roll to 106.[26] The meeting of 4 October 1774, a few days before the election, increased the roll to 124[27] but this last total did not reflect all activity since the previous October. Scottish electoral law required that a title be registered in the Register of Sasines (the record of land transfers) a full year before a vote could be claimed on it, and much legal work had been going on. In January 1774 the 'triple alliance' learned of rumours that their opponents, who included Glencairn, Dumfries, Auchinleck, Sir Thomas Wallace and John Dunlop, were making up to 100 nominal votes. Together with an initially reluctant Eglinton, Cassillis and Loudoun accelerated their own vote creation programme. A legal search made for their benefit in June 1774 showed the extent of their work.

---

[23] Scottish R.O., SC40/68/3, pp. 98–120, 121–31 (Haddington Sheriff Court Records), minutes of elections, 29 Oct. 1774 and 29 May 1777.

[24] *HP, 1754–90*, I, 471–2; for the Ayrshire election generally, see also F. Brady, *Boswell's Political Career*, (1965), pp. 56–74.

[25] Scottish R.O., GD267/22/7, George Home to Patrick Home, 14 Mar. 1774.

[26] Scottish R.O., SC6/78/2, pp. 133–6, 187–90 (Ayr Sheriff Court Records), minutes of freeholders, 6 Oct. 1772 and 5 Oct. 1773.

[27] Scottish R.O., SC6/78/2, pp. 167–172.

Between January and April the three nobles, with what allies and relatives they had among the gentry, had prepared the ground for making 137 votes. This activity was paralleled by a similar effort among those banded behind Sir Adam Fergusson who had prepared claims for 124 votes of their own.[28]

Buccleuch and Dundas had a small but significant influence on the struggle. At one level they could hope to influence individual voters, as Dundas did with Alexander Fergusson of Craigdarroch,[29] but they were also capable of more spectacular interventions. After 1768, Lord Auchinleck had largely withdrawn from involvement in Ayrshire politics, but in 1773 his anger at the ambitions of Kennedy's noble patrons led him both to rejoin the fray and to switch his allegiance to Sir Adam Fergusson. Then in March 1774, and quite surprisingly given his known aversion to nominal votes, he had begun making ten such qualifications to support Fergusson.[30] Some perceived that he had done this unbidden in direct response to the vote creation of the 'triple alliance',[31] but his furious son knew better. James Boswell had already sided with the alliance—'the ancient and respectable interest of Ayrshire', he styled it—believing that he had his father's permission to commit the family interest in their cause. The old man's action was a deep humiliation to him and years later he would publicly reveal that it stemmed from Dundas's private intercession with Auchinleck.[32]

In practice the early dissolution of Parliament meant that Auchinleck's new votes, together with the others commenced since January, were invalid at the election on 13 October. On the electoral roll as it stood Kennedy should have won, and indeed his friends carried the initial elections for preses and clerk. At that point Fergusson's supporters proposed putting the trust oath to those present. Introduced in 1714 as an attempt to weed out voters with nominal qualifications, this oath required voters to swear that they did not hold and exercise their vote in trust for another. It had never been fully effective but on this occasion its effects were spectacular. Fergusson had more nominal voters than Kennedy but all of them, perhaps tutored in an awareness of Lord Mansfield's decision on such qualifications, cheerfully took the oath. Five of Kennedy's voters demurred, however, and were struck off the roll, passing majority control to their opponents. Fergusson's allies then proceeded to enrol several friends and concluded by electing him with 60 votes to Kennedy's 47.[33]

Their work in Ayrshire necessarily brought Dundas and Buccleuch into contact with Dumfriesshire and Lanarkshire politics. The former was dominated by the

[28] N.L.S., MS. 4946, ff. 139–40, 169–70 (Mure of Caldwell papers), letters of Alexander Montgomerie of Coilsfield to Baron William Mure, 24 Jan. and 20 June 1774; MS. 5006, ff. 109–10, John Bell to same, 26 June 1774.

[29] Scottish R.O., GD77/200/12 (Fergusson of Craigdarroch papers), Dundas to Alexander Fergusson, 18 Oct. 1774.

[30] Brady, *Boswell*, p. 65; *Boswell for the Defence, 1769–1774*, eds. W.K. Wimsatt and F.A. Pottle, (New Haven, 1959), pp. 211–3; N.L.S., MS. 4946, ff. 139–40, Alexander Montgomerie to Baron Mure, 24 Jan. 1774; MS. 5006, ff. 109–10, John Bell to same, 26 June 1774.

[31] Scottish R.O., GD267/22/7, George Home to Patrick Home, 14 Mar. 1774.

[32] N.L S., MS. 16, ff. 1–2, Boswell to Henry Dundas, 20 Apr. 1782; J. Boswell, *A Letter to the People of Scotland* . . . (Edinburgh, 1785), pp. 60–1.

[33] Brady, *Boswell*, pp. 68–9.

aged 3rd Duke of Queensberry. The current M.P., Archibald Douglas, had resolved not to stand again and another local laird, Alexander Fergusson of Craigdarroch, wanted the seat, counting on the support of Sir James Johnstone and on old family ties with Queensberry.[34] As we have seen, Fergusson was a friend of Dundas and Buccleuch—he held a Midlothian vote—and the duke interceded on his behalf with Queensberry, who was known to favour the pretensions of Major Robert Laurie. Queensberry had in fact already firmly decided in Laurie's favour but for some time led Fergusson to believe otherwise, and the revelation of this deception was a bitter blow.[35] Buccleuch was second in line to the Queensberry title and the principal heir, the notorious libertine Lord March, was already 48. Buccleuch could reasonably expect soon to hold this second dukedom and consequently his and Dundas's advice to Fergusson was framed to avoid damaging that inheritance. If Fergusson realistically believed he could win, he should stand. If not, he should avoid any associations that might separate or weaken 'the present established interest . . . which you and I both wish to see come entire in to the hands of our friend'.[36] Fergusson did commence a canvass but he had little hope of winning and, perhaps mindful of his friends' wishes, did not carry his opposition to the election.[37] Ironically, given Buccleuch's calculations, Lord March, who succeeded as Duke of Queensberry in 1778, would live to be 85. Buccleuch would not inherit the title until 1810.

The dominant landholder in Lanarkshire, the Duke of Hamilton was a minor in 1774, his family interest supervised by tutors, principally Andrew Stuart, a prominent Edinburgh lawyer, and William Mure of Caldwell, a baron of the Scottish Exchequer. His widowed mother's remarriage to John, 5th Duke of Argyll, created a formidable alliance that stretched across Lanarkshire, Dumbartonshire, and Renfrewshire and could make ripples in the adjacent constituencies. In the 'Douglas Cause' before the Court of Session and the House of Lords both families had vainly opposed the claim of Archibald Douglas to that peerage and both now had to face Douglas's electoral ambitions.

Fergusson of Kilkerran had acted as counsel to the Hamiltons in the Douglas Cause and the Duchess of Argyll asked her son's tutors to use the Hamilton lands in Ayrshire to create votes in his support. This they cheerfully agreed to, despite the fact that Baron Mure was himself a Kennedy supporter in Ayrshire.[38] Although the three votes were not made in time for the election, it found the Hamiltons on the same side as the Dundases and they would have further contact in Lanarkshire.

Since 1754 Lanarkshire had been represented by men unconnected with the Hamilton family and its interest 'had been but little felt'. Only in 1768 had

---

[34] Laprade (ed.), *Robinson*, p. 18.
[35] Scottish R.O., GD77/224/3–5, letters of Buccleuch and Viscount Dalrymple to Fergusson, 15, 20 and 26 Sep. 1773; GD77/200/13, James Murray of Broughton to same, 22 Sep. 1773.
[36] Scottish R.O., GD77/224/6, Dundas to Fergusson, 21 Sep. 1773.
[37] Laprade (ed.), *Robinson*, p. 18.
[38] *Intimate Society Letters of the Eighteenth Century*, ed. J. Campbell, 9th Duke of Argyll (2 vols., 1910), II, 145–8; N.L.S., MS. 4946, ff. 169–70, Alexander Montgomerie to Mure, 20 June 1774.

Andrew Stuart stood with the family's support but he declared late and could not give his full attention to a close contest involving three candidates. At the last moment the two others, Daniel Campbell of Shawfield, the sitting M.P., and Captain John Lockhart Ross, a son-in-law of the Lord President, had joined forces and Ross was elected.

In defeat Stuart and Baron Mure set to work rebuilding the Hamilton interest in Lanarkshire, Renfrewshire and Ayrshire. Despite warnings that it 'might indispose the gentlemen of the county against the duke's family and interest', they commenced a major programme of vote creation in Lanarkshire, putting 18 on the roll at Michaelmas 1773.[39] They were not alone and by June 1773 it was known that Archibald Douglas was similarly making votes. Stuart advised the Duchess of Argyll to solicit government support, or at least neutrality, and she wrote both to Lord North and to Lord Suffolk, Secretary of State for the Northern Department. In the end she got neutrality, with Suffolk privately well disposed but unable to throw government weight publicly behind her cause.[40] By that summer there were three candidates for the county, Stuart, Campbell supported by Douglas, and Lockhart Ross. With the result unpredictable, the duchess even contemplated offering Campbell the Hamilton interest in the Linlithgow seat in return for his supporting Stuart in Lanarkshire.[41]

Through his wife, a Baillie of Lamington, Lord President Dundas had some influence in the county and both he and his brother Henry were very close friends of Stuart. There seems no evidence, however, that either could influence their in-law Lockhart Ross and by October 1773 it was rumoured that he had already joined Campbell. Stuart was not unduly concerned. He knew on good authority that the Dundases would not follow Ross into such a pact and he hoped to make an arrangement of his own with them. In any event, he was confident of the Hamiltons' voting strength and was privately working towards a compromise with one of the other groups.[42] The nature of this proposed compromise remains obscure, but Ross's junction with Campbell proved to be real enough and probably hinged on some agreement about Douglas's support for Ross's candidacy in the Linlithgow burghs.

The Dundases had still to declare their intentions in March 1774 when Stuart unexpectedly gained the votes of James Lockhart of Castlehill. Castlehill had learned that Queensberry had intervened in Lanarkshire, carrying Professor Dick from the Hamilton party with a promise of support to obtain the soon to be vacant sheriffship. Lockhart coveted this office for his brother, Robert Sinclair, and declared for the Hamiltons as the best way of securing it. Since Sinclair was a friend, the Dundases were expected to follow suit.[43]

[39] Argyll (ed.), *Intimate Society*, II, 160–4; N.L.S., MS. 8259, ff. 87–92 (Stuart Stevenson papers), 'State of the County of Lanark . . . in the year 1774', 13 Dec. 1783.

[40] Argyll (ed.), *Intimate Society*, II, 145–8, 168–72.

[41] N.L.S., MS. 4946, ff. 92–5, Duchess of Argyll to Mure, 1 Aug. 1773.

[42] Argyll (ed.), *Intimate Society*, II, 178–89.

[43] Scottish R.O., GD267/22/7, George Home to Patrick Home, 14 Mar. 1774; *View of the Political State of Scotland in the Last Century*, ed. C.E. Adam (Edinburgh 1887), p. 213.

The poll of 28 October saw 106 of 129 voters in attendance. As elsewhere, the unexpectedness of the election meant that many of the nominal votes in preparation could not be enrolled. Stuart and Mure had done their work well, however, and Stuart's 69 votes easily beat off the combined forces of Shawfield, Lockhart Ross, Douglas and their allies, who mustered 39.[44]

It is probable that the Dundases only took sides in Lanarkshire in June 1774 when the Argyll, Hamilton and Buccleuch interests entered a formal alliance concerning the Linlithgow burghs. The constitutions ('setts') of the 66 Scottish royal burghs had been mostly unchanged since the Union. Edinburgh had been allotted one M.P., with the remaining towns divided into 14 groups, five with four burghs and nine with five. At a parliamentary election, each burgh council chose a delegate and the delegates in a burgh group met to elect the Member. In four-burgh groups the delegate from the returning burgh had a casting vote in case of a tie. Bribery, virtually unknown in the counties, was common in burgh politics.[45] Linlithgow was grouped with Peebles, Lanark and Selkirk, and the four had been represented since 1772 by Sir James Cockburn. A wealthy merchant well able to stand the cost of greasing the palms of burgh magistrates, his candidacy had been pressed on the Hamiltons by Andrew Stuart's friend Sir George Colebrooke, himself an English M.P. and Lanarkshire landowner. Cockburn's election would not have met with the approval of Queensberry whose heir Lord March controlled Peebles, and this may explain the duke's subsequent interference in Lanarkshire.[46]

By early 1774 there were two candidates for the burghs, Cockburn and Lockhart Ross, the latter simultaneously contesting Lanarkshire. Ross had secured Lanark with the support of Archibald Douglas and Peebles through Lord March.[47] Early in 1773 he had indirectly approached Buccleuch for the duke's influence in Selkirk. Buccleuch, mindful of the difficulties then facing Fergusson of Kilkerran in Ayrshire, had decided to reserve his position with a view to trying to keep the burgh seat as a bolthole for his friend. He similarly declined a second application on Ross's behalf, this time from Archibald Douglas who influenced the Lanark council, although privately he contemplated an arrangement with them which would benefit Fergusson. In May or June 1774 Andrew Stuart, perhaps furthering his Lanarkshire struggle against Douglas and Campbell of Shawfield, broached with Buccleuch the possibility of an agreement over the burghs between the duke and the families of Argyll and Hamilton. Buccleuch and Dundas readily signalled their consent and the arrangement which was finally concluded in August was that Cockburn would contest the burghs with Hamilton support, but would be ready to resign the seat to Sir Adam if the latter failed in Ayrshire. Cockburn had required persuading, both because he resented being the second choice

[44] N.L.S., MS. 8259, ff.87–92.

[45] For burgh politics generally, see W. Ferguson, 'Dingwall Burgh Politics and the Parliamentary Franchise in the Eighteenth Century', S[cottish] H[istorical] R[eview], XXXVIII (1959), 89–108.

[46] N.L.S., MS. 4945, ff. 118–121, letters of Duchess of Argyll and John Ross Mackye to Baron Mure, 4 Dec. 1771.

[47] Scottish R.O., GD267/22/7, George Home to Patrick Home, 14 Mar. 1774.

candidate and because he felt that his past services gave him some expectation of a first preference from the Hamiltons.[48]

Even as the pact was settled, Lockhart Ross still looked for Buccleuch's support and this time solicited his relative Henry Dundas. The eventual reply was a mixture of friendly advice and understated threats, a style which would later become familiar to Scottish politicians. Buccleuch was now otherwise engaged and a continued contest would see Ross in a hard and expensive struggle: 'I own it often occasions me much regret that those with whom you are politically connected [Campbell and Douglas], seem anxious to embrace every opportunity of showing their disregard for those, whom perhaps in the long run you may think your best friends . . .'.[49] Dundas's homily may have encouraged Ross to assist the ubiquitous Fergusson in an unlikely (and unsuccessful) candidacy for the Tain Burghs seat. It is more probable that it persuaded him to stand aside from the Linlithgow contest, because on election day Cockburn's opponent was not Ross but James Dundas of Dundas, a West Lothian laird. This latecomer, with the vote only of the Lanark delegate, was easily brushed aside and Kilkerran's victory in Ayrshire allowed Cockburn to keep his burgh seat. Nonetheless, James Dundas had come perilously near to breaking the Hamilton family's grip on Linlithgow and their subsequent analysis concluded that Cockburn's retention of that town's vote 'was merely accidental'. Ominously for the future, his opponent had been heavily supported by Sir Lawrence Dundas of Kerse, who had been active in the burghs since at least February.[50]

This Dundas, a distant relative of his namesake Henry, had acquired a fortune as an army commissary in Germany in the Seven Years War. From 1768 he was M.P. for Edinburgh and his son Thomas sat for Stirlingshire. A nephew, also Thomas, sat for Orkney and Shetland, while an old military friend, Colonel James Masterton, sat for the Stirling burgh group. Sir Lawrence's extraordinary wealth bought him the Earl of Morton's property in the Northern Isles and his influence in several other Scottish and English parliamentary seats made him a figure of considerable importance at Westminster. His ambition aimed both at a peerage and at the leadership in Scots politics. This last would necessarily bring him into conflict with Dundas and Buccleuch and in time they would paint him, and others who had made their fortunes in commerce or imperial service, as parvenus and a threat to the traditional values of the Scottish landed classes. All this was a little way in the future, however. In the meantime he was already feared and resented by many of the local interests in the constituencies where his influence was felt.[51]

[48] Scottish R.O., GD224/30/6/2–6, 8 (Buccleuch muniments), letters of Henry Dundas and Andrew Stuart, [7 June]–23 Aug. 1774. Buccleuch muniments cited with kind permission of the Duke of Buccleuch and Queensberry, K.T.

[49] Scottish R.O., GD224/30/6/7, letters of Dundas and Lockhart Ross, 15 July–29 Aug. 1774.

[50] Scottish R.O., GD267/22/7, George Home to Patrick Home, 16 Oct. 1774; *HP 1754–90*, 508, 511; N.L.S., MS. 5390, ff. 178–83 (Stuart Stevenson papers), memorial of Walter Scott, W.S., respecting Linlithgow politics, [27 Feb. 1776]; N.L.S., MS. 4946, ff. 153–4 (Caldwell papers), Duke of Argyll to Mure, 24 Feb. 1774.

[51] *HP 1754–90*, II, 357–61; Murdoch, *People Above*, pp. 126–7; Murdoch and Dwyer, 'Paradigms', pp. 240–3.

Sir Lawrence's relationship with the Argyll and Hamilton families was confused and the evidence is rather contradictory. He was a friend of John Craufurd, one of the candidates for the Renfrewshire election who in turn was a friend of the Hamiltons. Craufurd was standing with the backing of the outgoing M.P., William McDowall of Castlesemple (whom he disliked), and Mure of Caldwell, a major landowner in the county. Even before February 1773, however, he had had an assurance that should he fail to win the county, Sir Lawrence Dundas would bring him in for another seat.[52] In practice this arrangement, which remains obscure, was unnecessary. Craufurd had the support of the Duke of Hamilton and he also obtained that rarity in contemporary Scots politics, a government letter endorsing his candidacy written by a plainly nervous Lord North.[53] Although he had anxious moments, Craufurd had little difficulty beating off the challenge from John Shaw Stewart of Greenock who withdrew before the election.[54] In Stirlingshire and Dumbartonshire matters were different, and Sir Lawrence Dundas and Argyll were locked in combat through proxies.

Stirlingshire, like Ayrshire, had a large electorate (83 were enrolled in 1773) and a pattern of landownership that made county politics a vigorous struggle between an independent, assertive gentry and a few noblemen. The most significant peer, William, 2nd Duke of Montrose, was blind and lived in England. In his absence, the Argyll family had supported James Campbell of Ardkinglass as M.P. since 1747 but his position had weakened after the death of the 3rd Duke of Argyll in 1761. In 1768 Campbell was defeated by Sir Lawrence Dundas, long a county landholder, who used his wealth and connections to entrench his son Thomas in the seat.[55] Now in the autumn of 1773 Campbell returned to the charge and, backed by Argyll, set to work making votes. The Dundases responded, beginning an elaborate programme of their own, and in a review of the situation in December they concluded that at the 1775 election they might have 62 votes to Campbell's 50.[56] Already, however, Sir Lawrence was under attack from another quarter.

The Stirling burgh group, composed of Dunfermline, Stirling, Queensferry, Inverkeithing, and Culross had been held for Dundas by Colonel James Masterton since 1768. Some time before Michaelmas 1773 a new candidate appeared. Previously unknown in the burghs, Colonel Archibald Campbell of Inverneil had made a fortune in East India and now set out to use it to take the seat.[57] Dundas saw the oppositions to him in Stirlingshire, its burghs and also one in his own seat in Edinburgh as being orchestrated by Argyll. Worse, Argyll's allies

[52] N.L.S., MS. 4946, ff. 33–4, Craufurd to [?Mure], 17 Feb. 1773.

[53] *Ibid.*, ff. 84–91, letters of Andrew Stuart to Mure, 22 and 31 July 1773.

[54] N.L.S., MS. 4945, ff. 124–5, Craufurd to Mure, 18 Jan. 1774; Laprade (ed.), *Robinson*, pp. 18–9; *HP 1754–90*, I, 494.

[55] J.R.M. Sunter, 'Stirlingshire Politics, 1707–1832' (University of Edinburgh Ph.D., 1972), pp. 216–22.

[56] *Ibid.*, pp. 227–34; N[orth] Y[orkshire] C[ounty] R.O., ZNK/X/3/11 (Zetland papers), memoranda from Thomas Dundas concerning Stirlingshire Roll, received 22 Dec. 1773.

[57] N.Y.C.R.O, ZNK/X/1/3/25, case for counsel's opinion [undated but late 1774]; *HP 1754–90*, II, 179–80.

claimed that they had government support in their attacks. Dundas's approaches to Lord North confirmed that this was untrue and he hoped that North might influence Argyll. North, however, faced with a struggle between friends, predictably opted for 'an absolute neutrality'.[58] Inevitably Sir Lawrence would be drawn to counter-attack Argyll and an opportunity was near at hand.

Since 1761 Dumbartonshire had been represented by Sir Archibald Edmonstone of Duntreath, a local gentleman and an Argyll relative, but by 1773 all was not well. Edmonstone was not giving the freeholders the attention they felt that they deserved[59] and resentment towards the Argyll family was growing. Robert Bontine of Ardoch complained that:[60]

> The A[rgyll] family have claim'd the sole management & direction of this county, their interest was formerly powerfull, the superior abilitys & attention of the late Duke, gave him a right to take the lead, especially at a time when the spirit of independence was not so prevalent, & the disunited sentiments of the inhabitants gave him an opening which his political genius converted to his own purposes . . . the present Duke in every respect unequal to his predecessor supports a languid interest by the abilitys of his brother Ld. Fredk. [Campbell] who . . . has been using every art & subterfuge which the law even seems to allow of to create votes in a new & unprec[ed]ented manner . . . Some even of the most leading men have declar'd that they only want a man of enterprize & they will support them.

Bontine contemplated standing himself and signalled his knowledge of plotting and discontent among the gentry to another laird, George Haldane of Gleneagles. Haldane, coincidentally married to a niece of Sir Lawrence Dundas, was enthusiastic and Bontine recognised him as a better candidate 'in the general system of making the county free and independent, which can only be accomplish'd by a sett of gentlemen drawing to one point . . .'.[61] In the event, open resistance to Argyll came from Lord Elphinstone who declared his son William a candidate in October 1773.[62]

Argyll began discreetly pressing friends to back Edmonstone but was alarmed to find that Sir James Colquhoun of Luss, an influential freeholder, was apparently indifferent. Colquhoun was persuaded to relent in November and Argyll continued his approaches to others.[63] Thereafter the evidence becomes contradictory. In

[58] N.Y.C.R.O., ZNK/X/1/2/191, 194 and 195, letters of Richard Rigby and William Norton to Sir Lawrence Dundas, 3–17 Dec. 1773. Transcripts courtesy of Dr Alexander Murdoch.

[59] Scottish R.O., GD47/551/1 (Ross Estate muniments), Robert Buchanan of Drumakill to Duke of Argyll, 18 Nov. 1773 (copy).

[60] N.L.S., Acc. 7282 (Graham of Gartmore papers), letterbook 4, pp. 35–7, [Bontine] to George Ramsay, 28 Feb. 1773 (copy).

[61] *Ibid.*, pp. 43–4, same to same, 27 March 1773 (copy).

[62] Scottish R.O., GD47/562/1, Sir Archibald Edmonstone to Buchanan of Drumakill, 23 Oct. 1773.

[63] Scottish R.O., GD47/551/1–2, letters of Argyll to Buchanan of Drumakill, 5 and 29 Nov. 1773; W. Fraser, *The Chiefs of Grant*, (3 vols., Edinburgh, 1883), II, 452–3; Scottish R.O., GD248/348/3/89 (Seafield papers), Colquhoun to [? Grant of Grant], 2 Dec. 1773. Seafield papers quoted with permission of the Rt. Hon. the Earl of Seafield.

December, Sir Lawrence Dundas was advised that the Elphinstones did not 'seem to have taken any fixed resolution' concerning Dumbartonshire and that in pursuing it they might be won as allies in Stirlingshire.[64] In February 1774, however, Argyll was writing that the Elphinstones 'who I look'd upon to be engag'd both in Clydesdale and Dumbartonshire are wavering'. He blamed this on Dundas's influence with them, warning the Hamiltons that if they did not use their new votes in Stirlingshire as a bargaining counter, Dundas would turn the Elphinstones against Argyll and Hamilton in both Lanarkshire and Dumbartonshire.[65] Thus it would appear that sometime between November and February either Argyll temporarily persuaded the Elphinstones to stand down, or Captain William Elphinstone, newly returned from East India, got cold feet. Argyll's subsequent intelligence proved exact and Lord Elphinstone resumed his attack with Dundas's support, this time with another son, George Keith Elphinstone, as candidate. A government survey in June reckoned Edmonstone would win.[66] This was not his perception, and at the November election he absolutely required the attendance of Sir James Colquhoun and friends to win by 26 votes to Elphinstone's 14.[67]

In Stirlingshire matters went better for the Dundases. After a spring and summer in which both sides made elaborate endeavours to create more votes, the manoeuvrings at the Michaelmas Head Court (4 October) produced little change. At the subsequent election (26 October) Dundas's friends easily took control of the meeting, electing Haldane of Gleneagles as their preses and then re-electing Thomas Dundas as their M.P. by 44 votes to a humiliating 19 for Campbell. The unexpectedly early date of the election proved very much in Dundas's favour. Five months later the margin would have been much closer.[68]

Sir Lawrence had similar success in neighbouring Clackmannanshire. One of six counties represented only in alternate Parliaments, it was paired with Kinross-shire and was due to elect a representative in 1775.[69] Dundas owned land in the county as did his brother-in-law Robert Bruce of Kennet, a Lord of Session. Both supported the candidacy of Kennet's brother-in-law Ralph Abercromby. He had been canvassing since July 1773[70] and was opposed by Colonel James F. Erskine. One of the Mar family, Erskine's likely objective in seeking election was the restoration of the peerage forfeited in 1715. Both sides had been making votes since 1765 but by late 1773 the Abercrombies had a majority on the roll. All too late the Erskines began an endeavour to create 15 new votes.[71] These would have turned the scale but the early election rendered them useless and in

[64] Sunter, 'Stirlingshire', p. 226, quoting from Zetland papers.

[65] N.L.S., MS. 4946, ff. 153–4, Argyll to [Mure], 24 Feb.1774.

[66] Laprade (ed.), *Robinson*, p. 19.

[67] Scottish R.O., GD248/51/2/74, Colquhoun to Sir James Grant of Grant, 6 Oct. 1774; *HP 1754–90*, I, 477.

[68] Sunter, 'Stirlingshire', pp. 228–42.

[69] The other pairings were Caithness with Bute and Nairnshire with Cromartyshire.

[70] Scottish R.O., GD124/15/1638 (Mar and Kellie papers), Abercromby to James Erskine, 29 July 1773.

[71] Scottish R.O., GD124/14/31/6, 'Schemes for freeholds in Clackmannan', 24 July 1765; GD124/14/3, memoir on Lady Erskine's vote creation; SC64/61/1 (Alloa Sheriff Court records), Freeholders' enrolments, 1766–75.

November 1774 Abercromby was elected by 15 votes to ten. It was a bad tempered poll, with several disputes over voting qualifications. Subsequently a duel would follow accusations of misconduct levelled against Kennet by Erskine.[72]

In the Stirling Burghs, Dundas's old friend Masterton was beaten. Both sides had spent lavishly. Colonel Campbell reportedly disbursed £17,000 and Dundas in an ill-advised letter in May 1774 instructed Masterton's agent to exert himself: 'don't be outbidden anywhere'. This did little good and Campbell gained the seat despite a last minute switch in which Dundas replaced Masterton as his candidate with Sir Alexander Gilmour. Protracted legal proceedings followed a blatantly corrupt election but did not change the result.[73]

Bad luck in Stirling threatened to follow Sir Lawrence to his Edinburgh seat. The city electorate consisted of 33 merchants and trades' representatives and had long supported the Argyll and Bute interests. Dundas had obtained the seat in 1768 partly in the absence of a government manager and partly because of the town's resentment at the way in which Stuart Mackenzie had recently interfered in its church patronages. While there had long been political tensions in the city between the merchants and the trades' incorporations, these were of only limited importance in 1774.[74] Sir Lawrence's main opponent was Colonel Erskine who now came to Edinburgh from Clackmannan and set up as a candidate, winning over three electors. Armed with a copy of Dundas's instructions to Masterton's agent (above) he claimed that this evidence of bribery disqualified him from election. Dundas was sufficiently worried to take legal advice but his allies meantime set up a friend, Lord Provost Stodart, as a third candidate. By giving him six votes, they put him ahead of Erskine and so in a position to claim that should Erskine overturn Dundas's election then the seat must pass to Stodart. It was a cunning ruse but in the event Erskine did not follow through his petition and Dundas, who had 23 votes, retained his seat. A fourth candidate, David Loch, received no votes.[75]

There were further, lesser defeats for Sir Lawrence. In April 1774 Alexander Fergusson of Craigdarroch had been promised Lord Galloway's support in Wigton and Whithorn, two of the four burghs in the Galloway group. In August Fergusson received Lord Stair's backing in New Galloway and Stranraer in return for undertaking to get an English seat for Stair's son Lord Dalrymple. Fergusson had difficulties and the final arrangement was that Dalrymple was to be elected for Richmond while William Norton, a friend of Sir Lawrence's, would have the support of Fergusson's allies in the Scots burghs. If Dalrymple could be found

[72] Scottish R.O., SC64/61/1, minutes of election, 3 Nov. 1774; Lord Dunfermline, *Lieutenant-General Sir Ralph Abercromby, 1793–1801*, (Edinburgh, 1861), pp. 23–4.

[73] *HP 1754–90*, I, 510; N.Y.C.R.O., ZNK/X/1/3/25, case for counsel's opinion [undated but late 1774].

[74] N.L.S., MS. 1639, ff. 96–9 (Ochtertyre MSS.); for the town's politics see A. Murdoch, 'The Importance of Being Edinburgh. Management and Opposition in Edinburgh Politics, 1746–1784', *S.H.R.*, LXII (1983), 1–16.

[75] N.Y.C.R.O., ZNK/X/1/3/25, case for counsel's opinion [undated but late 1774]; ZNK/X/1/3/26, petition by James Stodart to the House of Commons [undated but late 1774]; *HP 1754–90*, I, 502–3.

another seat, then Fergusson might at a later date hope for another chance at the Scottish seat. Dundas may have been party to Fergusson's original plan but he did not benefit from its eventual outcome. There was some confusion about the arrangement at the election, and the Wigton and Whithorn delegates voted for Henry Dashwood, Galloway's brother-in-law. Norton was returned with the casting vote of New Galloway, but there was an irregularity in that delegate's qualification and Dashwood exploited this to overturn the election on appeal. Fergusson understandably smelled duplicity in the actions of the Galloway family.[76]

Although Sir Lawrence Dundas had no direct conflict with Henry Dundas in 1774, Sir Alexander Gilmour's belated candidacy in Stirling showed a new alliance, and Sir Lawrence supported him in a simultaneous assault on the Haddington burghs, where he was also defeated. A petition to Parliament was unsuccessful.[77] Both burgh candidacies were a recognition of Gilmour's impending failure in Midlothian, where Henry Dundas had forged ahead. Having rejected a compromise offered by Gilmour a year earlier, Dundas was elected in October 1774 by 57 votes to 21.[78]

North of the Forth an unexpected and hard fought contest for the Dysart burgh group saw the incumbent James Townsend Oswald losing to John Johnstone, who deployed his immense wealth earned in East India.[79] Perthshire with its large electorate (141 by Michaelmas 1773) was in a situation comparable to those in Ayrshire and Dumbartonshire. The resident gentry, resenting the power of the Duke of Atholl, had unsuccessfully opposed his candidate at a 1773 by-election and were preparing to do the same at the general election.[80] Both parties were making votes and in June 1774 Thomas Graham of Balgowan, the gentry's candidate, anticipated an addition of 92 to the roll, of whom 48 were certainly for him. He had the active support of Douglas of Douglas and the Strathmore family, and the good wishes of Sir Lawrence Dundas.[81] Ultimately Graham abandoned his challenge as a mark of respect following Atholl's unexpected death days before polling and the late duke's candidate, Colonel James Murray, was elected unopposed.[82]

Further north, much of the electoral activity centred on Alexander, 4th Duke of Gordon. Henry Dundas had early had the support of Gordon and his few allies in Midlothian[83] and in 1771 the duke was reportedly 'determin'd to . . .

[76] N.Y.C.R.O., ZNK/X/1/3/24, 'State of facts relative to the election for the Galloway Burrows', [undated, but c. Nov. 1774]; *HP 1754–90*, I, 512.

[77] Scottish R.O., GD267/22/7, letters of George Home to Patrick Home, 16 Oct. and 21 Nov. 1774; N.Y.C.R.O., ZNK/X/1/3/35, journal of election expenses, 1774–6.

[78] Scottish R.O., GD235/8/4/11–12, Lady Arniston to Sir John Gordon, 13 Oct. 1773; *HP 1754–90*, I, 479.

[79] *HP 1754–90*, II, 687.

[80] Laprade (ed.), *Robinson*, pp. 6, 18.

[81] N.L.S., MS. 3590, ff. 73–4 (Lynedoch papers), [Graham] to [Earl of Strathmore], 23 June 1774 (draft); MS. 16123, ff. 193–4, state of Perthshire voters, [undated but 1773 or 1774].

[82] N.L.S. MS. 3590, ff. 83–6, copy letters of Graham to Murray, 29 Oct. and 8 Nov. 1774.

[83] Scottish R.O., GD235/8/4/13–14, Christian Dundas to Lady Invergordon, 4 Nov. [1771]; GD248/51/2/61A, Charles Gordon to Lord George Gordon, [Oct. 1774].

make as many barons [votes] as he could in every county in Scotland . . .'.[84]
Now, in 1774, George Home, a well informed Edinburgh lawyer and a friend
of Dundas, wrote:[85]

> The Duke of Buccleugh is laying a plan for taking the lead in Scotch affairs, he
> is at present rather antiministerial, tho' not so much so as to prevent his now
> and then receiving favours from the minister. He is interfeering in many of the
> elections in the South of Scotland, The D. of Gordon is doing the same for him
> in the North . . . I have had frequent opportunities of seeing him [Buccleuch]
> within these two years, he seems to have a sound understanding and is steady
> and active (tho' not violent) in the prosecution of his purpose.

Gordon was certainly 'interfeering' in the north and a relative, Lord Adam
Gordon, had an unopposed election for Kincardineshire. The family's main activities
were in the north east, however, where politics were and would remain complex.
Gordon had extensive properties in the shires of Aberdeen, Banff, Moray (Elginshire)
and Inverness. In the three former he was engaged in a bitter feud with James
Duff, 2nd Lord Fife, and in the latter he was pushing to remove the sitting M.P.,
Simon Fraser of Lovat. Lovat's family estates had been forfeited after the '45 but
his subsequent military career as a loyal Briton had done much to forward his
campaign for their restoration from government (he would succeed in 1774) and
he enjoyed much support among the county lairds. Further east, the young 7th
Earl of Findlater was a power in the Elgin Burghs, although his Morayshire
influence was far inferior to that of the Grants of Grant and their kindred.

The Grants, headed by Sir Ludovick and from March 1773 by his son Sir
James, were the focus of much politicking. Like Gordon, their central feud was
with Fife, who had opposed Sir Ludovick's brother General Francis Grant in
Elginshire from 1767. Fife and Grant were close relatives and at intervals friends
tried unsuccessfully to mediate.[86] The struggle proceeded with some bitterness
and much calculation. In March 1771 Gordon had opposed the election for the
Elgin Burghs of Thomas Lockhart, who was backed by the Grants, Findlater and
Lord Kinnoull, and he was expected to renew this assault.[87] Nevertheless within
weeks Gordon, Grant and Findlater were discussing an alliance against the common
enemy.[88] Findlater's relationship with Gordon was uneasy—the Elgin Burghs
would remain a bone of contention—but he was a firm friend to the Grants. By
early 1772 all three were in alliance and their attentions focussed on Elginshire.
In March Gordon ordered his lawyers to create votes to support the Grants and
he expected reciprocal support from them for the double candidacy of his brother,
Lord George Gordon, in Banffshire and Inverness-shire.[89] James Grant was

[84] Scottish R.O., GD248/349/1/22, Sir Ludovick Grant to Mr Grant, 25 Sep. 1771.

[85] Scottish R.O., GD267/22/7, George Home to Patrick Home, 14 Mar. 1774.

[86] Scottish R.O., GD248/348/2/36, Fife to [? James Grant of Grant], 10 July 1771;
GD248/348/4/116–7, Sir John Dalrymple to James Grant of Grant, 14 Jan. 1772.

[87] Scottish R.O., GD248/348/3/58, Thomas Ogilvie to [? James Grant of Grant], 5 Mar. 1771.

[88] Scottish R.O., GD248/348/2/31, Kinnoull to [? same], 31 May 1771.

[89] Scottish R.O., GD248/348/4/118, 121, letters of Gordon to James Grant of Grant, 12 Mar.
and 5 July 1772.

grateful: 'I wish Lord George all success and I shall contribute to it what is in my power . . . You should make all [the votes] you possibly can in both counties'.[90]

At Michaelmas 1772 the Elginshire freeholders split, holding two separate head courts. At their meeting the Grant party struck off all Fife's votes, creating several of their own. Fife took the matter to the Court of Session, where he was defeated in February 1773.[91] Even as this case proceeded, Grant was encouraging Findlater to make votes in the county but Fife's almost immediate victory in an appeal to the Lords, who found his roll of electors to be the legal one, threw matters into turmoil. The Grants faltered, with one adviser urging a compromise with Fife while Sir James resolved to be at no further expense. Optimism returned with the determination of Francis Grant to fight on and the hope that 'a proper exertion' must defeat Fife.[92] Grant of Ballindalloch, a relative, was firm in his advice to Sir James; the election was two years off and 'whoever . . . makes the greatest number of good votes will without doubt carry the election'. This became the Grant-Findlater strategy, and they also began approaches to Sir Hector Munro, the M.P. for the Inverness Burghs. An Elginshire landowner, it was hoped that he might be induced to give his support in the county in return for the influence wielded by the Grants in Forres.[93] These approaches became urgent in January 1774, when it became plain to the Grants that they could not win unaided and that his four votes would hold the balance. Munro was friendly with Fife but was guided by Stuart Mackenzie and it was to the latter that Ballindalloch appealed, without success. By early 1774 further vote creation was under way, involving litigation, and Munro's importance grew.[94] The unexpected dissolution ended the Grants' hopes. Government influence through Stuart Mackenzie settled Munro's support for Fife and the Grants were reduced to frantic expedients, including an appeal to Argyll to intercede with government and a failed plan to reduce Fife's support by timing the Banffshire and Elginshire polls for the same day. In the end they did not contest the election and Fife's brother was returned.[95]

Gordon's ambitions in Banffshire met a similar fate. Even with Grant support he was having difficulty in making votes and in February 1774 the Court of Session found against the claims of eight of his supporters to be enrolled.[96] Government anticipated a close contest with a local gentleman, Ferguson of

[90] Scottish R.O., GD248/50/3/59, Grant to Gordon, 15 July 1772 (copy).

[91] Scottish R.O., GD248/50/3/75, Francis Grant to James Grant of Grant, 10 Dec. 1772; GD248/50/4/17, letters of Ludovick Grant to same, 17 Feb. and 1 Mar. 1773; *HP 1754–90*, I, 480.

[92] Scottish R.O., GD248/50/4/34, 35, 39, 41–2, letters of Ludovick Grant to James Grant, 1 Apr.–10 May 1773.

[93] Scottish R.O., GD248/50/5/13, 21, Ballindalloch to [Grant], 24 Apr. 1773, Francis Grant to [same], 15 June.

[94] Scottish R.O., GD248/51/1/3, 84–5, Ballindalloch to [same], 19 Jan. 1774, Charles Gordon to same, 21 Mar. 1774; GD248/51/2/30, Sir James Grant to Ballindalloch, 7 Sep. 1774 (copy), with appended letters 7 June–1 Sep.

[95] Scottish R.O., GD248/51/2/42, 52, 79, 76, 90, Francis Grant to Sir James Grant, 4 Oct. 1774; Sir James Grant to Argyll, 11 Oct. 1774 (copy), Argyll to [?Grant], 19 Oct. 1774, James Grant to Sir James Grant, 18 Oct. 1774, Ludovick Grant to same, 26 Oct. 1774.

[96] Scottish R.O., GD248/50/4/19, Ludovick Grant to James Grant of Grant, 1 Mar. 1773; GD248/51/1/9, same to same, 23 Feb. 1774.

Pitfour, holding the key. In the event Fife's re-election was unopposed, with Gordon's allies lamenting that things could have been otherwise had the dissolution been later.[97] Gordon cannot have helped his relationship with Findlater in Banffshire by his support, from March 1774, for the Elgin Burghs' candidacy of his relative Colonel Staats Long Morris. Findlater and Grant had put much effort and expense into tightening their grip on Elgin itself and in this seat at least there was now no pretence of co-operation with Gordon.[98] Grant put his full weight behind Thomas Lockhart and against Morris but it was not enough. Morris won over Burnett of Kemnay who directed the Inverurie magistrates—'he must have been highly bribed to make him such a rogue', wrote Lady Findlater—and with Banff and Kintore this gave him the election.[99]

Gordon could draw further satisfaction from the Inverness-shire result. Simon Fraser had been returned with Gordon support in 1768 after agreeing that at the next election he would either support Gordon's candidate or find him a seat elsewhere.[100] In practice Gordon and the Grants were prepared to evict Fraser if necessary. In mid-1772 Fraser was informed of Gordon's preparations but was not alarmed.[101] The independent county gentlemen had little taste for a Gordon candidate and the Grants heard rumours in July 1773 that the Duke of Argyll and Sir Alexander MacDonald were to join to support Fraser and that government favoured him.[102] Consequently, when the dissolution came, Lord George Gordon pressed all his friends to attend, 'in case the Frasers should not chuse to elect the person their chief is engaged to'.[103] Already, however, Fraser was secretly negotiating a deal with Lord George to have him chosen for the English pocket borough of Ludgershall. This was eventually arranged by Fraser's friend North, and Lord George stood down, loftily writing that the Duke of Gordon 'has agreed, in consequence of this provision for me, to allow him [Fraser] to be again returned to Parliament for Inverness-shire'.[104]

Despite his insensitive dealings with Findlater and his friends' defeats in Banffshire and Moray, the Duke of Gordon had much to be pleased with in 1774. He could believe, as some did, that only the early dissolution had saved Lord Fife from serious defeats. Time had yet to reveal the resilience of Fife's position. Meanwhile the duke could muster a Westminster support as respectable

[97] Laprade (ed.), *Robinson*, pp. 5, 20; Scottish R.O., GD248/51/2/56, James Ross to [? James Grant of Corrimony], 11 Oct. 1774.

[98] Scottish R.O., GD248/51/1/90, John Ross to Sir James Grant, 23 Mar. 1774; GD248/50/5/2, Lady Findlater to [same], 3 Feb. 1773; GD248/51/1/2, 14, Findlater to same, 5 Jan. 1774, and copy reply, 28 Feb. 1774.

[99] Scottish R.O., GD248/51/2/48, letters of John Ross to Sir James Grant, 8 Oct. 1774 and Grant to Lady Findlater, 9 Oct. 1774 (copy); GD248/51/2/87, Lady Findlater to Sir James Grant, 24 Oct. [1774]; *HP 1754–90*, I, 505.

[100] *HP 1754–90*, I, 485.

[101] Scottish R.O., GD135/149 (Stair muniments), volume containing letter of Fraser to Sir John Dalrymple, 5 Aug. 1772.

[102] Laprade (ed.), *Robinson*, pp. 5–6; Scottish R.O., GD248/50/4/63, Ludovick Grant to Sir James Grant, 12 July 1773.

[103] Scottish R.O., GD248/51/2/49, Lord George Gordon to same, 9 Oct. 1774.

[104] Scottish R.O., GD248/51/2/61, same to same, 12 Oct. 1774.

as the grouping around his ally Buccleuch. The madness of Lord George Gordon lay unseen in the future.

It is time to try to draw together some general conclusions from all this electoral activity. When the Scottish Commons elections ended, seven petitions were pending[105] but only that for the Galloway Burghs actually unseated a member. The rest were either rejected or dropped. Dundas and Buccleuch had run a successful campaign of their own, returning a corps of followers to Westminster. At this period they still acted as equals and it would be several years before the duke, for reasons that are still unclear, retreated to the background. Meantime their ambitions were manifest, and in April 1775 one observer reported 'Buccleuch's imagining that he should be Prime Minister for Scotland, and that Harry Dundas was to act along with him'.[106] This did not happen and there is little mystery about why. With only limited interventions by ministers in the Scottish elections, the overwhelming bulk of the constituencies returned government supporters. Government had as yet no need for the services of a Scottish manager and it would be another four years before disaster in America, dwindling government support in Parliament and his own debating skills combined to put Henry Dundas in a position where Lord North was forced to accord him the prime role in Scottish affairs. Dundas would use this period to perfect a pose as the natural leader of the Scottish political nation and to participate fully in an ideological campaign against the nouveau riche and nabobs edging their way into Scottish society and politics. Lord Fife and Sir Lawrence Dundas were particularly stigmatised in this campaign and the Buccleuch party were soon embroiled with the latter in a struggle for the Edinburgh constituency which would last for the rest of the decade.

It was in its corruption that the general election of 1774 made its most important mark. Venality in burgh elections was nothing new and the general acquiescence in it would continue for a few years yet. Attitudes to what had happened in the counties were very different, however. There had been considerable friction within the political nation at the time of the 1768 election but this was as nothing compared to the feelings vented in 1773 and 1774. As we have seen, in county after county the Scottish gentry were furious at the tide of fictitious votes unleashed upon them by their larger neighbours in what were commonly perceived of as attempts to break the independence of the electorate and reduce the constituencies to the status of aristocratic pocket burghs. After 1768 there had been calls for changes in the election laws and from 1774 these demands became much louder. Even as the Lord Advocate Sir James Montgomery attended his own election for Peebles-shire it was known that he planned 'immediately to prepare a draught of an Act to cutt off parchment lairds who have no property . . .'.[107] The age of political reform in Scotland was about to begin.

[105] For Clackmannanshire, Dunbartonshire, Nairnshire, Edinburgh, and the Elgin, Tain and Wigtown burgh groups.
[106] *Boswell: The Ominous Years 1774–1776*, eds. F.A. Pottle and C. Ryskamp (New Haven, 1963), p. 130.
[107] Scottish R.O., GD248/51/2/90, Ludovick Grant to Sir James Grant, 26 Oct. 1774.

The New Scottish County Electors in 1832: An Occupational Analysis

J.I. BRASH

University of Western Australia

In spite of all the research done into the Reform Acts there is one perennial question which has never been answered except in the most general terms, 'Who obtained the vote in 1832?'. The difficulty is not with knowing who had the vote after 1832. There are often, particularly in England, registers of electors and pollbooks from which the voters can be identified. The problem is distinguishing those who had votes before 1832 from those who owed their enfranchisement to the Reform Acts. An exception is found in the Scottish counties where, owing to the distinctive character of the system of county representation before 1832, there is an opportunity to examine a discrete body of voters enfranchised for the first time under the provisions of the Scottish Reform Act. They formed 90 percent of the immediate post-1832 constituency and can be distinguished from the old voters. As a contribution to the question of who obtained the vote in 1832 the object of this study is modest: to present an analysis of the occupations of approximately two-thirds of the new Scottish county constituency in order to obtain a clearer sense of what sorts of men qualified for the vote.

Under the previous, complicated and restrictive franchise based on the feudal concept of the superiority the number of electors was very small.[1] According to an estimate in 1830 the total number of 'old freeholders', fiars (proprietors) and liferenters of superiorities, was 3253; the largest of the counties, Aberdeen, Fife, Lanark and Perth, had between 180 and 240 voters, the smallest, Clackmannan, Cromarty and Nairn, fewer than 20.[2] Even these figures were inflated: where a fiar and a liferenter were enrolled on the same qualification both may have been counted but only one could vote; and there were many individuals qualified in more than one county. Reformers claimed that there were probably no more than 2,500 individuals with county votes, and that half of those held fictitious qualifications.[3]

Because the old constituency had been so small the Scottish Reform Act had proportionately a much greater impact on both the size and the composition of

---

[1] The best account is W. Ferguson, 'The Electoral System in the Scottish Counties Before 1832', *The Stair Society, Miscellany II* (Stair Soc., XXXV, 1984), pp. 261–94.

[2] [H. Cockburn], 'Parliamentary Representation of Scotland', *Edinburgh Review*, LII (1830), 210–11.

[3] Durham University Library (Earl Grey MSS., 2nd Earl), Papers on Parliamentary Reform I, no. 77.

the county electorate than their respective acts had in England and Wales or Ireland.[4] Although the initial enrolment in the 30 counties established for the purposes of representation in 1832 was just over 33,000, and numbers in individual counties were often tiny compared with those in England, the Reform Act had brought about an immediate increase of at least ten-fold and probably more. Consequently, the overwhelming majority of those whose claims were successful at the first registration were enrolled for the first time, in contrast to the English counties where less than half the electors could be considered new.

It was one of the distinctive features of Scottish county representation before reform that by an act of 1681 a roll of the county freeholders was maintained, whereas in England and Wales there was no electoral register until 1832.[5] The roll was revised annually at the meeting of the Michaelmas head court, and as an essential preliminary when the freeholders met to conduct a county election. The Reform Act allowed freeholders to continue to exercise their rights of voting on superiorities (but only for their own lifetimes or for as long as they retained their qualifications) and provided for their transfer to the new register of electors.[6] A few requalified under the changed provisions but their numbers are insignificant for the purposes of this analysis. Consequently, the 'old freeholders' can be treated as a distinct group, identifiable in a number of ways: (a) from the rolls of freeholders recorded in the surviving minute books of their meetings; (b) from the designation under which they were sometimes entered in the sheriffs register of electors, for example as 'freeholder under the old qualification' or as 'proprietor of superiorities' or 'liferenter of superiorities'; (c) when that information is not included in the register the date of their entry identifies them, because they are shown as enrolled together on a date distinct from those on which new voters were enrolled; and finally (d) in some printed lists of electors in 1832 their names are marked or they are listed separately.

The Scottish Reform Act has not been studied as exhaustively as the English legislation. Its drafting has been severely criticized by Ferguson, the scheme of redistribution has been unfavourably assessed by Dyer, and there has been some work on its more immediate effects on electoral politics.[7] There has been no previous attempt to establish beyond broad generalizations who was actually enfranchised. The right of voting in counties was granted to proprietors of subjects with a minimum annual value of £10, which could be land, houses, business premises, or other forms of property such as feu-duties. Such voters included

---

[4] For the latest estimates of the increase in the English and Welsh electorate as a result of the Reform Act see F. O'Gorman, *Voters, Patrons and Parties. The Unreformed Electorate of Hanoverian England, 1734–1832* (Oxford, 1989), pp. 178–80.

[5] Ferguson, 'The Electoral System in Scottish Counties Before 1832', p. 270.

[6] 2 & 3 Will. IV, c.65, clause vi.

[7] W. Ferguson, 'The Reform Act (Scotland) of 1832: Intention and Effect', *Scottish Historical Review*, XLV (1966), 105–14. M. Dyer, ' "Mere Detail and Machinery", The Great Reform Act and the Effects of Redistribution on Scottish Representation, 1832–1868', *Scottish Historical Review*, LXII (1983), 17–34; *Papers on Scottish Electoral Politics, 1832–1854*, ed. J.I. Brash (Scottish History Soc., 4th ser. XI, 1974); I.G.C. Hutchison, *A Political History of Scotland 1832–1924. Parties, Elections and Issues* (Edinburgh, 1986), chapters 1–2.

both the owner of a landed estate and the small village proprietor or feuar whose house and garden barely met the minimum valuation. The largest single body of new voters consisted of tenant farmers who could qualify on a lease for 57 years or longer of land with an annual value of £10, or on a lease of 19 years if the land had an annual value of £50; and by a late addition similar to the Chandos clause in the English act tenants could qualify who had been in actual personal occupancy of the land for 12 months and paid £50 a year in rent whether they had a written title or not.

It is commonly estimated that under the provisions of the Scottish act one man in eight was registered to vote at the general election in 1832, or, I would suggest, one in six in the burghs, and one in 11 in the counties if the old freeholders are included. However, such estimates take no account of the considerable regional differences in Scotland at the beginning of the 1830s, in the distribution and level of economic activity, in patterns of urban settlement, in the values of land and houses, and generally in the distribution of poverty and prosperity.[8] The ratio between the number of county voters and the adult male population in 1832 varied enormously across the country, but within a broad regional pattern in which the extremes were represented by the prosperous counties of the south east and the western isles from Islay to Lewis with their large and mostly impoverished populations. Across southern, central and eastern Scotland, where approximately three-quarters of the population and nine out of every ten county voters were located, the ratio ranged from one in six to one in 12. In the northern and highland counties the ratios were much higher, ranging from one in 21 to almost one in 60. In most counties from Stirlingshire and the Lothians to the Borders the ratio was from one man in seven to one in nine; Selkirk was lower at one in six, Renfrew and Haddington slightly higher at ten, Bute and Dumfries higher still on 11 and 12 respectively. In central and eastern Scotland there was one voter to every nine men in Fife, every ten in Clackmannan (though only six in the joint-county of Kinross), Perth, Forfar and Kincardine, 11 in Aberdeen, 12 in Elgin and Nairn, though one in 21 in neighbouring Banff. In counties to the north and west the ratios were higher still: one in 23 in Argyll, 34 in Inverness, 30 in Ross and Cromarty, 32 in Caithness, 46 in Orkney and Shetland, and 58 in the ducal fief of Sutherland. Moreover, within counties there were considerable differences so that, for example, while voters were relatively scarce in the highland counties of Argyll, Inverness and Ross and Cromarty, they were even scarcer in the islands that formed part of these counties. In the Hebrides from Islay to Lewis there was in 1832 a population of approximately 90,000 but only 275 voters, of whom 43 were old freeholders, 108 tenant farmers and 28 parish ministers. In the islands of Argyll there were probably 58 adult male inhabitants to each of 121 electors. A quarter of the county population lived on Islay and Mull, yet only just over one in ten of the county voters was qualified there. And in Inverness-shire the island electorate was even smaller in proportion to the adult male population.

---

[8] I. Levitt and C. Smout, *The State of the Scottish Working Class in 1843* (Edinburgh, 1979), presents an excellent account of regional differences.

The total of 96 voters on Skye, Eigg, Barra, North and South Uist and Harris (a quarter of them old freeholders) was equivalent to about one in 100 of adult males. In Lewis, part of Ross and Cromarty, there were 58 voters, most of them (46) qualified in or near Stornoway, the one town of economic importance in the Outer Hebrides. For each man on the register there were 58 others who did not qualify, five times the average in Scottish counties and almost ten times more than in the most favoured of the southern counties.[9]

Research into Scottish electoral history in the 30 years or 40 years after the passing of the Reform Act suffers from a paucity of sources. Whereas in English counties and boroughs there are frequently long runs of electoral registers and rich collections of printed pollbooks, in Scotland such materials are comparatively rare. There was no provision in the Scottish act for the publication of either the burgh or the county registers, an important though generally unnoted difference between the English and Scottish legislation. Clause 55 of the act for England and Wales required that 'the clerks of the peace shall cause to be written or printed copies of the registers of electors for their respective counties'. The Scottish act provided only that the register should be open for public examination for a short period each year. The sheriff clerk was required to keep a correct copy of the register at a convenient place in the head burgh of the county and to make it available for inspection without charge during the ten business days immediately following 20 June.[10] It was not until the County Voters Registration (Scotland) Act of 1861 introduced a new mode of registration that for the first time provision was made for copies of the county electoral roll to be printed after correction at the annual registration court, the cost being covered by a small assessment on the county rate.[11]

Lists of the voters in Scottish counties between 1832 and 1861 have survived in three main forms: (a) the sheriffs' manuscript registers or certified copies of them made for use at polling stations during an election; (b) printed lists, normally produced by one of the political parties for canvassing the voters, though occasionally found in local directories; and (c) private manuscript copies of the register. In one of these forms, sometimes more than one, there are lists of electors for most of the 30 counties that sent a Member to Parliament from 1832.[12] A few cover lengthy periods, the majority one year only. It is hardly surprising that 1832 is the year for which the fullest record has survived, providing a sufficient number of lists for an adequate sample of voters to be obtained.

---

[9] These estimates have been arrived at through a re-working of data in the 1831 census and in 'The Report from the Select Committee on Election Expenses', Appendices (E), (F) and (G), *British Parliamentary Papers*, 591, pp. 193–6 (1834), IX, 263, adjusting for errors in the number of electors recorded for 1832, e.g. the omission of old freeholders in the counties of Aberdeen, Forfar and Sutherland, and for the occasional understating of the county population by attributing to a parliamentary burgh the entire population of the parish in which it was situated, which also explains the apparent decline in the population of some districts of burghs in subsequent returns.

[10] 2 & 3 Will. IV, c. 65, clause xxii.

[11] 24 & 25 Vic, c. 83.

[12] The 34 Scottish counties returned 30 Members to Parliament; in 1832 eight counties were formed into joint-constituencies: Clackmannan and Kinross, Elgin and Nairn, Orkney and Shetland, and Ross and Cromarty.

Lists of the 1832 voters, and later lists from which they can be extracted, are available for 21 and a half of the constituencies (see Appendix 1 for details). Sheriffs' registers from 1832 (originals or certified polling copies) have been found for eight counties: Clackmannan and Kinross, Inverness, Kirkcudbright, Peebles, Ross and Cromarty, Selkirk, Stirling and Wigtown. For two others most of the 1832 electors have been identified from later registers. From a copy register of Argyllshire electors after the 1834 registration 979 of the original 995 voters (including old freeholders) have been identified; and from a Caithness register of 1835, 204 of the original 221 voters. With one exception the registers form part of the massive deposit of sheriff court records in the Scottish Record Office, the register for Kinross-shire 1832–63 being held in the Perth and Kinross District Archives in Perth.

For ten counties and two others which formed part of joint-constituencies there are printed lists: Aberdeen, Ayr, Clackmannan, Fife, Forfar, Kincardine, Midlothian, Orkney, Perth, Renfrew, Roxburgh and Stirling. In addition, although the earliest surviving register for Lanarkshire was not published until after the 1839 registration, from dates of enrolment it has been possible to identify 72 per cent of the voters registered in 1832. Finally, there is a manuscript list of the voters in the joint-constituency of Elgin and Nairn, prepared before the 1832 election as a survey of voting strength in the county. Most of these lists were produced by one of the local parties for canvassing and organizing the new and greatly enlarged electorate. In Perthshire the reformers took the initiative in printing a register of the voters, whereupon the conservatives asked if they could purchase 200 copies in return for a share of the cost. It is indicative of the extent of partisanship at the first election that, although 700 copies had been printed and there were plenty to spare, Robert Graham of Redgorton refused to sell any to the opposition, who had to produce their own.[13] A list published in Orkney appears to confirm that it was not expected there would be an official publication of the register. After the first registration the sheriff clerk, it seems, arranged for a list of the voters in the county and in the burgh of Kirkwall to be printed and distributed to all electors, but he insisted that issuing the list was 'gratuitous and forms no part of the duty of the Sheriff Clerk'. Another untypical example is the printed register of Roxburghshire voters, in which it is stated that the information was taken from the registers by the sheriff clerk William Rutherford, without suggesting that he did so as part of his official duties or that he was actually responsible for publishing the register.

A small number of the printed lists record how the electors voted at the first election. Printed pollbooks from Scottish counties are extremely rare, but for the neighbouring counties of Ayr and Renfrew there are lists published after the 1832 election recording the votes given, and from Clackmannan a register published on the eve of the 1835 election which records the votes electors still on the roll in 1832.

[13] National Library of Scotland, MS. 16137 (Graham of Lynedoch Papers), ff. 35–7, George Gardiner to Robert Graham of Redgorton, 18 Nov. 1832.

If all the information in the surviving record had been usable, the sample which forms the basis of the analysis would have consisted of 26,733 voters, or 80 per cent of the county electorate in 1832, which according to contemporary but not always reliable parliamentary returns numbered 33,115, about 10 per cent of them old freeholders.[14] As the object was to analyse occupations the printed register for the county of Aberdeen, which records qualifications but few occupations, had to be excluded.[15] The printed record of voting in the Ayrshire election suffers from the same defect, and includes only those who voted or paired off. However, among the papers of James Dobie, a writer and electoral agent in the town of Beith, there is a list of the claimants in the registration court convened at Irvine in September 1832. Dobie's list, which covers eight populous parishes in the north of Ayrshire, identified the occupations of 30 per cent of the county electors.[16] After adjustment for the exclusion of Aberdeen (2449) and the unusable districts of Ayrshire the sample was reduced to 22,553. Because 2,154 of these were old freeholders the sample of voters enrolled for the first time in 1832 is 20,399, probably just over two-thirds of the new county constituency.

For other counties either no 1832 registers have been found, or the earliest available, as in Haddington (1834) or Linlithgow (1836), do not indicate which were the 1832 enrolments.[17] For several counties no records of electors from the period 1832 to 1861 have yet come to light: Banff, Berwick, Bute, Dumfries, Dumbarton, Shetland and Sutherland.[18] In spite of these gaps the sample is representative of all Scottish regions. In the south west Dumfries and central and southern Ayrshire are not included but Wigtown and the Stewartry of Kirkcudbright are. In the south east the omission of Berwickshire is compensated for by the inclusion of Peebles, Roxburgh and Selkirk. Central and eastern Scotland are well represented: Stirling, Clackmannan and Kinross, Perth, Fife, Forfar and Kincardine. The highland districts from Argyll and Perthshire to Inverness and Ross and Cromarty, including the western isles, are well covered. Most important of all, the counties included in the sample present a considerable variety of general and local economic and social conditions which are reflected, though imperfectly, in the composition of their electorates.

The information contained in the registers is not uniform. The sheriff's register is the most comprehensive, the entry for each elector consisting of his number in the register, the date of his enrolment, his name, his occupation or designation, his qualification, for example as 'proprietor of house and garden', and where his

[14] See note 9; 33,300 would be closer to the correct figure.

[15] The Society of Genealogists, London, holds a copy of the Aberdeenshire list.

[16] Glasgow University Archives, DC1/564 (Beith Parish MSS.), 'List of Claimants for regtn of voters . . . placed before the court at Irvine'. The eight parishes are Ardrossan, Beith, Dalry, Kilbirnie, Kilbride, Kilwinning, Largs and Stevenston.

[17] Scottish R.O., GD 364/1/166, (Hope of Luffness papers), *Haddington County List of Electors Sept. 1834*; National Lib. Scotland, R.244f, *List of Voters of the County of Linlithgow, Made Up From the Sheriff's Register, as Adjusted in the Year 1836* (Edinburgh, 1837).

[18] The National Register of Archives (Scotland), Survey No.7 (Askew of Ladykirk papers) records a copy of the Berwickshire pollbook for 1832; I have not seen it. In Scottish R.O., GD 171/1258/15 (Forbes of Callendar papers), John Marshall to William Forbes of Callendar, 6 Nov. 1839, refers to a recently printed roll of the Dumbartonshire electors, but I have not yet found a copy.

qualifying property was situated; including in the case of a tenant farmer the name of the farm he held. Some printed registers, for example those for Midlothian in 1832 and Lanarkshire in 1839, contain as much detail as one would find in the sheriff's register. Others record no more than the elector's name and occupation, and the name of the estate, farm, village or town where his qualification was located. Some indicate that the elector was qualified as a proprietor or as a tenant, though sometimes as already noted this information is given but not the man's occupation.

An important issue concerns the quality of the occupational information when as here it depends on the claimant's self-description. O'Gorman takes the view that there were community checks on false or inflated claims.[19] In Scottish counties it was the parish schoolmaster who distributed and received claim forms, and then posted the list of claimants at the parish church, so neighbours and the registration procedures themselves probably helped keep the aspiring voters honest. It therefore seems reasonable to accept that the occupations claimed by electors represent their calling at the time of enrolment. Nonetheless, when using these descriptions one has to acknowledge that they are not as clear-cut and unambiguous as they seem. It is difficult to distinguish between masters or self-employed and employees (even though one assumes the latter were always a minority), or between those who had retired and those who were still active in their occupation. Occasionally the same individual appears in different guises. Three men enrolled as proprietors in the parish of Kilbirnie, Ayrshire, are described in Dobie's list as 'grocers'; in a local list of the votes given at the 1832 election they are 'merchants'; and in a similar list from 1835 two are once again 'grocers' and the third a 'spirit dealer'.[20] The occupations are closely related and the variants in the polling lists probably represent the perceptions of the compiler. It is more common for electors occupations to be consistent between lists.

Given the character of the basic information (and the tiny numbers in many occupations), oversophisticated analysis was deemed to be inappropriate. The primary object was to organize the data into comprehensible and manageable categories with which a profile could be constructed of the sample of 20,399 new voters, and of the separate county electorates. The number had to be small enough to identify general and common features, and large enough to convey the diversity of the electorate and the distinctive characteristics of individual counties. It was crucial not to lose the sense of difference by subsuming too many distinct occupations in a small number of over-standardized classifications. I have used nine categories, which represent mostly types of economic activity. A tenth category not actually required for this analysis would consist of the 2,154 old freeholders in the sample counties. The following table presents a general analysis of the new county voters. Table 2 presents an analysis county by county.

[19] O'Gorman, Voters, Patrons and Parties, pp. 200–1.
[20] Glasgow Univ. Archives, DC1/708 (Beith MSS.), A List of the Electors of Kilbirnie Who Voted at Dalry on the 24th and 25th December 1832 (Beith, 1832); and DC1/621, A List of the Electors of Kilbirnie Who Voted at Dalry on the 30th June and 1st July 1835 (Beith, 1835)—both published by the Reformers of Kilbirnie.

Table 1: *Scottish County Electors 1832*

1.	Proprietors & Miscellaneous	3,446	16.89%
2.	Agriculture	10,632	52.12%
3.	Professions & Service	1,378	6.76%
4.	Merchants & Dealers	742	3.64%
5.	Shipping & Fishing	253	1.24%
6.	Manufacturing & Mining	1,210	5.93%
7.	Retail Trades	1,142	5.60%
8.	Artisanal Trades	1,176	5.76%
9.	Labour & General Work	420	2.06%
Total		20,399	

1. *Proprietors and Miscellaneous*: In what is essentially an occupational analysis this is partly a residual category. It is not comparable with 'gentry' in previous English analyses. Few large or titled landowners, or higher ranking military and naval officers, figure among the new electors; they most frequently appear in the registers as old freeholders. Here the category comprises those whose qualification as proprietors is known, or can be assumed, but not their occupation if they had one. Most were proprietors of land, but to underline the difficulty of creating unambiguous categories some, for example in the dairying districts of Ayrshire and Lanarkshire, were almost certainly owner-occupying farmers.[21] In the Orkney list only two electors described themselves as farmers, yet other evidence suggests that many of the proprietors were small landowners who farmed their own land.[22] There were also those who claimed under various designations, as feuars (359) or portioners (258), whose occupations if known would often place them in another category.[23]

2. *Agriculture*: 10,404 farmers made up by far the largest single occupational group among the new electors, 52 per cent overall though in the sample counties the proportion ranged from over three-quarters of the electors in Argyll to only a quarter in Clackmannan. Most were tenants, whose enfranchisement it should be noted was rarely contemplated during the early stages of formulating the Scottish reform legislation.[24] Others, notably in Kinross, parts of Lanarkshire and

[21] *New Statistical Account of Scotland* (15 vols., Edinburgh, 1845) [hereafter cited as *N.S.A.*], V, Ayr, p. 589 (Beith), p. 226 (Dalry); VI, Lanark, p. 36 (Lesmahagow), pp. 304–6 (Avondale).

[22] *Ibid.*, XV, Orkney, pp. 28, 53, 67, 150, 155; all refer to large numbers of small landowners, though given the backward state of agriculture many of them probably too poor to qualify.

[23] The £10 proprietors, whatever their occupation, were often referred to as the 'village feuars', as feuing was commonly how land was made available for house building in towns and villages, and some of them enrolled under that designation. Definitions of a portioner suggest he was the proprietor of a small piece of land arising from the subdivision of property among co-heirs. In several counties, especially Kinross, Lanark, Roxburgh and Stirling it was a common term for a small proprietor; there were 66 on the roll for Kinross where they comprised one in five of the new electors.

[24] There is no reference to tenants in T.F.Kennedy's 'Memorandum of Proposed Reform in Scotland, sent to Lord John Russell, November 1830', *Letters Chiefly Concerned with the Affairs of Scotland from Henry Cockburn . . . to Thomas Francis Kennedy 1818–52* (1874), pp. 258–66; nor in Durham Univ. Lib., Earl Grey MSS., Papers on Parliamentary Reform I, nos. 72–73 (Cockburn's plan and bill); but compare National Lib. Scotland, Adv. MS. 9.1.8., f.11, Francis Jeffrey to Henry Cockburn, 13 Feb. 1831.

Stirling were owner-occupiers;[25] while some tenants of farms qualified as village proprietors. In the highland counties, especially Inverness, there were military and naval officers who described themselves as tenants of lands and farmers, though in this analysis they have been classed as professionals. In addition to farmers the agricultural category includes 228 electors in a variety of rural callings. Of these the most numerous are 159 millers (often an ambiguous designation), the rest an assortment of occupations: nurseryman (17) and seedsman (3), factor (9), forester (5), gamekeeper (6), shepherd (8), thatcher (4), dyker (3), two ploughmen and two molecatchers, a crofter, a farm servant, a farrier, a horse breaker and a stabler.

3. *Professions and Service:* This category consists predominantly (80 per cent) of the traditional professions of the church (515), law (271), medicine (157) and education (192), many in occupations already frequently represented among the old freeholders. To these have been added military and naval officers who were not old freeholders (85) and a miscellany of occupations which were often to achieve professional status later in the nineteenth century or since, or which might be regarded as service occupations (in finance, management, or local government), bankers (22) and accountants (11), architects (7), veterinary surgeons (3), surveyors (various) (20), engineers (various) (10), managers and agents, and local officeholders including three provosts and six town clerks.

4. *Merchants and Dealers:* 568 described themselves simply as merchants; the remainder dealt in a variety of goods: agricultural produce, cattle, horses, building materials, cloth, stockings, leather, wine and provisions.

5. *Shipping and Fishing:* This group of occupations made a distinctive contribution to the electorates of such counties as Clackmannan, Fife, Caithness, Ross and Cromarty, Orkney and Wigtown.

6. *Manufacturing and Mining:* The classification has been by industry. Of the 1,210 electors in this category almost three-quarters were engaged in the manufacture and finishing of textiles, in wool, flax or cotton depending on locality, including 219 manufacturers, a general term for textile manufacturers, and 461 weavers, the largest industrial occupation represented in the sample. The remainder were divided between coal, iron, quarrying, leather, brewing and distilling, and a miscellany of manufactures from paper to gunpowder.

7. *Retail Trades:* Mostly the retailers of food, clothing, and other goods and personal services, from innkeepers and bakers to shoemakers and hairdressers.

8. *Artisanal Trades:* Mostly in the building and construction trades, wrights, masons and blacksmiths, and including some fine arts trades such as engraving, and carving and gilding.

9. *Labour and General Work:* An essential category for the identification of a significant body of labourers, gardeners, carters and carriers, and a number of miscellaneous workers.

The greatest diversity is found in groups 3–9, which can be described,

---

[25] The number of small owner-occupying farmers was a distinctive feature of Kinross: *N.S.A.,* IX, Kinross, p.71. Of 170 farmers in the 1832 register 73 were proprietors. In Lanarkshire, of 936 farmers 165 were proprietors.

ambiguously in some cases, as the non-agricultural occupations. They include 6,321 new county voters in 249 occupations and comprise 31 per cent of the sample. To make greater sense of the welter of information the occupations were arranged in three groups according to the number of electors in each: (i) those with 20 electors or more, equivalent to an average of one in each county in the sample; (ii) 5–19 electors; and (iii) 1–4 electors.

Size of occupation	Number of occupations	Number of Electors	%
20 +	52	5,491	86.9
5–19	60	566	8.9
1–4	137	264	4.2

The third group provides fascinating detail but is ultimately of limited significance. The more interesting and useful finding is that virtually 87 per cent of the electors in categories 3–9 were employed in a core of 52 occupations. The following is a summary of these occupations, including the number of electors in each and the size of the core in each of the seven categories (for summaries of the other occupations see Appendix 2):

3. *Professions and Service*: minister of religion 504, physician/doctor 47, surgeon 110, advocate 32, Writer to the Signet 57, writer 164, schoolmaster 185, military or naval officer 85, banker 22. (1206/1378, 87.5 per cent).

4. *Merchants and Dealers*: merchant 568, cattle dealer 21, timber merchant 21, hosier 20. (630/742, 85 per cent).

5. *Shipping and Fishing*: shipowner 73, shipmaster 37, sailor 35, fisherman 28, fish curer 20, salmon fisher 29. (222/253, 87.7 per cent).

6. *Manufacturing and Mining*: manufacturer 219, weaver 461, cotton spinner 23, calico printer 23, bleacher 51, tanner 27, brewer 58, distiller 51, paper manufacturer 21, coalmaster 36. (970/1210, 80.2 per cent)

7. *Retail trades*: innkeeper 236, vintner 93, spirit dealer 23, grocer 169, baker 165, flesher 100, tailor 62, shoemaker 174, watchmaker 24. (1046/1142, 91.6 per cent).

8. *Artisanal trades*: wright 335, mason 262, blacksmith 208, carpenter/joiner 81, builder 42, millwright 23, slater 39, cooper 42, saddler 31, nailmaker 20. (1083/1176, 92 per cent).

9. *Labour and General Work*: labourer 102, carter 97, carrier 65, gardener 70. (334/420, 79.5 per cent)

The 20,399 new electors formed a small minority among adult males in the counties. In most occupations men with votes were the exception, as a comparison with the occupation tables in the 1841 census confirms.[26] Nevertheless, there were few economic activities in which men engaged not represented somewhere among

[26] '1841 Census, Occupation Abstract, part II, Scotland', *British Parliamentary Papers* (588), pp. 85–8 (1844), XXVII, 385.

Table 2: *The Structure of Scottish County Electorates 1832*

		Ayr(a)	Argyll	Caithness	Clackmannan(b)	Kinross(b)	Elgin & Nairn	Fife	Forfar	Inverness	Kincardine	Kirkcudbright	Lanark(c)
1. Proprietors		189	77	27	65	81	68	409	197	56	79	135	359
	%	21.26	8.79	17.09	13.66	21.83	11.04	20.73	16.12	11.76	11.55	15.31	20.05
2. Agriculture		322	678	56	119	171	416	733	760	296	465	597	952
	%	36.22	77.40	35.44	25.00	46.09	67.53	37.15	62.19	62.18	67.98	67.69	53.15
3. Professions & Service		47	47	20	36	27	43	137	65	79	34	39	114
	%	5.29	5.36	12.66	7.56	7.28	6.98	6.94	5.32	16.60	4.97	4.42	6.37
4. Merchants & Dealers		36	12	15	33	15	21	75	32	17	19	19	83
	%	4.05	1.37	9.49	6.93	4.04	3.41	3.80	2.62	3.57	2.78	2.15	4.63
5. Shipping & Fishing		18	5	20	41	0	7	57	14	3	12	3	0
	%	2.02	0.57	12.66	8.61	0	1.14	2.90	1.15	0.63	1.75	0.34	0
6. Manufactures & Mining		98	11	5	52	22	3	214	68	3	17	11	100
	%	11.02	1.25	3.16	10.92	5.93	0.49	10.85	5.56	0.63	2.48	1.25	5.58
7. Retail Trades		70	16	3	52	24	18	135	36	12	28	34	90
	%	7.87	1.83	1.90	10.92	6.47	2.92	6.84	2.95	2.52	4.09	3.85	5.03
8. Artisans		66	26	11	52	17	33	164	31	9	21	36	65
	%	7.42	2.97	6.96	10.92	4.58	5.36	8.31	2.54	1.89	3.07	4.08	3.63
9. Labour & General Work		43	4	1	26	14	7	49	19	1	9	8	28
	%	4.84	0.46	0.63	5.46	3.77	1.14	2.48	1.55	0.21	1.32	0.91	1.56
TOTAL		889	876	158	476	371	616	1973	1222	476	684	882	1791
	%	100	100	100	100	100	100	100	100	100	100	100	100

(a) Represents 30% of the new electors in Ayrshire in 1832.

(b) The joint-constituency of Clackmannan and Kinross has been disaggregated to show the distinctive character of Clackmannan as well as the differences between the two parts of the constituency.

(c) Represents 72% of the new electors in Lanarkshire in 1832.

Table 2: *continued*

		Midlothian	Orkney	Peebles	Perth	Renfrew	Ross & Cromarty	Roxburgh	Selkirk	Stirling	Wigtown	TOTAL
1. Proprietors		127	58	25	544	240	15	244	45	367	39	3446
	%	11.27	38.67	9.73	18.41	19.80	3.41	20.68	19.48	22.11	5.04	16.89
2. Agriculture		491	29	164	1653	514	277	481	89	787	582	10632
	%	43.57	19.33	63.81	55.94	42.41	62.95	40.76	38.53	47.41	75.29	52.12
3. Professions & Service		118	16	22	162	57	56	104	19	99	37	1378
	%	10.47	10.67	8.56	5.48	4.70	12.73	8.81	8.22	5.96	4.79	6.76
4. Merchants & Dealers		60	20	5	97	40	17	46	12	48	20	742
	%	5.32	13.33	1.94	3.28	3.30	3.86	3.90	5.19	2.89	2.59	3.64
5. Shipping & Fishing		0	12	0	6	9	26	1	0	5	14	253
	%	0	8.00	0	0.20	0.74	5.91	0.08	0	0.30	1.81	1.24
6. Manufactures & Mining		58	2	7	137	153	2	72	25	134	16	1210
	%	5.15	1.33	2.72	4.64	12.62	0.45	6.10	10.82	8.07	2.07	5.93
7. Retail Trades		111	7	20	139	104	19	101	15	84	24	1142
	%	9.85	4.67	7.78	4.70	8.58	4.32	8.56	6.49	5.06	3.10	5.60
8. Artisans		104	6	13	180	65	24	96	24	98	35	1176
	%	9.23	4.00	5.06	6.09	5.36	5.45	8.13	10.39	5.90	4.53	5.76
9. Labour & General Work		58	0	1	37	30	4	35	2	38	6	420
	%	5.15	0	0.39	1.25	2.48	0.91	2.97	0.87	2.29	0.78	2.06
TOTAL		1127	150	257	2955	1212	440	1180	231	1660	773	20399
	%	100	100	100	100	100	100	100	100	100	100	100

the county voters, and while the numbers in many occupations were tiny, a feature of the sample is its occupational diversity, from landed proprietors, professionals and manufacturers, to artisans, shopkeepers, gardeners and labourers. When considering who obtained the vote in 1832 it is salutary to learn that there were more labourers on the electoral roll than bankers or advocates—except that there were many more labourers to start with, and those among them who had votes were truly exceptional. It is impossible to say how any individual acquired the property on which he qualified, whether by inheritance, purchase or marriage, but irrespective of his occupation, a man who held the minimum £10 qualification could have his name entered in the register of voters if he chose to submit a claim. It is undeniable that the majority of county voters belonged to the middling ranks of Scottish society, but it would be difficult to apply any simple or general class label to an electorate that included labourers, coalminers, servants, ploughmen and molecatchers.

Table 1, showing the total number and percentage of electors in each of the nine categories, presents a general profile of the new county electorate, but as can be seen in Table 2 no one county matches this profile, though some large ones, such as Perth, Fife and Lanark which together contribute a third of the sample, come close. There are considerable differences between counties in the distribution of the nine categories into which electors have been classified. Of these the largest by far is Agriculture representing the most important economic activity common to all counties in some form. Over half the new voters were farmers (10,404), so the differences in their distribution provide a convenient way of distinguishing between counties. In Table 3 the counties are ranked according to the percentage of their electors in Agriculture. It suggests that the answer to the question of who obtained a county vote in 1832 will depend upon which county one is examining.

Table 3: *Percentage of New Electors in Agriculture in Rank Order*

Argyll	77.40	Stirling	47.41
Wigtown	75.29	Kinross	46.09
Kincardine	67.98	Midlothian	43.57
Kirkcudbright	67.69	Renfrew	42.41
Elgin & Nairn	67.53	Roxburgh	40.76
Peebles	63.81	Selkirk	38.53
Ross & Cromarty	62.95	Fife	37.15
Forfar	62.19	Ayr	36.22
Inverness	62.18	Caithness	35.44
Perth	55.94	Clackmannan	25.00
Lanark	53.15	[Orkney	19.33][27]

[27] The percentage shown for Orkney should be disregarded. It results from the small number of the 150 new electors who can actually be identified as engaged in agriculture as proprietors or tenants. There are 58 in category one for whom no occupation is known. There were 25 others but they were identified as tenants from a later canvassing list; Orkney County Library, 'List Showing Electors in Orkney . . .' [c.1837]. Caithness comes well down the rank order because in a small constituency there were proportionately large numbers in the professional, merchant and fishing categories.

To understand why the counties differ so much it is necessary to consider the three principal determinants of the composition of a county electorate. The first was the county's economy. However incompletely or unsatisfactorily, each electorate reflected the main economic activities in the county. The second was the nature of urban settlement in the county (to which should be added the influence of large, perhaps external, centres of population such as Edinburgh or Glasgow). And the third, closely linked to the second, was the extent to which towns were separately represented in Parliament or formed part of the county constituency. In 1832 a number of hitherto unrepresented towns were raised to the status of parliamentary burghs, either in their own right or as part of a district of burghs. Nevertheless, in many counties, especially outside the highland and northern region, there were numerous large villages, and many more towns than could have been accommodated in any number of districts of burghs. In Ayr, Renfrew, Lanark, Stirling, Clackmannan and Kinross, Midlothian, Roxburgh, Selkirk, the southern and eastern parishes of Perthshire, and above all in Fife, these settlements were frequently significant centres of manufacture and trade. Admittedly, they often had a close and sometimes dependent relationship with the surrounding countryside to which they provided goods and services, but they contributed substantially to the number of county voters in 'non-agricultural' occupations, and could be the focus of both political and religious dissent.

The presence, or indeed the absence, of such settlements has influenced the ordering of counties in Table 3. Counties high in the table are generally those where agriculture, irrespective of type or quality, dominated the economy. And in counties such as Argyll, Wigtown and Kirkcudbright the separate representation in Parliament of small burghs tended to increase the agricultural character of the electorate by reducing the number of £10 voters eligible to vote in the county. Conversely, in the lower part of the table there are counties where the proportion of agricultural voters has been reduced by the numbers of voters in non-agricultural occupations, especially in unrepresented towns within the county, as seen notably in the influence of Alloa, Kincardine and the hillfoot towns of Alva, Menstrie and Tillicoultry in Clackmannan, where shipping and shipbuilding, coalmining, brewing, distilling, and the manufacture of woollen goods, combined to give it the least agricultural of electorates.[28] In Fife, even although Dunfermline, Cupar, Kirkcaldy, St Andrews and nine other burghs were separately represented (including several small ones that notoriously survived 1832), the county electorate remained one of the least agricultural, with probably the richest and most diverse body of non-agricultural voters. The explanation is that there were numerous other small unrepresented towns in the county, so that most parishes had electors in a variety of occupations, and there were few where farmers comprised a majority of voters. Although the electors of Fife make up only 9.7 per cent of the sample, they include 21 per cent of all weavers, 17 per cent of masons, 17 per cent of wrights, 16 per cent of labourers, 15 per cent of smiths, and over 22

[28] J.I. Brash, 'The Voters of Clackmannan in 1832', *Forth Naturalist and Historian*, XVI (1993), 108–10.

per cent of the shipping and fishing category. In other counties with a mixed economy there were strong internal contrasts, for example between the industrializing districts of Lanarkshire, exemplified by the coalmasters and ironmasters in the parishes of Old and New Monklands, and the Upper Ward of the county where there were 14 parishes in which the new voters consisted of 195 farmers (84 per cent compared with the county figure of 53 per cent), 15 proprietors, 12 ministers and five schoolmasters, and only four other individuals. In 1832 the royal burgh of Selkirk was thrown in to the county constituency. With the woollen manufacturing town of Galashiels it dominated the small electorate, as shown by the county's low ranking in Table 3; but in the large upland parishes of Ettrick and Yarrow 92 per cent of the new voters were farmers, the only others being two parish ministers and two schoolmasters. In neighbouring Roxburgh, where the inhabitants of Kelso, Melrose and Hawick overshadowed the constituency, the percentage of farmers in the rural districts was 80 per cent or double the figure for the county as a whole.

As one would expect the first and second categories in Tables 1 and 2 confirm the dominance of land and agriculture in the electorates of most counties. Nevertheless, it is the electors in other categories, especially those of a less universal character, that more clearly convey the differences between counties. Electors in the main professional occupations were enrolled in every county, but not in the same proportions. The most common were the parish minister, the surgeon, the local writer (solicitor), and the schoolmaster. In the highland and northern counties (Argyll, the highland districts of Perthshire, Inverness, Ross and Cromarty, Elgin and Nairn, Caithness and Orkney) the clergy were especially prominent: in Argyll, Ross and Cromarty, Caithness and Orkney half or more of the professional group were parish ministers. In Inverness three-quarters consisted of 30 ministers and 30 of the 85 military and naval officers in the sample, whereas in Midlothian, under the influence of Edinburgh, there was a much more diverse body of professionals on the roll, especially from law and medicine.

Merchants were another group represented in the registers of every county, especially in the more economically developed districts. In the highland and northern counties they were prominent only in the electorates of Caithness and Orkney and at Stornoway in Ross and Cromarty, in close association with shipping or fishing interests. In Caithness two important groups of electors were 15 fishcurers and 14 merchants, one of whom, James Miller of Leith, was tenant of two curing stations. Shipping and fishing added a distinctive element to the electorates of several counties. Of 73 shipowners 30 were qualified in Alloa or Kincardine in the county of Clackmannan, 29 were enrolled in Fife and seven in Stornoway. Several coastal counties, Ayr, Clackmannan, Fife, Orkney, Ross and Cromarty, and Wigtown had shipmasters (37), sailors (35), and associated shipbuilding craftsmen on their rolls, in addition to which there were fishermen (28) in several districts, as well as salmon fishers in Ross and Cromarty (11), Kincardine (7) and Caithness (4).

The registers of several counties included electors from manufacturing or mining, but especially from the textile industries. In addition to the numerous manufacturers and weavers of wool, linen or cotton, there were the related occupations that identify local specialization: flaxdressers and spinners in Fife, Forfar, and to a lesser extent Perthshire, cotton spinners, calico printers and bleachers in Renfrew and Stirling, and the concentration of stockingmakers (as well as hosiers) in Roxburgh. The influence of Glasgow is seen in the presence of six city merchants, including James Buchanan and James Dennistoun, in the parish of Auchtergaven in Perthshire, where they owned the cotton mills at Stanley, and similarly of John, James and Kirkman Finlay, merchants, and proprietors of the Ballindalloch cotton mills at Balfron in Stirlingshire. By comparison with textiles, the contribution of coal and iron to county electorates was small, especially when one considers the many thousands employed in these industries. Coal was mined in many districts from Ayr to Fife and left traces in the electoral registers of several lowland counties. There are 36 coalmasters in the sample (15 of them in Lanarkshire, six in Fife, six in Stirling, and five in Midlothian) as well as the managers and overseers of pits (10) and 16 miners. There are eight ironmasters (six in Lanarkshire, including five Bairds of Gartsherrie, and two in Midlothian), seven ironfounders and two managers of the Carron Ironworks. In sharp contrast, manufactures were poorly represented in the registers of highland and northern counties, apart from 15 distillers, mostly on Islay, in Argyll, and in Caithness. Between them they could muster only two textile manufacturers and two weavers. Other electors placed in the manufacturing category were usually in business outside the county. In Argyll by 1832 steam navigation on the Clyde provided easier access to the district of Cowal; a dyer, a brickmaker, a candlemaker, as well as two merchants, a writer, and three proprietors (all from Glasgow or Paisley) were qualified there in the parishes of Dunoon and Kilmun on properties which they had probably acquired as holiday residences.

Electors in the retail and artisanal trades are found in all registers but again in very different proportions, from almost 22 per cent in Clackmannan to less than 5 per cent in Argyll and Inverness. They probably comprised the majority of electors in the many towns that formed part of county constituencies in lowland and southern Scotland, and in towns such as Dalkeith in Midlothian and Kelso in Roxburgh they present a variety of occupations that in themselves suggest local prosperity. The situation was very different in the highland counties where there were few unrepresented towns of importance. There were generally fewer electors in retail trades than in lowland counties, and in Argyll, Inverness and Ross and Cromarty half of those were innkeepers. Though artisans were not so numerous among the electors as elsewhere, there were usually more of them than of retailers, especially masons, wrights, carpenters and joiners, and smiths, suggesting that in these counties there was a greater need and better opportunities for men in the building trades than in shopkeeping.

Electors in the final category of labour and general work figure in the registers of most counties outside the highland and northern counties. They were most numerous in districts where there were manufacturing towns and villages, in the counties of Ayr, Renfrew, Clackmannan and Fife, but also in Midlothian, where there was an exceptional enrolment of 30 gardeners, Roxburgh and Stirling. In the northern counties this group of electors was notably absent; there was not a single labourer and only three gardeners and four carriers on the rolls.

In summary, the composition of county electorates was most varied in central and southern Scotland, where there were many unrepresented towns and villages and a wide range of economic activities. In the highlands and north of Scotland generally there were fewer electors, relatively more of them in agriculture and fewer in most of the 'non-agricultural' categories; in particular localities, shipping, fishing, and the distilling of whisky, added distinctive components to the electorate; but over large areas of the highlands the dominant pattern was one where those who obtained the franchise in 1832 consisted overwhelmingly of tenant farmers, a few proprietors, the parish minister, and an occasional schoolmaster, though more commonly an innkeeper. This pattern it should be said was also common in the more rural districts of lowland and southern counties such as Lanark, Roxburgh and Selkirk, and especially in the south-west where the electorates of Wigtown and the Stewartry of Kirkcudbright appear in many respects to have more in common with the highland counties than with the counties of the central lowlands. But although one can make broad regional comparisons between electorates, when individual counties are examined one finds as much variety as uniformity. At least 79 per cent of the 20,399 voters in the sample were engaged in agriculture or one of the 52 core occupations in categories 3 to 9; but beyond that there is a surprising diversity in the occupations, and I suspect the social backgrounds, of the electors. When considering who was enfranchised by the Scottish Reform Act it would seem best to avoid generalization. Although the franchise was restricted to the owners, lessees and tenants of qualifying properties, to the exclusion of the majority of men and all women, the county electors in 1832 formed a not altogether unrepresentative and varied cross-section of adult male occupations in Scotland.

APPENDIX 1: *Registers and Lists of Electors.*

Argyll:
Scottish R.O., SC54/22/129, Copy Register of Electors 1834–35.

Ayr:
Ayrshire Election. List of the Names and Designations of the Electors who Voted at the First Election of a Member to Serve in Parliament for the County of Ayr under the Reform Act, 24th & 25th December 1832 (Ayr, 1833): Public Libraries Ayr and Kilmarnock.

Caithness:
Scottish R.O., SC14/64/1, Copy Register of Voters corrected to September 1835.

Clackmannan:
Scottish R.O., SC64/63/27, Register of Electors 1832; and *Register of Voters in the County of Clackmannan Including the Parishes of Alva, Tulliallan, and Culross*

1832–3–4. (Alloa, [1834]) [author's own copy]. This register, edited J.I. Brash, was reprinted by the Clackmannan Public Libraries, Alloa, 1993.

Kinross:
Perth and Kinross District Archives, Sandeman Library, Perth, CC2/1/6/3, Register of Electors 1832–62.

Elgin and Nairn:
National Library of Scotland, MS. 747, 'Constituency of The Combined Counties of Elgin and Nairn 1832'.

Fife:
National Lib. Scotland, 5.1178 (14), *List of the Registered Voters For the County of Fife November 1832* (Cupar, 1832).

Forfar:
Scottish R.O., GD16/40/59 (Airlie MSS.), *List of Freeholders and Registered Electors in the County of Forfar, November 1832* (Forfar, 1832).

Inverness:
Scottish R.O., SC29/71/1, Register of Electors 1832.

Kincardine:
National Lib. Scotland, Acc. 4796 Box 205, (Fettercairn papers), *Roll of the New Constituency of Kincardineshire 1832* (Aberdeen, 1832).

Kirkcudbright:
Scottish R.O., SC16/68/1, Register of Voters for the Stewartry of Kirkcudbright 1832.

Lanark:
Lanark District Library, *Roll of Freeholders of the County of Lanark, As it Stood in 1831; and List of Electors of Said County As Corrected At the Registration Court of 1839* (Glasgow, 1840).

Midlothian:
National Lib. Scotland, Ry.IV.e.2 (4), *Register of Voters in the County of Mid-Lothian 1832* (Edinburgh, 1832).

Orkney:
List of Voters In the Burgh of Kirkwall and County of Orkney Under Act 2 and 3 Gul. Cap. 65, Register 1832 (Kirkwall, 1832): County Library, Kirkwall.

Peebles:
Scottish R.O., SC42/44/5, Register of Electors 1832.

Perth:
National Lib. Scotland, Y.59.d.26, *Register of Voters in the County of Perth, 1832* (Perth, 1832).

Renfrew:
Scottish R.O., GD22/2/158 (Cunningham Graham papers), *Red and Black List of Electors in the County of Renfrew Showing How They Voted at the First Election under the Reform Act* [Paisley, 1833].

Ross and Cromarty:
Scottish R.O., SC34/25/1, Register of Electors 1832.

Roxburgh:
National Lib. Scotland, MS. 2951 (Spotiswoode papers), *Registered Voters of the County of Roxburgh . . . Comprehending the Old Freeholders. With An Appendix Containing the Names of all the Rejected Claimants and The Electors of the Burgh of Jedburgh The Whole Taken from the Registers etc. by Wm Rutherford Sh[eriff] Clerk* (Jedburgh, 1832).

Selkirk:
Scottish R.O., SC63/61/1, Register of Electors 1832–61.

Stirling:
National Lib. Scotland, 1935.16 (19), *Roll of Electors for the County of Stirling 1st December 1832* (Edinburgh, 1832); Scottish R.O., SC67/61/5 (Stirling); SC67/61/13, 14 (Falkirk); SC67/61/21 (Lennoxtown); and SC67/61/29 (Drymen). Copy Registers of Electors 1832 (four polling districts).

Wigtown:
Scottish R.O., SC19/64/1, Register of Voters 1832.

APPENDIX 2: *Summary of Occupations in categories three to nine with 5–19 voters*

3. *Professions and Service:* Solicitor in the Supreme Court 6, solicitor 9, university academic 7, preacher 11, accountant 11, agent 19, bank agent 6, clerk 6, town clerk 6, architect 7, surveyor/land surveyor 14, road surveyor 6, road contractor 9, civil engineer 5.

4. *Merchants and Dealers:* auctioneer 8, horses 8, coal 5, provisions 8, wine 6, spirits 5, leather 5, cloth 13, grain 13, meal 11.

5. *Shipping and Fishing:* shipbuilder 7, boatman 5.

6. *Manufacturing and Mining:* cotton manufacturer 10, mill spinner 7, flax spinner 15, flax dresser 8, stockingmaker 17, dyer 18, skinner 7, currier 11, maltster 12, candle manufacturer 5, gunpowder manufacturer 6, coal manager 10, quarrier 19, ironmaster 8, ironfounder 7.

7 *Retail Trades:* cowfeeder 7, tobacconist 14, druggist 6, ironmonger 18, bookseller 11, draper 7, shopkeeper 7.

8. *Artisanal Trades:* cartwright 12, wheelwright 8, cabinetmaker 15, coppersmith 5, tinsmith 7, plasterer 7, painter 6.

9. *Labour:* tollkeeper 13, coal miner 16, sawyer 18, limeburner 5, servant 8.

Summary 1–4 voters

3. *Professions and Service:* barrister 1, sheriff-substitute 1, Clerk to the Signet 1, veterinary surgeon 3, musician 3, artist 1, miniature painter 1, bank clerk 1, Secretary of the North British Insurance Company 1, manager 3, contractor 3, editor *Stirling Journal* 1, librarian 1, provost 3, baron bailie 3, sheriff's clerk 1, commissary clerk 1, session clerk 2, beadle 1, collector of gas rates 1, postmaster 2, chamberlain 1, steward 2, butler 1, mail contractor 1, Lord Treasurer's Remembrancer 1, barrackmaster 1, asylum keeper 1, measurer 1, land measurer 1, engineer 4, mining engineer 1.

4. *Merchants and Dealers:* flour 1, hay 1, potatoes 3, seed 1, lime 4, iron 1, slate 1, stoneware 3, hardware 1, tea 4, cheese 2, wool 3, flax 2, lace 1, merchant tailor 2.

5. *Shipping and Fishing:* pilot 1, ferryman 3, blockmaker 1, ship's carpenter 2, rope/sailmaker 4, shipwright 1, chandler 1, ship's agent 4, shoremaster 1, tenant of drydock 1.

6. *Manufactures and Mining:* manufacturer's agent 3, weaver's agent 3, wool carder 4, wool spinner 4, mill manager 3, warper 1, yarnmiller 1, lintmiller 2, stocking weaver 3, silk throwster 1, damask manufacturer 1, print cutter 3, printer 3, waulker 4, thongmaker 2, maltman 3, mashman 1, ploughmaker 1, coachmaker 1, and manufacturers of bandages 1, baskets 1, boxes 1, bricks 2, powder 1, haircloth 2, hats 1, matches 1, salt 2, snuff 1, straw 1, glass 1, pottery 2, alum 3, acid 1, starch 3, agricultural implements 1, and coal agent 2, limemaster 4, manager Carron Ironworks 2, brassfounder 1, moulder 2.

7. *Retail Trades:* barber 4, hairdresser 4, perfumer 2, clockmaker 3, stationer 3, haberdasher 2, glover 1, confectioner 1, jeweller 3, optician 1, pawnbroker 1, fishmonger 1.

8. *Artisanal Trades:* squarewright 2, glazier 3, plumber 3, printer 2, turner 3, upholsterer 3, reedmaker 1, tinplate worker 1, cutler 1, gunmaker/smith 4, carver 1, carver and gilder 1, engraver 2, bookbinder 2, silversmith 1, goldsmith 2, lapidary 1.

9. *Labour:* workman 1, roadman 4, lock keeper 1, hillman (colliery) 2, hostler 3, mail/coach guard 3, coachman 1, sheriff's officer 4, messenger-at-arms 3, messenger 4.

Index

Computing Parliamentary History: George III to Victoria

Parliamentary History
Special Issue One (1994)

Edited by John A. Phillips,
University of California, Riverside

JOHN A. PHILLIPS,
Introduction - QUASSHing M.P.s and Electors:
New Perspectives on Parliamentary History
DONALD GINTER
Unofficial Division Lists of the British House of Commons,
1761-1820: A New Data Base and its Implications
GARY COX
The Developments of Collective Responsibility in
the United Kingdom
JOHN A. PHILLIPS and CHARLES WETHERELL
Parliamentary Parties and Municipal Politics:
1835 and the Party System
CHERYL SCHONHARDT-BAILEY
Linking Constituency Interests to Legislative Voting
Behaviour: The Role of District Economic and Electoral
Composition in the Repeal of the Corn Laws
WILLIAM C. LUBENOW
The Liberals and the National Question: Irish Home Rule,
Nationalism, and the Relationship to
Nineteenth-Century Liberalism

Available • 146 pages • 0 7486 0488 X • £12.95

Parliament and the Atlantic Empire

Parliamentary History
Special Issue Two (1995)

Edited by Philip Lawson,
University of Alberta

Available • 102 pages • 0 7486 0628 9 • £12.95

The Age of Transition:
British Politics 1880-1914

Parliamentary History
Special Issue Four (1997)

Edited by E.H.H. Green,
Magdalen College, Oxford

This forthcoming issue will include articles by
Andrew Adonis, E.H.H. Green, John Lawrence,
Margaret O'Callaghan and Duncan Tanner

Available March 1997

HOW TO ORDER

These special issues are available from bookshops
or can be ordered direct from our distributor:
Marston Book Services,
PO Box 269, Abingdon, Oxon OX14 4SD
Tel: 01235 465600, Fax: 01235 465655

THE ENGLISH HISTORICAL REVIEW

First published in 1886, **The English Historical Review** is the oldest journal of historical scholarship in the English-speaking world. It deals not only with British history, but with almost all aspects of European and world history since the classical era.

With contributions from around the world, each issue includes major Articles, Notes and Documents and Debates on medieval and modern themes. The journal also features an unrivalled range and quantity of reviews of books published worldwide.

THE
ENGLISH
HISTORICAL
REVIEW

Edited by
J R Maddicott,
J Stevenson

Assistant Editor
H A Bolick

FREE ISSUE OFFER

❑ Please send me a FREE sample issue of *The English Historical Review*, without obligation to subscribe.
❑ I would like to subscribe. Please send me an invoice.

Subscription Details
Volume 111, 1996 (5 issues)
Annual Subscriptions

	UK	Europe	R.o.W.	USA/Can
Standard	£83	£88	£91	$155
Student	£43	£48	£47	$80
Single issues	£21	£21	£23	$39

ISSN 0013-8266

Name:

_____

Address:_____

_____

_____

Return to: Julia Wood, Addison Wesley Longman Higher Education, Edinburgh Gate, Harlow, Essex CM20 2JE, UK
Tel +44 (0)1279 623212
Fax +44 (0)1279 623862,
e-mail: julia.wood@awl.co.uk

LONGMAN Parliamentary History

Articles for 1996 include:

The Transformation of Knighthood in Early Thirteenth-Century England
Kathryn Faulkner

Unexpected Contacts: Lithuanian Emigration to and Integration within Western Courts, c.1316-c.1400
S.C. Rowell

The International Mercenary Market in the Sixteenth Century: Anglo-French Competition in Germany, 1543-50
David Potter

Popularity, Prelacy and Puritanism in the 1620s: Joseph Hall Explains Himself
Kenneth Fincham and Peter Lake

'Pagans or Paragons?' Images of the Cornish during the English Civil War
M.J. Stoyle

British Conservatism and Class Politics in the 1920s
David Jarvis